TRAILS TO TIBURÓN

THE SOUTHWEST CENTER SERIES

TRAILS TO TIBURÓN

THE 1894 AND 1895 FIELD DIARIES OF

W J McGee

TRANSCRIBED BY
Hazel McFeely Fontana

ANNOTATED AND WITH
AN INTRODUCTION BY
Bernard L. Fontana

THE UNIVERSITY OF ARIZONA PRESS
TUCSON

First printing
The University of Arizona Press
© 2000 The Arizona Board of Regents
∞ This book is printed on acid-free, archival-quality paper.
Manufactured in the United States of America
05 04 03 02 01 00   6 5 4 3 2 1

Library of Congress Cataloging-in-Publication Data

McGee, W. J., 1853–1912
  Trails to Tiburón : the 1894 and 1895 field diaries of W J McGee /
transcribed by Hazel McFeely Fontana ; annotated and with an
introduction by Bernard L. Fontana.
    p. cm. — (Southwest Center series)
  Includes bibliographical references and index.
  ISBN 0-8165-2030-5
  1. Tohono O'Odham Indians. 2. Seri Indians. 3. McGee, W. J.,
1853–1912—Diaries. 4. Tiburón Island (Mexico)—Description and
travel. I. Fontana, Bernard L. II. Title. III. Series
  E99.P25 M34 2000
  972.1'7—dc21
                    99-006917

British Library Cataloguing-in-Publication Data
A catalogue record for this book is available from the British Library.

To the spirit of adventure and discovery

CONTENTS

Figures

MAPS

Acknowledgments

Bringing W J McGee's field notes of his 1894 and 1895 journeys from Arizona to Sonora into print is a project that began more than four decades ago, in 1956, and during the course of that time we inevitably became indebted to numerous individuals, many of them, sadly, no longer alive. Among these are Margaret Blaker, archivist for the now-defunct Bureau of American Ethnology at the Smithsonian Institution; Ronald L. Ives, geographer and cartographer extraordinaire, who supplied encouragement, maps, and material for one of the appendices and who died February 26, 1982; Klotho McGee Lattin, W J McGee's daughter, who died November 17, 1985; Elsie McGee Ellis, W J McGee's grandniece; Don Roberto Thomson, grandnephew of Pascual Encinas and son of Louis Keith Thompson, one of McGee's companions in 1895; Matthew W. Stirling, director of the Bureau of American Ethnology; Frank H. H. Roberts, Jr., director of the Bureau of American Ethnology; David C. Mearns, chief of the Manuscripts Division of the Library of Congress; and Licenciado Luis Encinas, governor of the state of Sonora.

We were also aided in identification of plants and animals and in other ways by Charles H. Lowe, Jr., and Paul S. Martin, both retired from the University of Arizona; Raymond M. Turner, retired from the U.S. Geological Survey; Steven J. Prchal of Sonoran Arthropod Studies, Inc.; Richard S. Felger of Drylands Institute; and Curtis M. Hinsley, Jr., of Northern Arizona University.

All photographs are reprinted by permission of the National Anthropological Archives, Smithsonian Institution, and are identified by catalog number in the caption. Photographs in the introduction and "Papago Trip, 1894" journal were taken by William Dinwiddie; photographs in the "Second Expedition, 1895" journal were taken by John W. Mitchell.

INTRODUCTION

By the end of the nineteenth century, a self-taught and now largely forgotten scientist had climbed to the pinnacle of the fledgling field of American anthropology as one of its most powerful and outspoken proponents. Unlikely though it may seem, chief among the trails leading to that summit were those headed to a remote, dry, and forbidding place in the Gulf of California known as Shark Island, or, more properly, Isla Tiburón. The field notes presented here for the first time are an important part of that story.

The Career Trail

The scientist's name was William John McGee, "Don" to members of his immediate family and close friends. He came to identify himself on many dozens of publications and in official correspondence as "W J McGee," deliberately dropping the periods from his initials—an affectation that continued for the rest of his adult life and was acknowledged by his peers.[1]

W J McGee was born April 17, 1853, on a rural farmstead near Farley, Iowa, the fourth of nine children of James and Martha Ann Anderson McGee. The house in which he was born and grew up was, in the words of his sister Emma, "a very modest structure made of logs which were cut from the trees in our woods. The lumber used for finishing the cabin, my father purchased from the Dubuque and Sioux City Railroad Company. . . . They used little frame shanties to house the men employed on the road, and as there were no sawmills at that early date, to cut the trees into lumber, my father was glad to obtain one or two of these small buildings to aid in the construction of a humble home in which to rear his family" (E. McGee 1915: 14).

Although McGee's mother was a schoolteacher, most of his learning occurred at home rather than in the classroom, and it appears he had fewer than eight years of formal education. Besides working on his father's farm, he tried his hand as an inventor and salesman of farm machinery, a blacksmith, and a surveyor before he discovered his true loves: geology and anthropology. In 1876, when he was just twenty-three years old, the neophyte observer began to examine carefully the geological strata that could be seen in wells in the vicinity of Farley. It was a time when geologists were beginning to debate in earnest the glacial history of North America, a history revealing some of its secrets in deposits such as those McGee was encountering. Excited by what he was seeing, the budding scientist stretched his horizons to include a geological and archaeological survey of all of northeastern Iowa.

In 1877, McGee joined the American Association for the Advancement of Science (AAAS), and at the following year's meeting he offered remarks on Iowa geology and on aboriginal crania found in his home state. He began publishing the results of his surveys in scientific journals,[2] at the same time corresponding with professionals and nonprofessionals who had established their reputations in the field. In 1880, thanks to the influence of an Iowa congressman, McGee was paid to write a report on the building stones of Iowa for the tenth United States census.

McGee met—and favorably impressed—John Wesley Powell at the 1878 AAAS meeting. Powell, by then famous for his 1869 and 1871–72 expeditions down the Colorado River through the Grand Canyon and for his surveys in the West, had been working in Washington to bring about the creation of the United States Geological Survey (USGS). Although geologist Clarence King became the director of the USGS when it was established in 1879, and Powell was chosen instead to direct the newly created Bureau of American Ethnology (BAE), the latter remained an influential figure in geology. King resigned from the USGS in 1881, and Powell became his successor. The next year, McGee was hired as one of many USGS assistant geologists. As his publications suggest, from then until Powell left the USGS in 1893, the youthful Iowan's calling in that agency was highly productive.

While McGee was recognized as having "remarkable powers of observation" and as being a workaholic (Hinsley 1976: 350), it certainly did not hurt his Washington, D.C., career when in 1888 he married Anita Newcomb, daughter of Simon Newcomb, who at the time was one of the best-known astronomers in the United States and a person of high status in the Washington social scene. If Emma McGee is correct, Lincoln biographer, novelist, editor, and critic William Dean Howells (1837–1920) designed the future Mrs. McGee's wedding dress and was a guest at the couple's wedding.

Not that the Newcombs approved of the marriage. Anita's mother disapproved of the Iowa farm boy, and the senior Newcomb simply ignored McGee's existence—all the more inspiration for McGee to continue pulling hard on his own bootstraps. Even Anita, while she remained her husband's staunch ally and promoter for fifteen years until their relationship disintegrated, was not going to lose her identity in that of her husband. She enrolled in Columbian University's School of Medicine in Washington, D.C., in 1889, earning her M.D. in 1892 and doing postgraduate work at Johns Hopkins. She and McGee had three children: Klotho, born in 1889, who later married and had two sons; Donald, who died in infancy; and Eric Doolittle, who remained unmarried and committed suicide in 1931. The latter event was doubly tragic for Anita, because after McGee's death, her son, at her insistence, had changed his name to Eric McGee Newcomb to satisfy her vain hope that the Newcomb family name would be perpetuated.

Anita enjoyed a remarkably successful career as a physician, a source of pride to her husband. In 1898 she was appointed acting assistant surgeon of the

U.S. Army; she organized the Army Nurse Corps; and in 1904, she was appointed by Japan's minister of war as superior of nurses during Japan's conflict with Russia, an assignment that won for her the Japanese Order of the Sacred Crown and a pair of Russo-Japanese war medals.

W J McGee's wagon had become securely hitched to John Wesley Powell's star, and when Powell left the USGS to assume full-time directorship of the Bureau of American Ethnology in 1893, his protégé—by then a seasoned warrior in the battles of Washington politics who had made himself well known in scientific circles—went with him. McGee signed on as "Ethnologist in Charge" of the BAE, and in charge is what he became. Powell's health began to deteriorate badly in 1894, and from then until Powell died in 1902, McGee was in fact, if not in name, the bureau's director, writing annual reports for Powell's signature, making personnel and policy decisions, deciding publication priorities, and, incidentally, making his own choices regarding fieldwork.

Although McGee had dabbled somewhat seriously in archaeological pursuits before 1894, his real strength had been in geology. To establish his *bona fides* as an ethnologist would require at least a modicum of work among living Indians. Thus the stage was set for two treks that would eventually take him to Tiburón and to a properly credentialed place among the nation's anthropologists.

The Philosophical Trail

For most scientists building their intellectual edifice during the last three decades of the nineteenth century, "Law," wrote Harvard historian and philosopher Henry Adams (1961: 232), "should be Evolution from lower to higher, aggregation of the atom in the mass, concentration of multiplicity in unity, compulsion of anarchy in order."

These tenets were certainly congenial to the thinking of John Wesley Powell and, by extension, that of W J McGee. The mindset of the two men had been influenced both directly and indirectly by the ideas of English philosopher Herbert Spencer and wealthy upstate New York lawyer and financier Lewis Henry Morgan. Morgan, often regarded as the "Father of American Anthropology," had developed and presented his ideas about human cultural evolution in three highly influential books: *League of the Ho-dé-no-sau-nee, or Iroquois* (1851), *Systems of Consanguinity and Affinity of the Human Family* (1870), and *Ancient Society: Or, Researches in the Lines of Human Progress from Savagery through Barbarism to Civilization* (1877). He postulated that humankind had moved inevitably through well-defined stages of development that began with lower, middle, and upper savagery and had then proceeded to lower, middle, and upper barbarism. The movement finally culminated in civilization and, one is tempted to say, in the legal and financial professionals of upper New York state. According to this scheme, there remained societies abroad in the world whose members had not progressed to the status of civilization and who represented one of the lower stages.

Morgan's framework of unilineal cultural evolution—itself no doubt a congenial reflection of popular American mores of the time—had a profound effect on the course of American anthropology. Nearly all nineteenth-century anthropologists embraced it or some variation of it, while many anthropologists of the first four decades of the twentieth century invested considerable time and energy in its repudiation.

For Powell, and for McGee, the locus of human cultural evolution lay in the mind. Peoples' behaviors, as well as products fashioned by them, were projections of their minds. Simple stone tools, therefore, were evidence of simple minds and a simple stage of culture. "Material culture, kinship systems, languages, folk-lore—all were inherently interesting, but they were ultimately only the data of science, the outward manifestations that revealed the operations of the underlying agency" (Hinsley 1981: 126).

This, then, was the philosophical path on which McGee trod in 1894 and again in 1895 in the Sonoran Desert of Arizona and Sonora. He went into the field with a ruling hypothesis as part of his intellectual baggage. He was in search of the primitive, seeking, like Morgan and others before him, origins of aspects of human behavior—and validations of what had become anthropological dogma. It is to his everlasting credit, however, and no doubt a tribute to his background as an objective observer of geological phenomena, that little in his field notes betrays the strong biases and prejudices that he assuredly carried with him. Whether describing geology and topography, plants, people, or other animals, McGee drew word pictures—and occasionally real pictures—of these as he encountered them. Most speculations, as well as the creation of magisterial theories, could wait for publication. The field notes, like the photographs, would provide "facts." The meanings of those facts could be pondered better in a Washington office than while coping with the daily tribulations of travel in an alien world.

Quite unconsciously, McGee also took with him into the Sonoran Desert a tradition of field exploration and observation whose roots might be traced back at least to the so-called voyages of discovery of the sixteenth century. It was then that, for Europeans at least, a "New World" began to be opened. Seagoing explorers and adventurers, in addition to mapping bodies of water and lands previously unknown to them, sometimes recorded on paper what by the eighteenth century had become conceptualized as "natural history," including people, other animals, plants, and geological formations. During Sir Francis Drake's 1577–79 circumnavigation of the globe and his 1585–86 voyage to the Caribbean and North America, for example, artists who accompanied him, and perhaps even Drake himself, rendered colored drawings and provided written descriptions of people and their activities and artifacts as well as of such things as birds, trees, and sea lions. The Drake Manuscript in the Pierpont Morgan Library in New York City consists of 199 separate images of West Indian plants, animals, and Indian life, all of them bound together in the eighteenth century with a title page proclaiming them as *Histoire Naturelle des Indes* (Natural History of the Indies). The illustrations are captioned in late-sixteenth-century French (Klinkenborg 1988).

The eighteenth century witnessed an outpouring of voyages of discovery emanating from western powers. Jean François de Galaup, Comte de la Pérouse (1741–88?), was sent by the French government in 1785 on an expedition for scientific, geographic, and commercial purposes, one that in 1786 took him from Alaska to Monterey in Alta California. His crew included geologists, botanists, and artists. There were similar eighteenth-century expeditions for Spain, the most notable of them led by Alejandro Malaspina. And England had its famed Captain James Cook as well as Captain George Vancouver. It was not for nothing that Vancouver's flagship was called *Discovery*.

The explorer whose career capped those of his many predecessors was Alexander von Humboldt (1769–1859). This German scientist and geographer, who had studied geology, biology, and political science at the University of Göttingen, not only explored Mexico, Central America, and South America from 1799 to 1804, but consorted among the intelligentsia in France and Germany, lectured often, and wrote profusely. His five-volume *Cosmos* (1846–1862) was nothing less than an effort to describe the entire physical universe. Humboldt's name became synonymous with geography and exploration, and his influence was felt by countless explorers who followed in his intellectual wake. John Wesley Powell, explorer of the Grand Canyon, geologist, and would-be ethnologist, was firmly in the Humboldt tradition. It is not surprising W J McGee would find himself there as well.

McGee's 1894 and 1895 journeys, and their published results, must be understood within the context of his time. From seagoing ventures to overland expeditions, arduous travel, rather than in-depth study, became the principal means of effecting discovery. In the late nineteenth century, academicians and the reading public alike remained enthralled by encounters—however brief and superficial—with the "other," with people, landscapes, flora, fauna, climatic conditions, and experiences that were, for them, exotic. The more physical difficulties involved in achieving these discoveries, the more likely they were to be crowned with popular interest and with belief in their authenticity. Both scientific peers and general readers esteemed those who had gone where no others had been known to precede them. There was excitement in finding out about the "other," including people and places, and there was the tacit understanding such discoveries could be made, as they had been since the days of Sir Francis Drake, through strenuous, if passing, observation. Such observations, moreover, were not bound by the constraints of academic compartmentalization. The backgrounds, temperaments, and training of these earlier explorers inclined them less toward specialization than generalization. "Natural history," like "geography," was all-encompassing.

Desert Trails

There can be little doubt that McGee had no people other than the Papago Indians—Tohono O'odham (Desert People), as they call themselves—in mind when he set out on his 1894 field expedition. Only "Papago Trip" appears on the first page of his 1894 field notes, dated October 24, and it is six days later, after his arrival in Hermosillo, Sonora, when the word "Seri" is first written.

McGee apparently chose to make the Papagos the object of his first serious field study of American Indians because of his communication with David D. Gaillard, an Army officer who had accompanied the International Boundary Survey during its 1893 re-marking of the border between Sonora and Arizona (Hinsley 1976: 425). Gaillard had published an article on the Papagos in *American Anthropologist* in 1894 before McGee embarked on his journey, and later, in 1896, he wrote a popular article about the Sonoran Desert and its Papago dwellers for *The Cosmopolitan* (Gaillard 1894, 1896).

On the other hand, McGee seems not to have been aware of earlier visits to Papagos by Dutchman Herman F. C. ten Kate, the first professional anthropologist to spend time among them. Before 1894, ten Kate was the only anthropologist who had included Papagos in his working itineraries. He had spent a few days with them in 1883 and again in 1888 (ten Kate 1995: 637, 674–79). Interestingly enough, in 1883 ten Kate had visited Papagos living at San Xavier and had then ridden the train south through Nogales and Hermosillo all the way to Guaymas, nearly the entire route to Hermosillo being the same one followed at a more leisurely pace by McGee with horse and wagon in 1894. In 1888, in addition to visiting San Xavier, ten Kate also paid visits to Papagos in the villages of Fresnal and Coyote, which were to be seen again by McGee nearly seven years later. If McGee knew about the Dutchman's field trips among Papagos, however, he remained uncharacteristically silent on the subject, both in his notes and in print. Ten Kate's publications concerning Papagos were either written in languages McGee did not read (he seems to have read only English) or they consisted of physical anthropological data of little interest to him.[3]

McGee apparently believed that the Papagos most likely to be "primitive" and little influenced by outsiders would be those living south of the international boundary in Mexico. As he discovered, precisely the opposite proved to be the case. Papagos in Sonora were far more closely bound to the cash economy than were Papagos living in parts of Arizona (Powell 1897: xxxiv).

The Personnel   The 1894 expedition was organized in October on the San Xavier Papago Indian Reservation nine miles south of Tucson, Arizona. McGee obtained the use of a wagon (an ambulance), a team, and at least one saddle horse from John M. Berger, who was then the government farmer, de facto the Indian agent, on the reservation.

McGee was accompanied from Washington by BAE photographer William Dinwiddie. He hired E. P. Cunningham as his teamster and a Papago named Jose Lewis as his interpreter. Except for Cunningham, whose traces have been lost to history, they were a remarkable group.

William Dinwiddie was born in Charlottesville, Virginia, in 1867.[4] When he was fourteen years old, he was hired as an assistant electrician in the U.S. National Museum in Washington. Three years later he became a customs inspector in Corpus Christi, Texas, after which, from 1886 to 1896, he was employed in the BAE as an "ethno-photographer" and assistant archaeologist. When the 1894 expedition got back to Tucson toward the end of November, McGee returned at once to Washington while Dinwiddie remained "for a few days for the purpose of completing collections on the Papago reservation at San Xavier" (Powell 1897: lxii). It appears Dinwiddie used the time to take additional pictures at San Xavier, and he

J. M. Berger (center), at San Xavier del Bac, Arizona, with village residents discussing plans for the December 3 Feast of San Francisco Xavier. Others include Carlos Rios (fifth from left), Francisco Rios (sixth from left), Jose Juan Cristobal (seventh from left), Ok-sa-ga-wa (eleventh from left, seated foreground), Juan Capon (twelfth from left), and Octaviano Núñez (?, first on right). Taken ca. November 22, 1894. (2761)

seems also to have visited Prescott, Arizona, as well as the Phoenix Indian School, where he took still more photographs (Dinwiddie 1899b). By January 1895, he was back in Washington, where McGee put him to work developing the approximately six hundred photographs taken during the expedition. Dinwiddie also labeled the artifacts they had collected among Papago and Seri Indians. These tasks, in addition to his arranging a portion of the Papago and Seri materials "for display at the [1895 Cotton States and International] Atlanta Exposition" kept him busy through June of 1895 (Powell 1897: xlii–lviii).

In 1896, while working with famed anthropologist Frank Hamilton Cushing on an archaeological site at Key Marco, Florida, Dinwiddie accused Cushing of faking a shell artifact, an accusation precipitating a major imbroglio and leading to Dinwiddie's being fired from the BAE (Gilliland 1989: 99–105; Hinsley 1981: 205).

The photographer's departure from government service led him into a career as a journalist and publicist. He started as an illustrator and correspondent with the *New York Herald;* briefly became a photographer for the Baltimore & Ohio Railroad; and moved on to cover the Cuban and Puerto Rican campaigns in the 1898 Spanish-American War. In 1899–1900 he was a correspondent in the Philippine Islands for the *New York Herald* and *Harper's Weekly,* and he covered the second Anglo-Boer War in South Africa for *Harper's* in 1900. He next was Sunday editor of the *New York Herald,* followed in 1902 by a stint as editor of the *Manila Cablenews* and as governor of the province of Lepanto-Bontoc in the Philippines. Dinwiddie's overseas assignments were rounded off in 1904–5 when he reported on the Russo-Japanese War for the *New York World, Harper's Weekly,* and *Leslie's Weekly.*

Back in the United States once more, McGee's 1894 traveling companion became associate editor for the *New York World;* associate editor for the Hearst Syndicate; editorial writer for the *St. Louis Post-Dispatch;* advertising and publicity manager for the Lehigh Valley Railroad Company; and manager of personal relations for the Busch Estate in St. Louis. During World War I he discovered American clays to replace German clays in the manufacture of lead pencils and graphite crucibles, and in 1921 he dabbled in the manufacture of crucibles. Before he died at his home in Rockville, Maryland, in June of 1934, "Mr. Dinwiddie," as McGee always referred to him in his field notes, published countless articles and at least one book, *Puerto Rico; Its Conditions and Possibilities* (Dinwiddie 1899a). The Virginia lad who had started as an electrician's apprentice had done all right for himself.

Jose Lewis, the well-suited Papago interpreter who accompanied the 1894 expedition and who in the process became McGee's principal informant concerning Tohono O'odham culture, was passingly literate in English.[5] Where he was educated is unknown, but vague O'odham oral tradition suggests he was born in the Tohono O'odham village of Vainam Kug (Iron [Pipe] Stands) in the 1860s or '70s. He may have died in the Pima Indian village of Blackwater on the Gila River Indian Reservation in the 1920s. What is known is that after his journey with McGee, Lewis, who inexplicably became "Jose Lewis Brennan" on manuscripts by him, became an informant for John N. B. Hewitt at the Bureau of American Ethnology. Hewitt is listed as the 1897 "collector" of "Papago Material of Jose Lewis Brennan, Piman Stock," manuscripts written in Lewis's hand and now in the National Anthropological Archives of the Smithsonian Institution.[6] The texts are written both in O'odham and in English translation and include a small Papago-English dictionary; material relating to the Papago berdache and "backward people," or "contraries"; political organization; the Tohono O'odham salt-gathering expeditions; warfare; disease; and other topics. Some but by no means all of these have since appeared in print (Bahr 1975: 34–50, 72–101; Bahr et al. 1974: 66, 114, 120, 243, 272; Brennan 1959, 1991; Underhill et al. 1979: 38–47). Bahr (1975: x) observes: "The oldest known Piman-English text of ritual oratory was written by a Papago, Jose Lewis Brennan, in 1897, who transcribed the richest collection of Piman oratory ever made."

Much of the transcription to which Bahr refers was actually done by Lewis in 1901–2, when he served as "interpreter" for anthropologist Frank Russell among the Pima Indians on the Gila River Indian Reservation. Russell's book, *The Pima*

Jose Lewis, right, stands next to an horno, or beehive oven, at San Xavier del Bac, ca. November 23, 1894. (2770a)

Indians (initially published in 1908 as an Annual Report of the Bureau of American Ethnology), with its lengthy Pima texts, is as much Lewis's book as Russell's (Fontana 1975: xiv–xv). Thus, inadvertently or otherwise, in 1894 McGee initiated the training of a Native American ethnographer of his own people.

McGee's Papago interpreter on his 1895 expedition was Hugh Norris, whom he first met and whom Dinwiddie photographed in 1894, when Norris was twenty-four years old. He was the son of Juana Norris and Ban-se-gak (Dry Coyote). Norris, who demonstrated his good sense by declining to accompany McGee on his sea voyage to Tiburón Island, became a well-known interpreter at San Xavier and in Tucson, frequently called on by local courts to exercise his bilingual talents. Norris's relationship with McGee did not end in 1895. He served once more as McGee's interpreter, this time in November 1900 on a BAE-sponsored trip to southwestern Arizona and northwestern Sonora (McGee 1901: 130). He and his family also operated a small retail store, an early-twentieth-century version of the convenience market, in their home on the Papago Indian Reservation not far west of Mission San Xavier del Bac.

Hugh Norris at San Xavier del Bac, ca. November 23, 1894. (2728a)

According to historian Lori Davisson (1986: 339), Norris "attended school in Albuquerque, but returned to Arizona to work as a blacksmith at the Roadside mine. Norris eventually graduated from the Tucson Indian School and joined the Papago police. He patrolled the San Xavier Mission for twenty-two years and served another fifteen years as chief of police at Sells (the hub of the Papago Indian Reservation west of Tucson). Chief Norris proudly recalled that he never used his gun to bring in a prisoner, although he did get into a fight one time on Meyer Street in Tucson with a man who called him an 'old woman' because he didn't drink."

Norris achieved a modicum of national notice when he was acknowledged by best-selling author Harold Bell Wright (1929: ix–x) as one of his two guides, interpreters, and consultants in compiling a book of Papago legends and lore. Wright told his readers that Norris's Indian name was Muh-leef Chee-awch (Running Young Man), and that Norris was a "strict Roman Catholic." Indeed, McGee's 1895 and 1900 interpreter became so widely known and respected among non-Indians in southern Arizona that a popular footpath leading to the summit of Wasson Peak, the highest point in the Tucson Mountains, was named the Hugh Norris Trail in his honor. Norris died November 14, 1934 (Brown 1960).

The career of the photographer on the 1895 expedition, John Walter Mitchell, has remained elusive. He performed yeoman's service during the party's trying days on Tiburón, and McGee named an arroyo in Seri country on the Sonoran mainland in his honor (McGee 1898b: 19). His photographs, however, are far below the quality of those taken by Dinwiddie on the earlier trip.

The topographer in 1895 was Willard D. Johnson, a longtime friend of McGee's who was sent on loan from the USGS to the BAE.[7] McGee had met Johnson in 1882 when both worked for the USGS in Utah. McGee went to Washington in 1883, but Johnson, who always preferred the field to the office and independence to bureaucratic confinement, went to the Mono Lake region in California, mapping and illustrating geologist Grove K. Gilbert's work there. He later surveyed for three years in Massachusetts, perfecting the system of plane table surveying he had begun in Utah. Between 1889 and 1891 he headed the Colorado Division of the newly formed (and soon disbanded) Federal Irrigation Survey, afterwards directing USGS field operations in Colorado, South Dakota, Wyoming, and the San Francisco region. In 1895, his rank having been reduced back to topographer, he joined his old friend McGee in what turned out chiefly to be an Arizona-Sonora misadventure.

The tragedy connected with Johnson's participation in the 1895 expedition concerns the disappearance of his maps. According to McGee, and it is borne out in his field notes, "the whole of Seriland, the interior of which was never before trodden by white men, was examined, surveyed, and mapped; indeed, the survey was of such character as to yield the first topographic map of a broad belt in Sonora extending from the international boundary to Sonora river. The area covered by this survey is about 10,000 square miles. Forty-seven stations were occupied for control, and a considerably larger number of additional points for topographic sketching" (Powell 1898: xliv).

McGee reiterated elsewhere, "the Topographic surveys of the 1895 expedition covered a zone averaging 50 miles in width, extending from the international boundary to somewhat beyond Rio Sonora. Mr Johnson, by whom these surveys were executed, was on furlough from the United States Geological Survey, and his resumption of survey work prevented the construction of finished maps, except that of Seriland (plate I), which forms but a small fraction of the area surveyed. The results of the remaining, and by far the greater, part of the topographic surveys are withheld pending completion of the inquiries concerning the Papago Indians" (McGee 1898b: 15).

The inquiries concerning the Papagos seem never to have been completed, and not only were most of Johnson's maps left unpublished, but they have since been lost. Searches in all archives where they might reasonably be expected to be found have yielded nothing. Nor have Johnson's heirs, if he had any, been located.

After 1895, Johnson continued his work with the USGS, studying the water supply system in the High Plains around Meade, Kansas, and returning to Utah to examine the origins of the mountain ranges there. He was still writing letters on USGS letterhead in January 1907, when he applied for membership in the Association of American Geographers. He gave his permanent address as Lonepine, Inyo County, California.[8] The record then falls silent. Thanks to McGee, however, Johnson's name is enshrined as that of the highest mountain, Pico Johnson, in Sonora's Sierra Seri.

Itinerary and Observations, 1894   Throughout the course of both his 1894 and 1895 field trips, McGee kept detailed notes in three small field notebooks that, along with most of his other personal papers, have been preserved in the Library of Congress. Copies of those notebooks were sent on microfilm to the University of Arizona Library in Tucson, where Hazel Fontana, almost miraculously, was able to divine their contents and to prepare a readable transcript of them. The original diaries were transcribed as faithfully as possible, retaining the original grammar, punctuation, and spelling. McGee's handwriting, especially in the field, was often barely more than a scrawl. His sister even commented on her brother's poor handwriting in print after he died:

> I am of the opinion that Don never won any laurels for being a good penman. He usually wrote a plain, fairly legible hand, as good I am sure, as most people of the present day. But if Grandfather Anderson [McGee's mother's father] were living now, he would probably count all achievements as of little worth, because his penmanship did not come up to the standard of perfection prized by the old man. (E. McGee 1915: 55)

Earlier, McGee had gotten a note from an uncle which read, in part, "Your [post]-card found us about as usual. I am truly shocked at your careless chirography, especially when you write a card. It is almost inhuman to postmasters and their clerks since it is their duty to read all the cards lest something vulgar may be written on them" (E. McGee 1915: 56).

Although McGee's 1894 Papago field notes do not begin until October 24, by which time he was already about sixty miles south of Nogales, Arizona, and the international boundary, other sources fill in gaps of the preceding days. Two Dinwiddie photos were taken on October 3 of what were labeled a "Mexican Casa" and a "thatched casa"; locations were not given, but almost certainly were in southern Arizona. McGee says he and Dinwiddie began the fieldwork in September, and that in October "the party worked its way southward through the valleys of Santa Cruz and San Luis," suggesting that their route took them south of San Xavier to Amado Junction and from there southwestward along Sopori Creek to Arivaca and a valley in the vicinity of the San Luis Mountains (Powell 1897: xxix).

> The international boundary having been crossed temporarily [at Sásabe], two days were spent at Poso Verde, an exclusively Papago village on the headwaters of the Río Altar, and detailed studies of the various ethnologic features were made, attention being given also to collecting art products and procuring photographs showing art operations. The significant fact was developed that all the Papago of Poso Verde repudiate accultural religion and profess only aboriginal beliefs, though the influence of early Spanish survives in a form of baptism, sometimes by visiting priests, though generally (and preferably) by their own shamans in more primitive fashion. (Powell 1897: xxix)
>
> Here the leader [McGee] and interpreter [Lewis] remained several days, collecting information concerning the distribution of the Papago villages and rancherías, while Mr Dinwiddie was sent back to Tucson to make necessary changes in outfit. A few days later the party reassembled at Arivaca, Arizona, where surveys were made of extended prehistoric works. Thence the expedition moved eastward to the frontier at Nogales, where after some delay authority for extending the operations on Mexican soil was courteously accorded,

in response to representations made through the local officials to the federal officers of the Republic of Mexico. Leaving Nogales, the party proceeded southward, visiting several villages formerly occupied by Papago Indians but now abandoned, and finding rancherías occupied by representatives of the tribe at various points. (Powell 1897: lxii–lxiii)

A Tohono O'odham woman with an olla on her head walks toward the spring at Pozo Verde, ca. October 16, 1894. (2764-b-1)

Dates on Dinwiddie's photos make it clear they were at the Mexican customs house in Sásabe on October 13 and were in the Papago village of Pozo Verde on October 16. A sketch map in the National Anthropological Archives (MS. map, BAE MS. Cat. No. 2363) is labeled, "Los Ruinos, Arivaca Cañon, 2 miles above Arivaca—Pima Co., Ariz.—Surveyed by W J McGee & Wm Dinwiddie, October 17—1894." This archaeological site, probably a prehistoric ruin, was next to a windmill on N. Bernard's ranch.

Leaving Arivaca, the party headed east to Nogales, no doubt over the old Arivaca road to Amado, before turning south up the Santa Cruz Valley to Potrero Creek and the international boundary. Dated photos indicate the expedition was in Nogales, Sonora, on October 20 and 21, and by October 23 it was at least forty miles south of Nogales en route to Magdalena. The group had simply followed the main road paralleling the railroad tracks to San Ignacio, sixty miles from the border. They then continued on the road to Hermosillo, Sonora's capital city, where McGee learned about the Seri Indians, who surely must have sounded far more primitive to him than the few scattered families of Papago laborers he had encountered up to that point. He made arrangements to visit the Seris where they were temporarily camped next to Rancho San Francisco de Costa Rica, one of several ranching properties near the Gulf of California owned by Pascual Encinas, a prominent Sonoran rancher.

McGee's field camp at Pozo Verde, Sonora, ca. October 16, 1894. Left to right: teamster E. P. Cunningham, W J McGee, interpreter Jose Lewis. (2764-d-2)

L̸ooking north toward the border town of Nogales, Sonora, October 21, 1894. (Mex. 109: 3576[37])

McGee spent parts of November 2 and 3 at Costa Rica, interviewing a Spanish-speaking Seri through an English- and Spanish-speaking Mexican interpreter. Dinwiddie took photographs of Seris, many of them posed for the occasion. In total, McGee was with the Seris a maximum of sixteen hours, probably even less. Moreover, much of what he learned about Seris during that brief stay was from the hopelessly prejudiced perspective of his helpful and gracious Mexican hosts, men who by then had been battling these "savage" Indians for more than four decades.

When Spaniards first made their way into Seri territory in the sixteenth century, there may have been as many as five thousand Seris. In addition to their living along the Sonoran coast from as far south as Guaymas to as far north as the mouth of the Río de la Concepción, their inland range may at one time have extended as far east as the Río San Miguel where, in 1679, the mission of Nuestra Señora del Pópulo was founded for them by Jesuit missionaries. It is about a hundred air miles from Pópulo to the Gulf of California (Eckhart 1960: 37–39; Felger and Moser 1985: Map 1.1).

In pre-European times, Seri Indians had lived by hunting, gathering, and fishing. They were what anthropologists have since referred to as a nonagricultural band people; while the various theoretical implications of that status remain an ongoing source of discussion among anthropologists, the fact is that Seris produced none of their own food or materials for clothing and shelter but relied solely on what nature provided in their desert and ocean environment (Sheridan 1982; Spicer 1962: 14–15). When Spanish domestic livestock came into the Seri region, the stage was set for perpetual conflict. Seris, not surprisingly, began to harvest Spanish cattle as they had wild deer, pronghorns, and desert

M̸ariano Ballestere drives a burro loaded with fodder for the McGee expedition horses, near Imuris, Sonora, October 23, 1894. (Mex. 109: 3582[40])

bighorn sheep. Also not surprisingly, the owners of the livestock took exception to this aspect of Seri behavior, and a murderous cycle of raiding and vengeance warfare between Seris and outsiders was set in motion that lasted to the end of the nineteenth century. One especially egregious series of episodes of Seri and Mexican hostility occurred between 1855 and 1865, when Pascual Encinas, to whom McGee became indebted for whatever small success his expeditions may have had, decided to put a stop to the Seris' killing of his cattle by killing as many Seris as possible. Encinas believed he reduced the remnant Seri population by half during what became known as the Encinas War.[9]

When McGee arrived in Seriland, Seri numbers, by then probably fewer than three hundred, had collapsed to a pathetic remnant of their former size. He was seeing survivors of an endless war of attrition, descendants of a once-independent people who had been diminished to abject dependence on hostile neighbors who sometimes hunted them as they would wild game. It is even likely the Seris with whom McGee met, if not starving, were suffering from serious malnutrition. He noted the distended bellies of some of the children but failed to grasp in clinical terms what that may have indicated.

Late on November 4, McGee returned to Hermosillo. If the dates on Dinwiddie's photos are correct, Dinwiddie remained at the Costa Rica Ranch on November 5 taking pictures of Encinas family members. On November 7, the entire group headed back toward the United States, this time forsaking the road next to the railroad tracks and moving diagonally north-northwest to Caborca over an old route that had been the shortcut between Sonora and the goldfields of northern California. The road connected isolated ranches and mines in an especially arid part of Sonora that has remained remote and sparsely populated since 1894, a place where vast expanses are still without paved highways.

From Caborca he traveled east to Pitiquito and Altar, and from Altar, instead of heading up the Altar River valley to the Arizona-Sonora border at Sásabe, McGee took a more direct northerly route that brought him into the United States at the Papago settlement of San Miguel. Although this was Papago country, it was not until an executive order was issued on June 16, 1911, that part of the area around San Miguel was set aside as a reservation. And it was not until another executive order was issued on January 14, 1916, that San Miguel and other desert villages in Arizona were encompassed by the 2,700,000-acre Papago Indian Reservation created as a noncontiguous addition to those established earlier at San Xavier (1874) and Gila Bend (1882).

McGee returned to San Xavier and Tucson by heading north up the Baboquivari Valley along the west side of the Baboquivari Mountains. While his last diary entry for 1894 is November 17 at the village of Fresnal, we know from Dinwiddie photos that he was still in Fresnal on November 18, in the village of Little Tucson on November 19, and in the village of Coyote Sits (Ban Dak) on the west side of the north end of the Quinlan and Coyote Mountains on November 20. From there, on the same day, he followed the path eastward that is now paralleled, and partially covered, by Arizona State Highway 86. He, Jose Lewis Brennan, and Dinwiddie remained at San Xavier at least through November 24.

McGee's 1894 field notes, like those he kept in 1895, are filled with observations concerning the geology and topography of the country through which he was passing. He was also especially interested in the desert flora he was seeing for the first time. Lacking scientific names for the plants and not having a botanist's vocabulary, he did his best in layman's terms to describe what for him were exotic plants. By his 1895 expedition, not only did his botanical descriptions improve somewhat, but he collected voucher specimens for the National Herbarium, carefully making a record of these in his notes.

Itinerary, 1895   The route taken by McGee from San Xavier to Sásabe during November 10–12 remains somewhat uncertain. It seems probable, however, that he followed the road from San Xavier south to Amado and from Amado southwest through Arivaca to Sásabe as he had done the previous year. From Sásabe he seems to have taken a slightly different route south to Altar than the one he had followed north in 1894. In Altar he made sure his papers were in order and that he had the necessary legal permission for his Sonoran sojourn. From Altar he went west to Caborca in a fruitless effort to lease from a Frenchman residing there one of the latter's boats docked in the Gulf of California, in order to reach Tiburón.

In 1894, McGee had learned about the great prehistoric site of Las Trincheras southeast of Caborca, and he was anxious to examine it and have Johnson make a map of it. November 20 through 24 were spent at Las Trincheras, where Johnson did, in fact, make a map—since lost—of this terraced site. From Trincheras the expedition headed directly south to Rancho Costa Rica along the Río Bacuache.

During the intervening year, the Seris McGee was now intent on visiting had become involved in more hostilities with outsiders, including Papago Indians who had been hired by Mexicans to guard coastal ranches (McGee 1898b: 120–21). The result was that the Seris fled from McGee and his party, and while Seris doubtless saw them, McGee and his people never laid eyes on a single Seri in 1895 other than an elderly expatriate named Kolusio who lived in Hermosillo.

A portion of the Tohono O'odham village of Wa:k, with Mission San Xavier del Bac on the right, ca. November 23, 1894. (2789c)

McGee had a sloop built that the men used to transport themselves and their supplies and equipment from the mainland to Tiburón. The venture quickly became an adventure when for virtually the entire cold and windy month of December the enterprise became chiefly a matter of attempting to stay alive. They were forced to cope with shortages of water and food, and it became a struggle to stay dry and warm, as shoes, boots, and other footwear wore out. The desert and the rough waters of the Gulf of California became far more formidable obstacles than frightened and fleeing Seris.

Nothing, however, deterred McGee, the museum man, from "making collections." In 1894 he had acquired artifacts from Papagos and Seris through trade and purchase. This time, however, he simply helped himself to whatever the hapless Seris had left lying around in their campsites: pottery, stone tools, and even a large balsa raft stolen on the mainland. As if that weren't enough, he looted a fresh Seri grave near Kino Bay, retrieving the skeleton of an adult female that still had human tissue on the bones and was accompanied by personal belongings, which he also took.

McGee never associated concepts like *stealing* and *looting* with these activities. In keeping with his time, he perceived himself as an ethnologist in the field bent on scientific collecting among primitive peoples who were living in a state of savagery. Anthropologist Jacob Gruber (1970: 1298) put the matter succinctly:

> The savage was the vulnerable party; it was he who was so consistently in the focus of salvage ethnography. The loss of the savage, so real to the anthropologist, pointed up his value. Salvage provided the opportunity for human contact and human contrast. Here savagery met civilization, the presumed past met the present, stability met change. In the knowledge of the savage and the realization of his extinction we came to know that unless we know all men, we can understand no man. For throughout, in the stress for salvage, we feel that in the disappearance of the savage, in the irrevocable erosion of the human condition, we inevitably lose something of our own identity.[10]

By January 2, McGee was back in Hermosillo. He had had enough field experience, so he took the train back to Arizona and to Washington, D.C. Johnson and the others retraced their route to Arizona, "collecting objects and information among the Papago Indians, and completing the triangulation and topographic surveys. [Johnson] reached Tucson about the end of January" (Powell 1898: xliv).

Fruits of the Trails

With two field trips behind him and with publication of *The Seri Indians* in 1898, McGee had secured his place among American anthropologists. He used his Sonoran Desert observations in scientific papers concerning sheetflood erosion, the origins of agriculture, the beginnings of the domestication of animals, acculturation across hostile cultural boundaries, the origins of marriage, and the interrelationships among plants, animals, human beings, water, and soil.[11] What historian Curtis Hinsley has called "McGee's sharp eyes and colorful imagination" enabled him to write reports based on a "slim foundation of careful, sometimes brilliant observations, and a large dose of theory" (Hinsley 1976: 349).

Much in McGee's published volume on the Seri has been thoroughly discredited by later observers, but it nonetheless remains the inescapable bedrock on which subsequent studies continue to stand. The book's voluminous historical information compiled from published and manuscript sources remains sound just as the descriptions and full-page illustrations of Seri artifacts—like the photos of Seris themselves—are important contributions to knowledge of the Seri. And while he never intended it as such, McGee's volume offers classic insight, however unflattering, into the early culture of American anthropology. One might say that the late nineteenth century was anthropology's "Lower Savagery" period.

While McGee was involved securing his credentials among anthropologists, so was he intent on securing his place in American science generally and in solidifying his position in the Bureau of American Ethnology. By 1884 he had joined the Anthropological Society of Washington, publisher of *American Anthropologist,* subsequently serving as an officer for fifteen consecutive years, three of them as president. He was among the founders of the American Anthropological Association and of its journal, the new series of *American Anthropologist.* He was a charter member of the American Association of Museums; a charter member and one of the organizers of the Archaeological Institute of America; a one-time president of the National Geographic Society, which he had been instrumental in founding; a founder of the Columbia Historical Society of Washington; and a founder of the Geological Society of Washington. When the various Washington scientific societies banded together in 1898 as the Washington Academy of Sciences, only McGee was a member of all its dozen constituent organizations. So was he a member of Washington's prestigious Cosmos Club (Hinsley 1976: 355, 394, 475).

In November of 1900, McGee ventured off on what turned out to be his last anthropological field trip. As he summarized it in his own words:

> The party comprised W J McGee, in charge; De Lancey Gill, artist; Professor R. H. Forbes, of Tucson, a guest during part of the expedition; John J. Carroll and Jim Moberly, stockmen; Aurelio Mata, Mexican customs officer, and Ramon Zapeda, Mexican interpreter, with Hugh Norris, Papago interpreter. The entire route was from Phoenix to Gila Bend; thence via Ajo to Quitobaquito and Santo Domingo; thence to Sonoyta and southward via Quitobac, Cozon, and Las Tajitas to Caborca; next westward to the Gulf shore (at the point recently occupied by the now extinct Tepoka tribe), and thence back, mainly by new routes, to Santo Domingo. From this point the Old Yuma Trail was traversed to Tinajas Altas, and thence via Gila City to Yuma, whence the expedition pushed on to the Cocopa country, near the mouth of Colorado river, afterward returning via Yuma and the Gila valley to Phoenix. (McGee 1901: 130)[12]

The "Tepoka tribe" to which McGee refers was a label bestowed on one of the former bands of Seri Indians (Moser 1963: 14–15). Except for McGee's seeing a few
Papagos encamped next to the Mexican settlement of Santo Domingo and very
briefly visiting among Cocopahs living near the mouth of the Colorado River
(Alvarez de Williams 1975: 96–102), this 1900 expedition was as unproductive of
ethnological value as the 1895 trip had been. McGee's luck in finding Indians in
the field was not very good.

McGee's multitudinous activities—social, scientific, and political—in Washington were not enough to rescue him when his mentor, John Wesley Powell,
died in 1902. Samuel P. Langley, who was secretary of the Smithsonian Institution
from 1887 until his death in 1906, and who had never liked McGee or his brand
of science, selected William Henry Holmes to succeed Powell as director of the
Bureau of American Ethnology. The humiliation forced McGee out of Washington, and he moved to St. Louis, where he became chief of the anthropology
department of that city's Louisiana Purchase Exposition of 1904. He became like
a father figure to groups of people he assembled there from all over the world:
Ainu, African pygmies, Tehuelche, Japanese, Filipinos, Patagonians, and representatives of Indian tribes from throughout North America, Geronimo included. Here
"on the fairgrounds in the middle of America, . . . they reconstructed their village
lives and demonstrated their arts, crafts and ceremonies for the onlookers" (Hinsley 1976: 474; Rydell 1984: 160–67).

When the fair ended, McGee tried to organize support for a planned St.
Louis Public Museum, but the effort seems not to have gotten beyond an office
and some letterhead stationery. While still living in St. Louis, McGee headed back
to the Sonoran Desert, this time to the Tinajas Altas Mountains in southwestern
Arizona that he had visited in 1900. The reasons he gave for the trip were "partly
to purify his body and burn out the typhoid, partly 'to get away from my beloved
fellow-mortals until my affection for them is regenerated,' and partly to study
plant utilization of solar energy to produce water" (Hinsley 1976: 475).

It was while he was camped at Tinajas Altas in August that McGee had an
extraordinary encounter with a Mexican prospector who had become lost and left
without water for several days. McGee later wrote an account of rescuing this man
and the effects of his severe dehydration (McGee 1906). McGee's essay intrigued
desert explorer Bill Broyles, who set out in the 1980s to retrace the lost man's steps
and experience some of the same deprivations. He did so, and lived to write about
it (Broyles 1982).

The final productive years of McGee's life are summarized by Hinsley
(1976: 475–77):

> McGee returned to Washington and government work in March
> 1907, as an expert in the Bureau of Soils of the Department of Agri-
> culture. That summer, while camping in the California Sierras, he
> and Gifford Pinchot laid the plans for what became the conservation
> movement of the early twentieth century.[13] Pinchot later called
> McGee the "scientific brains of the conservation movement." In one
> respect McGee's final years in conservation constituted an anticlimax
> to his more illustrious years in geology and anthropology. In institu-

tional terms, certainly, he ended up as a mere "expert" in an obscure government research bureau. But McGee never measured personal value entirely in institutional terms, and perhaps we should not either. For in another sense he fulfilled his scientific life in these years.

By early 1909 McGee had become a member of the executive committee of Gifford Pinchot's National Conservation Commission, whose goal was nothing less than to conserve the nation's waterways, forests, mines, and irrigable lands. It was because of this group that the word *conservation* gained currency in the national consciousness. Pinchot credited McGee with

> formulating the plan for the [Theodore] Roosevelt Inland Waterways Commission. . . . As [Vice Chairman and] Secretary of this Commission . . . McGee played a part in the development of our rivers the importance of which it would be impossible to overstate. . . .
>
> His work in conservation dealt with navigable streams, water power, irrigation, potable water from wells and springs, and streams, the laws of streamflow, the whole subject of erosion, including as a single example the methods of avoiding erosion by contour plowing on hilly land, the protection of coal and oil lands from misappropriation, the saving of phosphate lands for the people, forestry, with particular emphasis on the Appalachian National Forest, the public lands, the whole question of country life, etc. . . . He was a great gentleman. (Washington Academy of Sciences 1916: 21–24)

On September 4, 1912, McGee died alone in his room at the Cosmos Club in Washington, with neither his estranged wife nor his children near him. It was characteristic of the agnostic McGee that he had willed his body to the Jefferson Medical College of Pennsylvania and his brain to Dr. E. A. Spitzka. At the same time Spitzka got John Wesley Powell's brain, which McGee had had since 1903. There had been a friendly rivalry between the two men over the size of their brains. Powell won: 1,488 grains to McGee's 1,410 grains (Washington Academy of Sciences 1916: 59–60).

It was also characteristic of McGee that he should have been keeping track of the progression of the prostate cancer that killed him and that his account—as objective as if he had been writing about someone else—would be published posthumously (McGee 1912). The first signs of the disease had manifested themselves in Sonora at the foot of the Sierra Seri in 1895.

According to Hinsley (1976: 476–77):

> McGee ended his life in science condemning wasteful, individualistic American capitalism and turning to the models of aboriginal Americans for alternative modes of organizing society and using resources. Gifford Pinchot recalled that McGee, a man of "constructive imagination," made him see that "monopoly of natural resources was only less dangerous to the public welfare than their actual destruction." Adopting the iconoclastic view of American history coming into vogue among progressive reformers, McGee came to believe that the

dreams of the founding fathers had been subverted as "the People became in large measure industrial dependents rather than free citizens." This had occurred because the national habit of giving away land and resource rights to individuals had developed into an unprecedented "saturnalia of squandering the sources of permanent prosperity. . . ."

. . . McGee called for a nobler patriotism, honesty of purpose, a warmer charity, a stronger sense of family, and a "livelier humanity, in which each will feel that he lives not for himself alone but as a part of a common life for a common world and for the common good. . . ."

. . . To his credit, McGee never lost faith. A champion of American individualism in science, technology, and commerce most of his life, McGee in the end foresaw and demanded its demise in order to return to what the desert had shown him: that man, like all life, must band together for the common welfare. For McGee this was the goal and final lesson of anthropology.

TRAILS TO TIBURÓN

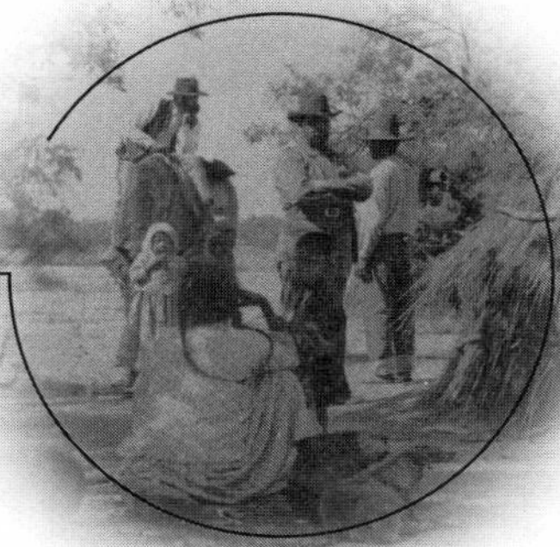

Papago Trip, 1894

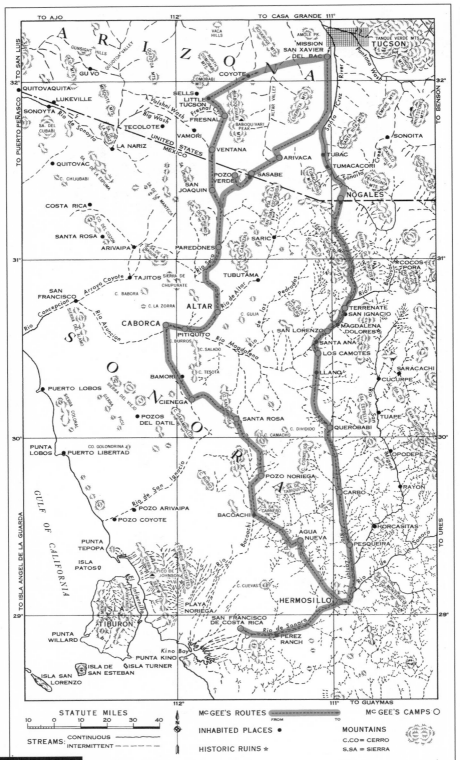

Route of the 1894 Expedition

Map by Ronald Ives

W J McGee

Bureau of American Ethnology
Washington, D.C.

Papago Trip, 1894.

If lost, finder will receive a reward of five
dollars ($5.00) for returning to above address.

OCT. 24, 1894. • TERENATE[1] TO SAN LORENZO.[2]
15 MILES (BREAKDOWN)[3]

The supposed mesa below the knob overlooking the river proves to be almost throughout its length a mass of rock, the usual crystallines, clad with pitahaya;[4] for here is another gorge analogous to that at Agua Caliente[5] though broader; and below it the mesas are no more at present. The bottom is luxuriantly wooded and weeded save in the fields, for which all the low water is taken. The weeds are enormous; wild sunflower [*Helianthus* spp.] is 2½ or 3 in. thick and 15–20 ft. high; weeds (like pampas grass) are an inch thick and twenty or more feet high;[6] and other weeds in proportion. They trammel the fields and grow along the ditches and fences in the utmost luxuriance and profusion, probably ⅓ of the available water and soil energy of this beautiful valley are expended in support of weeds. The reed, it is true, is used by the Indian in small quantity, and even by the Mexicans, being propagated by cuttings, but it remains a weed.[7]

After all, the mesas do not end completely, though they are low and narrow; for San Ignacio is on one of the finest of them. S. I. is a quaint, typical Mexican town, without a wooden roof save in a single new mill building of brick, and with this exception, and the church all of adobe, one story.[8] The church is chiefly of adobe and stucco, with a curious buttress of boulders, and an ornately carved door. It was photographed by Mr. Dinwiddie, and as he made ready two bystanders went down and sat on a low ledge supporting a wing; then a woman with a child-in-arms walked half a block to get in; then came some more men; then the señors and señoritas begin assembling by twos and singly, until a goodly representation of the population of quaint old San Ignacio were posing in the sun in front of the old church. An old beggar woman, walking on her hands, knees to chin, worked her way painfully toward the group, but too late.[9]

Below San Ignacio the mountains on the E. become more recent volcanics, and a true mesa looms in the background. In the west the mountains give place to swelling ranges of hills, which about San Lorenzo are not at all prominent. The mesa of San Ignacio soon disappears, showing a single broken metate and a circular mound as sole relics of the past. The dealer in Magdalena[10] says that many pictographs adorn the cliffs of the Cocospera [River] and that a few occur near Terenate on cliffs overlooking the Magdalena [River].

Directly opposite [east of] San Lorenzo, and only a little way beyond the river, rises a bald knob of red volcanic rock, probably identical with the slightly vesicular reddish lava in the spur jutting out of the river below Magdalena; and off to S.E. appears to be a long stretch of volcanic rock more modern than usual, culminating in the distant mesa no longer in sight.

A sprinkle of rain going into camp, heavy rain E.

*E*ighteenth-century mission church of San Ignacio de Caburica, Sonora, southeast elevation, October 24, 1894. (Mex. 109: 3583)

*T*he "old beggar woman" who was unable to join the group picture at the mission church, San Ignacio, October 24, 1894. (Mex. 109: 3587[68])

*T*ownspeople assembled by the mission church, San Ignacio, October 24, 1894. (Mex. 109:3584[19])

[THURSDAY, OCT. 25, 1894. • SAN LORENZO TO
LA CAMOTES.[11] • 18 MI. 15 FOR WAGON • 5 MI. DOUBLE]

On W. the river valley is broad, running away off to N.N.W. in a broad valley bounded on E. by a range of mountains of which the bald knob opposite is representative, and of which the distant mesa is a continuation; and on W. by a range with a culminating peak analogous to Baboquivara[12] called Cí-vo-ta by the Papago, Cióta[13] by Mexicans, it having been in the past an Apache watchtower, with which many definite traditions and still more legends are connected. The intermediate valley is a rolling land into which the "mesa" grades; it might be called a table lid but for the overlooking mountains; and it sweeps around the southern end of the Ciota range, and apparently far descends the Magdalena [River].

> th w
> *Cí-vo-ta*

The flora remains superb; great mesquites [*Prosopis* spp.] abound; the organ cactus [*Stenocereus thurberi*] comes in; two feathery palms,[14] giants in stature, grow apparently in an ancient priestly garden in old Santa Ana;[15] and weeds continue to prevail. No water in the Magdalena, but plenty at 25 ft. and a strong permanent flow at 40 ft. in Santa Ana station, a few feet above the lowest river bottom on old flood plain.[16]

Old Santa Ana is quite old, and many houses are in ruins; and it is noticeable that the ruins eventually assume the form of mounds, rounded in plan or elliptical according to the form of the structure, square or oblong. One mound carried a little monument bearing a cross. No prehistoric remains were found though it is probable that they would be revealed by search.

Mission Santa María Magdalena, Sonora, October 24, 1894.
(Mex. 109: 3586[21])

Mexican blacksmith shop, Santa Ana, Sonora, October 25, 1894. (Mex. 109: 3594[22])

Mexican house, a swinging cradle . . . and two children and a woman," on the road between San Lorenzo and Santa Ana, October 25, 1894. (Mex. 109: 3593[74])

No Papago at Santa Ana, old or new. Generally there are some at old S. A., but the group (of two or three families) have gone down the river 6 or 7 miles. At Santa Marta, a league below San Lorenzo, there formerly dwelt continuously a family of Papago, which was a nucleus for a nomadic group; but the son shot the father in a domestic difficulty some years ago, and the family were scattered, a part going to Cavorca.[17] A group of Yaqui[18] were at Santa Ana loafing around the station.

Below Santa Ana the road soon leaves the valley and ascends to the mesa on the S.E.; and at last the monotony of volcanic rock is broken, and a heavy bed of half-crystalline limestone crops out, dipping E. about 20°. No fossils were seen; the limestone is apparently rather argillaceous, with a little chert. From the mesa proper the Siota valley with its bounding ranges shows well; but the break in the range is broad, though a low sierra appears to be present, it W. of Comote's ranch. The valley is probably 20 mi. wide, and is here occupied by railway.

The sahuara [saguaro, *Carnegiea gigantea*] continues, and seems very much at home, young specimens in all stages of development being seen. On the mesa, or in the valley, greasewood[19] reappears, and in the grass patches the forms of the ants become vast, often 30–40 feet across.[20]

Clouds but no rain. It should be observed that last eve. there was a magnificent display of color in storm clouds in E., reflecting sunset colors, perhaps; and at the same time a rainbow of most gorgeous colors, especially the red; and the red and pink background brought out the green of the bald knob opposite and of the lesser knobs and swells, so that the mountains seemed clothed in the most luxuriant verdure.

And after nightfall we went down to the Yaki shelter to witness "la pasquala," an Indian dance with music and a sort of word play which is supposed to be highly amusing. The actor was absent, unfortunately, so we had to content ourselves with a musical performance. The instruments were a drum, a flute, and a violin. The violin was not seen, the operator remaining in the background. The drum and flute were operated by the same person. The former consisted of a shell cheesebox 18± in. in diameter and 3± in. deep, with heads of raw deerskin fastened to rings of wood (apparently) considerably larger than shell (¾ in. or 1 in.), then corded, exactly as with us except for lugs, with a thing which passes around rings. Both heads are alike; one hole (½ in.) in shell. It is tuned finally by heating before the fire. It is played sitting (squatting) on the ground, set on the left leg, and held by wrist and side of left hand, the beating being with right hand, and the fingering of the flute with the thumb and two fingers of the left. The flute is of reed, being made in two lengths, joined about the middle by a slide joint apparently. It is 20 or 21 inches long; the blowing end is fashioned exactly like a boy's whistle, notch and all, save that the end of the reed is not closed except by the piece of wood forming the wind aperture, and this seems to extend forward to a thin plate or sliver forming a reed. At 12 in.± from wind end there is a hole ½ in. in the bottom, on which the thumb is placed; at about 16 and 17 in. are two holes on top, played by fingers. The instrument is about ¾ in. in diameter. The drum gives time or rhythm alone in a beat at first simple (two light quick taps followed by a heavy), but later becomes more complex; it is played some time before the fluting begins. The flute gives a simple, short melody repeated over and over again with no change except in verve, and is said to be an imitation of the song of a bird, different bird songs giving different airs. The bird song is confessedly conventionalized greatly, but the skillful musicians are said to give the bird song with close fidelity.

The camp was not lighted save by the fitful gleam of the fire, which threw most of it in shadow, the principal operator sat near the blaze, facing it; the violin chimed in at intervals from the unseen background; the squaws and alternately fretting and suckling babies were occasionally seen in the glow of the starting fire or dimly in the starlight as the fire died away; and the companion of the musician, smoking Mr. Dinwiddie's cigarettes, wrapped in a gay serape, sat in the firelight; and all made a most effective picture.[21]

It may be added that the Mexicans here are a most simple-minded folk, probably 50 or 60% Indian, their mode of life differing little from that of the aboriginal tribes. A boy came up to camp with two eggs, which he desired to exchange for coffee; and the ranchero from whom we purchased "corn-hoy"[22] desired to dispose of a melon, also, for 20 cts. (Mex), 10 cts. in sugar and 10 cts. in cash.

FRIDAY, OCT. 26, 1894.
CAMOTES TO QUEROBABI.[23] • 42 MILES

The valley already noted continues, and it becomes evident that the eastern wall is a volcanic range, with many mesa-scarps, beginning with the butte, opposite San Lorenzo. The W. rim is again broken nearly opposite Llano,[24] the range being small between the two breaks, and made up of rather irregularly dispersed buttes, some so sharp as to suggest igneous rocks of considerable heterogeneity. The valley retains its plain character; Llano is well round. There is surprisingly abundant grass, with great ant forms, and abundant though not surprisingly large mesquites, and the sahuara extends well down the slopes to the plain. From Llano the road followed is quite direct E.S.E. for Querobabi, and a spur sits out from the eastern valley rim, Sierra Coraca [Caracahui]—, and the road crosses the foothills of the spur, which is made up of scattered sharp peaks. At one point rock is exposed— the typical blue limestone of E. Mex., eroded in the usual way into miniature mountains, of which a Kodak was taken. The debris seen during the day, however, indicates that the prevailing rocks are igneous. S.W. of Llano a low western rim of the valley rises again, in scattered buttes and ridges of little prominence. S. of the spur of Sierra Coraca the valley stretches away to E. again, and a spur coming up from S. divides it some miles N.W. of Querobabi. It is this spur which is described above; the main rim is more continuous and prominent. Querobabi is in the midst of a broad mesquite plain, with several ranches, a stone-walled reservoir, a few Papago houses, and a station a mile from the old town. Water at station is tanked from Llano.

No well-preserved antiquities seen. A mile or two S. of Camotes there are a number of vaguely defined mounds that would repay examination; and at southern extremity, on a natural elevation of some 20 ft., there is a stone monument, laid in mortar, carrying a plain, flimsy wooden cross. Another such occurs on the divide of the Sierra Coraca spur, the monument being triangular in plan, 6 ft. sides at base, 4½ ft. high, with cross broken out.[25] In Querobabi Valley, between station and old town there is a vague linear and rectilinear surface configuration suggesting fields, and a rude metate stone (not shaped) and a few stones evidently artificially shaped, were seen lying about; but all may be historic.

Living Papago were found in a small camp at the first waterway S. of Llano, perhaps 4 mi. from town, and also at Querobabi. At the former locality there are two families, brothers, with 7 persons seen and at least one absent. Two houses, both photographed. The more typical is about 9 ft. in diameter and 5 ft. high, supported by two mesquite posts and a cross beam, with about a dozen mesquite branches set upright in a circle in the ground with tops bent over to rest on the beam and interlaced to form a fairly strong lattice or basket-work roof. Then over all sage brush is laid in rude thatch fashion, and two loops, of slender mesquite boughs joined, are girded about, and a few more are bound over the top. The door is an open space about 27 in. wide and 30 high. The furniture consisted of two ollas, a fictile cup, three small ollas, stones with the embers of a fire almost in center of hut (but no smoke opening), a rude pillow and a few rags forming a bed, rolled up. The other house is larger and more pretentious, about 12 ft. across, rudely rectangular, and 5½ ft. high, with doorway full height. It is supported at one side by two mesquite crotches and crossbeam, at other side by a strong horizontal branch of the mesquite tree under which it is built. The thatching is the same as in the other house. In both cases the roof is used as a storehouse of miscellaneous articles, fabrics, pieces of rawhide, and ollas and jars not in use, as well as corn in ear and small bags of provisions of various sorts, the function of some of these things being in part the shedding of water and the improvement of the roof. In one case (smaller house) a store house is a rude receptacle stuck up in the mesquite tree shading the doorway. The child's cradle hung in the branches of the same tree; it consists of a rawhide rope and a few rags of civilized fabrics.[26] The chief kitchen in each case is out of doors near the door. Only one metate and grinder was seen, at the smaller house.[27] It is an elaborate mill of Mexican manufacture. The one other accultural article was a metal-rimmed sifter, through which the meal is apparently rubbed. Ollas and olla-stones[28] and fictile cups made up the rest of the kitchen outfit. In the larger house, apparently belonging to the younger brother, there were lying about an old tin can or two, a canteen, and a few other accultural articles with a predominance of primitive. This is a permanent residence of the two families, who plant a little corn and a few squashes, subsisting chiefly on mesquite beans, game, and cacti.[29]

*T*he more typical" of two Tohono O'odham houses at a two-family settlement four miles from Querobabi, Sonora, October 26, 1894. Jose Lewis is astride the horse; McGee stands with arms folded across his chest. (2779-p)

*T*he larger of the two Tohono O'odham houses near Querobabi, October 26, 1894. (2788h)

At Querobabi there are four or five families, permanent residents, with a headman or chief, who inherited his office; he is now an old man. There is no "doctor," and in case of illness a shaman is called from one of the settlements in the next valley westward.[30] About 25 individuals were seen. As at Pozo Verde,[31] they decry religion, yet all the children are baptized, part by a priest a day's journey away S.E., generally by one of their own people in primitive fashion.[32] All speak more or less Spanish, none English, none go to school or to church except on the occasion of baptism. We spent an hour through Lewis as interpreter, and tried a flashlight picture of the group. On leaving, distributed a few trifling presents and an invitation to breakfast.

[**SATURDAY, OCT. 27, 1894.**
QUEROBABI TO CARBO.[33] • **28 MILES.**]

Another visit to Papago village, Cho-hó-quent[34]-chut-a-wah'-fia (Cho-hó [grass—really a roadside weed] plenty well among = well among the weeds); Querobabi is the same; quero meaning the same weed, bá-vi, well (not to be confounded with bá-bo, stone),[35] gave a number of photos, etc. The houses and people were specially swept and garnished in anticipation, 5 men having accepted the breakfast invitation. It is Papago etiquette to approach a house, or group, or individual with indifference, their presence being ignored.[36] After a few minutes, conversation begins, as though a renewal of previous talk. There are no words for greeting or parting, and salutations and goodbyes are breaches of etiquette, though no longer serious if Spanish is used; for a veneer of Spanish courtesy is taken on with the tongue. In the same way handshaking is tolerated, though generally with scant grace; many of Lewis's old acquaintances parting from him with a handshake, and a few greeting him in the same way, generally after a moment's indifferent silence. Neither have they any word for gift or present, the word corresponding to "give"[37] covering loan, sale, handing over for examination, etc., and requiring repetition and gesture elaboration to be understood as conveying ownership. And when an invitation is extended, etiquette demands an indifferent silence of some duration, and a final ungracious acceptance. The breakfast invitation was really not accepted at all last evening; Lewis says a woman jocularly remarked that they (the women) would all go and leave the men at home, but this was merely a stage aside, though productive of much mirth. The formal acceptance was the presence of the five men. Then when they were invited to seat themselves at the canvas spread on the ground in lieu of a table, they ignored the remark and gazed about apathetically; after some two minutes, during which I was dishing up bacon and beans and Lewis explaining the custom, one diffidently advanced and the others soon followed. In several cases when the plate was passed the intended recipient gazed into vacancy a moment, with the outstretched plate before him, before ostensibly seeing it and reaching to take it. But the old Mexican carpenter showed no such compunction, seizing a whole handful of sugar and taking a spoon petulantly away from his better-bred Papago neighbor. Few of the Indians accepted a second help, and all impressed one as naturally courteous, despite the utter dearth of terms of courtesy.

It may be observed that when a favor is asked of a Papago, as to take his picture, he does not at once grant it, but puts on

A "flashlight picture" of Jose Lewis, left, and other Tohono O'odham men at Querobabi, October 26, 1894. (2762-L-1 or 2[?])

A Mexican carpenter and beggar, said by McGee to be seventy-nine years old, at Querobabi, October 27, 1894. "He had supper and breakfast with us in camp, and he did not know what bacon and yeast powder biscuit was, and he would not eat it. His only covering at night was the ragged blanket suspended from his shoulders." (Mex. 109: 3605[23])

a mantle of apathy, lasting some minutes; then it is generally granted, for the people are most kindly and good-hearted.

The chief purpose of the visit was to secure photos of houses and people. The houses are modelled after Mexican types, one being chiefly of adobe, with jacal[38] addition and shed, the others of jacal type, i.e., sheds walled with palo-mata spikes,[39] etc., and roofed with earth resting on weeds (the "grass" of the local name in large part) supported on sahuara segments and palo-mata branches lying on the cross beams. The bedding is primitive in quantity at least, consisting of a few serapes, blankets, etc., but mainly rags and tatters, remnants of old clothes. A group [picture] was taken first, including a young man from Hermosillo, with luxuriant hair well down on forehead, named Pedro Flores, who desires a copy of the group. The chief figure in the group is the lady of the house on left, Juana Rosara, with child at breast, and her family, with others, stand about. The picture of the house shows some of the same group with two or three of Juana's children and an invalid in blanket in this house suffering from disordered stomach consequent on pregnancy (she was "loaded" as the information was conveyed to me). Then, standing in the rear of the house, Juana, with the inexhaustible fount still flowing into the infinite capacity of that child, and several of her family, were taken; then several not including the big-headed boy in a waist-jacket who always wept vociferously when the camera was directed toward him. Next, standing in the same place, Juana's two eldest daughters (unmarried, judged 16 and 18; elder on right) were taken, Mariana Au-ra-ké-ras (the elder) and Laura (or Lora) Au-ra-ké-ras. The elder is exceptionally handsome and sprightly, with graceful, erect carriage—too handsome for a type. The younger, too, is considerably above the average. Juana herself is a better type; she looks 35 or 40. None know age even approximately. Next the partly adobe house was taken, with the owner, his wife, Francisca and others standing about. Then the owner and wife (Checo Marguerita looks 40–45, husband, Laura (or Lora) Martine, 35–40, wife), with two infants, were taken in the doorway; and later the wife's cousin, Francisca Martinas (unmarried, looks 19), with her godchild Marcie Martinas (looks 8 or 10), were taken. Francisca had baptized the child, without the aid of a priest, and thus acquired some title to her, apparently, and would not be photographed without her.[40] Francisca is a fair type of young Papago females, hardly so handsome of features as the average, and a little more robust and better developed of figure. She was seen at work last evening, washing with great industry, her waist removed and a Mexican chemise covering her shoulders and chest, displaying muscular and shapely arms and neck. Lewis was greatly surprised to see girls so old as the three, Francisca, Mariana, and Lora, unmarried. The chief unfortunately was absent; all want photos to be sent in his care. His name is Santiago, the Indian surname, if any, being unknown to his people. The custom of using Spanish prenames[41] is hardly fixed, though most of the Papago employ them; and when used, they are never changed throughout the lifetime of the individual. The Indian name, on the contrary, is changed frequently, through mere whim, through the death of another bearing the same name (when the name is abandoned by other bearers), through the defeat of a competitor in a race, etc.[42] It appears that very few children are baptized by the priests, partly at least because of inaccessibility, the nearest priest being at Opodepe, on San Miguel River, a long day's journey away. The people were eminently cheerful and curious, very few showing the least trepidation or restraint—except the small boy caught with the Kodak by Mr. Dinwiddie lying on a mat, who once more burst into dolorous wails; but he came promptly to me, with the most brilliant expression of joy on his face, when I offered him a dime; and the women and children, and even the men, were highly amused by the incident, laughing gleefully. It should be noted that they are quite affectionate, the mothers fondling and kissing their babies regardless of horribly dirty faces, and elder children being hardly less demonstrative to the little ones. The elder children, too, are kindly to one another, no trace of selfishness or ill temper being seen; and the adult girls are as gregarious as white damsels—last evening the three noted above, after an exchange of inconspicuous nudges and glances, went out evidently to attend calls of nature in a flock, evidently, again, going only around the corner, so short was their stay. There is a sense of hospitality, too, shown well by the women spreading a sheet of canvas on the ground near the fire for the white visitors; after which they withdrew from the foreground, grouping themselves, with one exception, on one side of the rude rectangle, rather in the shadow. A few of them smoked as the tobacco and cigarette papers went around, but they seldom took part in the conversation, and then but briefly; yet they paid close attention—my remark, that my wife eats as much as I, though I weigh 200 and she only 100, brought, when translated by Lewis, an immediate giggle from the women's side, and slower mirth from the men. Indeed their conversation generally is carried on for the group of Indians by one of their number, the others remaining silent; the selection appears natural, a change being made now and then; during the evening there were two spokesmen, one earlier, the other after the formal exchange of views, etc., was completed; the second relating to Lewis personally an account of the Yaqui revolution and the governmental suppression of sale of cartridges to all Indians.[43] The people here deny the possession of civilized religion, and pay no attention to sabbath—except that if they have money they join the Mexicans in drinking mescal on that day.

The road follows the broad valley, so broad that except for the bounding mountains in the distance it would seem a limitless plain. It is rather luxuriantly clothed with mesquite, and large patches of luxuriant, though golden, grass appear. Where rocky the palo verde prevails, and it is noticeable that the tree is no longer leafless; there are two varieties, one with an entire pea-like leaf, and a

*T*ohono O'odham children standing next to a walled shed at Querobabi, October 27, 1894.

*F*rancisca Martinas (right) and her godchild, Marcie Martinas, by a "partly adobe" house at Querobabi, October 27, 1894. (2745-b)

*H*ouse and some children of Juana Rosara at Querobabi, October 27, 1894. (2787-a)

*W*J McGee, right, and Tohono O'odham at Querobabi, October 27, 1894. Juana Rosara stands with family members, including, next to her, her eldest daughter, Mariana Aurakéras, and second daughter, Laura ("Lora") Aurakéras. (2787-d)

more common one with a mesquite-like leaf, very small.[44] The mountains are not conspicuous, though the rugged character of those on E. indicates volcanic character. Those near by on W. are a succession of buttes. A butte approximately within a mile or two, named Tavaca, is a conspicuous object, apparently arising abruptly from the plain thus. ⎯⎯⌒⎯ Among the rocks of the arroyos and ridges there are a good many pumice fragments, such as are used for metates; and the Papagos at Querobabi report that they got their largest metate from the nearest arroyo. Another metate was seen near Q., and still another, broken, midway to Carbo, with no other traces of settlement. From halfway to Carbo the road is near center of valley, and the soil assumes an alkaline character, and a fine, playa-like texture is displayed in the arroyos. A new cactus, that growing in great patches, with many dead stems, is prominent.[45]

> ## SUNDAY, OCT. 28, 1894
> ## CARBO TO PESQUEIRA.[46] • 27 MI. (TEAM LOST)

The plain of the Zanjon[47] continues broad and generally well-clothed with mesquite, palo verde, pitahaya, golden grass, and other vegetation; and the land grows greener, though no water is seen; but there are steam pumps and primitive windlass and horse-pulley arrangements at the dozen ranches seen. On the west the mountains approach somewhat and become more conspicuous and continuous; the profile rather strongly suggesting igneous rocks. In E. there is a first rather low series of buttes like that in W. yesterday though more continuous, and beyond, though not distant (probably cis-. San Miguel[48]) rises a parallel sierra of exceedingly rugose

WJ McGee "turning out" at 6:30 a.m. at Carbó, Sonora, October 28, 1894. (Mex. 109: 3616[93])

profile, one knob in particular sitting like a huge chair on a pile of benches, apparently relatively new volcanics; and beyond, in the blue distance, a somber, massive range, probably beyond the San Miguel [the Sierra Aconchi]. The rocks seen are a variety of crystallines, though some seem metamorphic. The road is most devious and dusty, with several crossings of the great arroyo of El Zanjon. A few metates were seen, but nothing indicative certainly of prehistoric rock work. Yaki live permanently at Noria Verde,[49] and probably at other ranches; no Papago.

> ## MONDAY, OCT. 29, '94.
> ## PESQUEIRA TO HERMOSILLO.[50] • 32 MI (BROKE KING BOLT)

The valley continues with unchanged character save that the variety of plant life increases; also its luxuriance. Two trees, closely similar, are prominent; one bears a sort of winter green pod of five lobes with brilliant scarlet beans in an apple-core-like pericarp, with no covering;[51] the other bears a hard, acorn-like pepper-pod with two seeds in it.[52] Both have whitish, hard-looking trunks and close branches, with abundant small, narrow, velvet-like dark green leaves, closely set on the branches, the whole forming a mass of rich green. The mesquite, too, grows greener; the palo verde takes on a fairly abundant foliage; and it is significant, perhaps, that certain general changes (with many exceptions) occur in the plants: 1, the thorns and spines are relatively less abundant; 2, the leaves are longer; and 3, the gray largely gives place to green.

The mountains on E. remain distant, and the front range breaks down, evidently at San Miguel, which thus makes a pass for itself, though not a conspicuous one; beyond the blue range remains massive and strong—probably forming collectively a Sierra Madre.[53] The foreground mountains look volcanic, old. On W. the mountains approach; they are a plexus of buttes rising from a general ridge, but becoming more mountain-like midway to Hermosillo. Here, or rather two or three mi. S. of Zamora, tepetate[54] occurs, not typically, but recognizably as a pudding stone of various pebbles in an abundant calcareous matrix, rather soft and friable; and on looking toward the mountains here a bold sierrita, already inferred to be limestone, was found to be made up of heavy inclined ledges, reminding one of the E. Sierra Madre. But farther southward the old type of scattered buttes, suggesting much worn igneous rocks, is resumed. Finally the rd. turns toward the range and actually crosses a pass in the range, the telegraph line crossing another. While the Sonora [River] cuts through a third, the range continuing S. and the broad valley noted above Santa Ana[55] sweeps on E.S.E. so far as can be seen from a commanding spur. Hermosillo nestles about the base of a butte 600 ft. high in the very center of the gateway through this range, the butte probably being the original bearer of the name.[56] Westward there is a vast stretch of plain with scattered buttes and short ranges rising from its surface; but no system can be seen. Rio Sonora runs at this season as a rather feeble stream to Hermosillo, but no water can be seen in the broad sandwash below town. The city is supplied with water from the river, and there is said to be a well, perhaps as a supplementary source. The range where crossed consists chiefly of a coarse-grained granite, with some

Looking over a portion of Hermosillo, Sonora. The Cerro de la Campana (Hill of the Bell) on the left, October 30, 1894. (Mex. 109: 3624[32])

finer-grained portions which are more obdurate and rise as peaks, the granite being predominantly gray with intercalations of darker granite, suggesting brecciation. This mass is frequently cut by dikes, or traversed by beds, of massive greenstone, perhaps diorite, just as at Nogales. In addition there are certain jaspery and nondescript rocks that may be metamorphosed sedimentaries. In the pass the rocks crop in ledges trending S.E. or S.S.E., oblique to range; and it is noteworthy that all the structure lines seen in this vicinity are parallel or approximately so, and oblique to the range.

[**TUESDAY, OCT. 30, 1894.**
IN CAMP AT HERMOSILLO. • 4 MI.]

In morning climbed the butte N. of telegraph pass to photograph city. It is about 450 ft. above camp, say 500 above city, composed of granite, generally coarse and gray with intercalations of greenish-gray granite on the lower slopes, fine and hard, ringing much however on crest. Here again the dikes or ledges of greenstone are noticeable. It is also noteworthy that in the foothills a good deal of tepetate occurs often as a cement for the pebbles. The photos, if successful, should illustrate well the type of country S.W. of Hermosillo—a region of old basin ranges, perhaps, now reduced to buttes, scattered or grouped, with vast torrential valleys between— a province that might appropriately be set apart as Western Mexican or Sonoran.

Luis explains that marriage is generally in the village, in order that parents and children may not be separated; but that in one case, near Quijotoa, two villages intermarry habitually. In this village the people have recently become converts to Mormonism.[57] In both cases it soon comes about that marriages occur between relations, and a considerable part of the marriages are more or less consanguineous. Generally certain prohibited relations are avoided; brother and sister do not marry; cousins of the first class (whose parents are children of same father and mother) do not marry; but beyond there seems to be no limitation.[58] One case of a father marrying his daughter is mentioned, though Luis charitably infers that the report of marriage was circulated to discourage suitors. The penalty for violation of the unwritten social code is simple, direct, and effective—the violators are "not respected."

Much is said hereabouts of the Neago Indians, who are said to be white, "whiter than you or I," often with blue eyes and red hair; they are said to all speak Yaki, and to be simply a branch of that tribe. There is much speculation as to their genesis.[59]

Luis visited a rancho, named Chanati, 6 miles down river, ½ mi. N. of channel where both Papagos and Seris are said to be located; no Seris were found, and the Papago say none have ever been there. There are two houses, with three families of Papago, about a dozen, possibly fifteen persons. They reside permanently; one cuts her hair round like the Yaki (as did the Hermosillo Papago seen at Vasquez). They dress like others, live in jacals like those near Llano, and do not farm. The men work occasionally for "the Governior," chiefly as vaqueros [cowboys], but subsist principally by hunting; the women make ollas for sale in addition to domestic duties. They describe another settlement of 8 families living 4 or 5 mi. S., probably near El Pozita, near a ranch. This group plant corn, melons, squashes, etc., on which, with mesquite beans and the like they commonly subsist; but in case of drought they work for or beg from the neighboring rancher, moving their habitation temporarily in order to do so the more efficiently. They also describe the village of Tonoga,[60] where there are 30 families; this we shall doubtless see.

WEDNESDAY, OCT. 31, 1894.
IN CAMP AT HERMOSILLO. • 4 MI.

The governor[61] was expected in his office, but remains junketing, with Secretary of State and other officers at Guaymas.[62] Called on the prefect of police with Mr. Forbes, exconsul, also one judge of supreme court.[63] All disclose the Seris cannot be visited without an escort of 10 or 15 armed men; in fact Hermosillo seems to be in a state of terror with respect to the Seris. Finally in despair of State aid,[64] by reason of the junket aforesaid, decided to go to the nearest ranch, that of Pasqual Encinas.[65] The prefect says there are some 70 men belonging to the tribe, with over 200 women and children, making a population of some 300; that they have no legal status, no right to the island of Tiburon, no arts or industries, but are just like animals, subsisting on raw fish and carrion. Occasionally a few visit Hermosillo to barter, when the State appears to exercise a sort of supervision over the sale, apparently to see that the poor Indian is not cheated. The Papago, on the contrary, are recognized as possessing civil rights, and are said to have title, e.g., to Pozo Verde.

THURSDAY, NOV. 1, 1894.
HERMOSILLO TO SAN FRANCISCO DE COSTA RICA. • 52 MI.

The route is somewhat S. of W., across the broad valley or torrential plains stretching to the coast, near the river course, on N. The flow is chiefly flood plain; within a mile of Señor Encinas's hacienda San Ignacio (3 mi. from town) there is a low "mesa" with creviced scarp, somewhat gravelly; the bottom being generally sandy at first. The mountain ranges are mostly within a few miles of Hermosillo ("Little Beautiful," or named after Gen. Hermosillo—Exconsul Forbes—formerly Pitic) and no definite arrangement can be seen save a linear extension N.–S., or rather N.N.W.–S.S.E. Generally the contours are rather sharp and irregular, suggesting igneous rocks. About 10 or 6 mi. out there is a low range on S., probably a mesa; about 10. mi. there is a more prominent range of igneous rock, perhaps 100 ft. high, apparently a lava stream not yet reduced or even eroded appreciably; it rises sharply from plain as if the earth were built around rather than from its mass. Then there is a long stretch without mountains some distant masses on N. with an isolated knob far N.W.—a vast, slightly undulating plain dotted with scant mesquite, equally abundant palo verde (chiefly mesquite-leafed, partly other), abundant pitahaya (which has a distinctive habit, more slender and abundant of branches than before) [*Stenocereus gummosus,* called "pitahaya agria" by Sonorans], occasional large patches of cholla,[66] a cholla-like tree cactus in which the branches are so long and slender as to make it appear a cross between cholla and palo verde,[67] and the star-section cactus called sina in considerable abundance [*Lophocereus schottii*]; also the poplar-leafed, purple-stemmed shrub noted from Llano.[68] Beyond the Perez ranch, 35 mi. from Hermosillo, there is a scattered range or group of peaks on S., rising sharply from plain; and 3 mi. W.N.W. of ranch there are two knobs which look like igneous jets pushed up through plain, from which they appear to rise sharply without talus. The sand of the plain grows fine and becomes dust; and toward Costa Rica the dust is fine and alkaline. Meantime the flora is more luxuriant, and among other plants the sahuara appears, scattered, rather stunted and ill-conditioned. The soil is of great fertility but water evidently scanty, at Costa Rica a good supply, slightly alkaline, is found at about 150 feet. The ranch is in the delta of Hermosillo or Sonora river, reached only during the annual freshet in July–August, rarely failing; the soil is rich, fine black loam, somewhat alkaline as indicated by slight efflorescence, with a labyrinth of wandering channels two or three yards wide and one deep. The prevailing vegetation is alité, which is said to be the best possible stock feed, better than true grasses.[69] The corn, beans, wheat, and other crops grown on Costa Rica ranch are of the greatest luxuriance, a stool of wheat (a selected sample) comprising 250 stalks, each of the great heads containing fully 50 grains on the average, the wheat being of the best quality. There is a considerable tract of mesquite here, dead because of a shift in current—evidently badly spoiled mesquite, since the ground water can not be very deep. The mesquite forest is quite thick, forest rather than orchard, though the trees are not so large as in Santa Cruz and Magdalena valleys.

[**FRIDAY, NOV. 2, 1894.**
IN CAMP AT SAN FRANCISCO DE COSTA RICA.]

We are guests of senior Pascual Encinas, owner of this ranch and several others (some concessions in recognition of his services anent the Seri Indians) together with other property galore. For more than twenty years he has been in contact with the Seri on the mainland and has several times visited Tiburon, at one time remaining over a week with a small party of vaqueros, engaged in prospecting. His first efforts were to convert and civilize the Indians, and his reward was slaughter of stock. He then notified the tribe that killing of cattle or horses would be punished by killing Seris; they continued the slaughter, and he began, personally and with the aid of his vaqueros; there were several engagements during a period of some years, the Seris losing about 250, mostly men (between 60 and 70 in a single action), and he losing one vaquero killed, 2 wounded, and half a dozen horses, one killed under him. His determined stand gradually did its perfect work, the killing of cattle was discontinued, and the Seris came to look on senior Pascual with affectionate admiration—or as nearly affectionate admiration as their sentiments and vocabulary permit. For some years he has gone among them fully unarmed, though seldom alone, and he has little fear, though he would not go on Tiburon with[out] at least two or three companions. He is, however, a man of exceptional, and indeed remarkable, intrepidity. He explains that the Seris use poisoned arrows, and that several of his horses were killed by means of these arrows, the wound being slight, but the animal becoming ill and dying within a few hours.[70] He considers them absolutely devoid of religion, and says they have no ceremonial except the puberty ceremonial for girls. He witnessed such a ceremonial on one occasion. A patch of ground was cleared, enclosed in boughs, and used as a dancing floor. At one end there was a sort of bower in which a young girl was seated. On inquiry he was informed that the purpose of the fiesta was to advertise the fact that the girl was menstruant and a woman.[71] He says they make excellent rafts of bamboos or reeds with which they cross the strait between the mainland and Tiburon and visit other islands;[72] also that their ollas are remarkably large, up to a barrel in capacity, extremely thin of wall, and small necked.[73] Their habitations are of the rudest; generally a depression is occupied or made by removing stones, a low ring of stones is put about it, and boughs of trees are arranged rudely about, a standing tree or two commonly utilized, and one or more shells of the green turtle used as a roof.[74] Their food is fish, shell-fish, water fowl, etc., largely eaten raw; on land they eat in addition the bura (large deer), small deer, wild hog or peccary, rabbit,[75] etc., as well as horses, mules, burros, cattle, swine, etc. belonging to rancheros, taking the carcasses of animals dead of disease and for days or a week and eating of the carrion raw, carrying away the remainder after gorging themselves. They catch deer, rabbits, etc. with the aid of dogs, though sometimes they run the animal down alone, their fleetness being unexampled.

Señor Pascual is over 70, a sufferer from cataract so severe that his vision is of shadows, his hearing defective; yet he volunteered at once to go to the ranch from his hacienda near Hermosillo, making two fifty-mile drives and spending two days there; he even offered to go to the coast, or to the island if a vessel could be obtained. He does not speak English, but fortunately Señor Alvemar-Leon,[76] who speaks Pacific Coast perfectly, was at his hacienda and consented to join the party. On reaching the ranch Señor Pascual sent a message to the Seris rancheria, and soon a dozen of them, including their interpreter Pelado (nick-name only)[77] were there. They seemed pleased to see him, and we walked up to the rancheria. This was the first of a half dozen visits.

Señor Pascual says the Indians have no mortuary ceremonies, though "they cry like the devil" (a typical bit of Señor Alvemar's interpretation) when one of their number dies, the women particularly, and paint their faces, black or white, the mourning lasting sometimes a fortnight. The body is generally buried, either in a shallow grave or low cairn or bushes are thrown over it. Señor Pascual saw the body of a chief's son treated in this way.[78]

There are a number of Papago here, though the men are absent hunting with the exception of one old man. Mr. Dinwiddie and Lewis have seen the rancheria and the people present. There are also a number of Yaki, most of the laborers or peons on the ranch being of that tribe. This is All Souls Day, and the Yaki have shrines erected for prayers for los muertos [the dead], and nearby are tables spread with food and delicacies for the worshipers. The shrine consists of a cross and usually an arch of paper fragments with a few flowers, tied to a bow of

wood, probably a sahuara segment. In one of the domiciles there is a more elaborate shrine consisting of a picture of the virgin (borrowed from the ranch) with a
white spread table and a burning candle before it, an arch being arranged above
and in front. Here two dancers were seen last evening, in front of this shrine, dancing to music and shaking gourd rattles in rhythm. Tomorrow comes the Paskola,
which is one of the events of the year among the Yaki.[79]

Went to Seris rancheria in accordance with pre-arrangement to take pictures. The tribe seems to have no words or gestures of greeting, though they are
less formal than the Papago, beginning conversation at once. They are not sullen
or taciturn, rather vivacious and sociable; and they took considerable interest in
the photograph, arranging themselves cheerfully, albeit clumsily, for the group
picture. Afterward individual photographs were taken of several, beginning with
the men. They posed readily, in some cases with alacrity, removing their short
shirts and putting on pelican-skin aprons without hesitation,[80] though there was
mirth and jeering among the tribe as well as among the Yaki onlookers. The men
are of splendid stature, with good chests, generally good though rather slender
arms, somewhat contracted waists, moderately broad hips, and slender, sinewy
legs, and lower leg particularly being noticeably thin. Faces are more mobile and
expressive than among the Papago, features stronger. Beard is rare and scanty; a
few have scattered face hairs, Pulado has a faint moustache, one man moustache
and chin, both feeble, two or three others weak moustaches. The scalp hair is luxuriant, long, coarse and straight, generally jet black though a few show a tawny
tinge. The axillar hair is short and scant, and one man in removing cotton dress
and substituting pelican skin accidentally (though indifferently) displayed fairly
full and somewhat curly pubic hair. The masculine costume is an apron or short
petticoat of cotton cloth, in imitation of the pelican skin, together with a short
shirt barely reaching the waist, a belt or cord or skin holding the petticoat, and a
strip of skin showing above the belt; few wear hats, and one or two wore sandals;
the legs are bare, save in the case of Pulado who wears civilized garments and one
other who wears trousers of the Yaki pattern and material—white sailor-like
trousers, large at bottom, short of waist, with the breech-clout outside. The children of say 5 years and upward to about 15, with the boys to 16 or 17, wear the
petticoat of cotton goods, or rarely pelican skin of the original character; nothing else. Smaller children wear nothing though the nursing infants are usually
covered with rags of cotton goods or pelican skin, and the youngest babes are
swathed in all sorts of stuff, the heads being usually tied up. A sense of modesty
appears now and then, however; when Mr. Dinwiddie was photographing a small
group a mother had her 3-year old girl stand up; but when he was about to repeat,
and asked to have the child stand up again, the mother first tore off a bit of rag
and tucked it under the cord abut the child's waist as an apron; the modesty in
this case being a second thought. Several children have such cords about their
rather protuberant bellies, the cords slipping down in front nearly to the pubis.
The women are usually suckling or pregnant, and sometimes both. Their costume
is more diverse than that of the men. All wear long dresses in lieu of the pelican
skin apron, which was probably longer for women than for men; these are of calico or sheeting or other cotton goods. All wear also a short shirt like that worn by

the men, or else waist or jacket of some sort, usually so short as to expose a zone of skin above the waist as well as the more pendant breasts. This garment is easily lifted by suckling mothers, and this is done with no show of restraint or modesty. Candelaria, the best dressed of the rancheria, wore waist and skirt of calico, and beneath an underskirt and short chemise of white muslin. On photographing, Juana Maria, the matriarch, bared her upper person and put on the pelican skin robe without the least hesitation, and there was little hesitation among other women of middle age. Candelaria objected, but yielded to Señor Encinas's instructions. She, like most of the other women and one of the men, had her face painted, the colors used being black, white, blue and red.[81]

W J McGee stands in the center of a group of Seri Indians at Rancho San Francisco de Costa Rica, Sonora, November 2, 1894. Mashém ("Pelado") stands just left of McGee; the largest Seri in the group, El Mudo, stands ninth from right. (4275)

Seri Manuel Miranda and W J McGee at Rancho San Francisco de Costa Rica, November 2, 1894. McGee holds two olla stands and a yucca brush in his left hand. (4260)

"A small group" of Seri Indians at Rancho San Francisco de Costa Rica, November 2, 1894. (4276a-1)

Candelaria, the Seri woman who objected to posing half-naked, Rancho San Francisco de Costa Rica, November 2, 1894. (4265)

The Seri's rancheria is in a state of good cheer, and the faces are smiling. Yesterday a horse died of some disease, and the Seris, being notified, "got away it in ten minutes," eating the fat and entrails and some of the meat raw, and carrying the rest away to "ripen" in the sun or be cooked; on every hut strips and fragments of the meat may be seen, and in many ollas the larger bones are slowly cooking. Knives were used in part, and the meat was torn in various ways. A squaw was seen industriously pounding the edge of a hoof to remove it, using a rudely discoidal pebble (which was acquired), and resting the leg on a large stone, altogether unshapen; in the same way the leg bones were broken and the legs boiled in an olla, the skin and hair with the rest. This morning a pig of some 75 pounds weight was found dead of disease, and three Seris boys seized on it with avidity and bore it away to the rancheria, where soon after fresh pork was being eaten raw, cooked, or dried in the sun. A variable lot of dogs, scrub curs of all sizes, colors, and forms, run about the camp, eating of everything within reach, and fleeing only before the children with lassos; one of these was a small white bitch, thin and scrawny as if diseased, and well advanced in gravidity; this vile cur annoyed one of the women, who gave it a resounding kick, sending it flying two or 3 yards; the dog screamed in pain and terror, and continued yelping and howling piteously until, within a few seconds, a premature birth began, and a ¾ developed puppy, appeared, enclosed in the placenta; some of the horde saw the puppy, and at once a chase began for the bitch, the boys with their little riatas [lariats], the girls with stones and sticks, all laughing and shouting in glee, in which the women (there were women about) joined; the dog ran here and there, still yelping. Finally the expression on the face of a ten-year old boy changed from one of simple sportiveness to one of serious purpose, and he ran more energetically toward the bitch; another saw the change, and he too joined in the serious chase; thus the mirth changed to work, and all partook of the new excitement; but the first boy was victor, and seizing the half born puppy, jerked off the attending placenta, and followed by one or two others rushed away with his prize, evidently with the intention of eating it.[82] So, between the horse, the pig, the pot of burned beans we gave them, and the two-dollars worth of sugar cane I distributed among them, the Seris fared sumptuously.

Seri boys carrying away the carcass of a dead pig, Rancho San Francisco de Costa Rica. (4276b-10)

Palado's wife is sick, chronic dysentery apparently complicated with malaria, accompanied by pregnancy, being the trouble. Before learning of the chronic condition I undertook to cure her. The first dose, given last evening, was a moderate one of brandy and blackberry given in a little water. She took it reluctantly, and when I returned an hour later complained of feeling worse; pains in back and arms, etc. Still later she felt as if she was about to have a miscarriage. I gave her bacon and hardtack for supper. This morning she is evidently better, though she denies it; and a second dose was taken without reluctance. She may recover.

The greater part of the day was spent in taking vocabulary from Palado, with assistance of Señor Alvemar-Leon. It is hard work for Palado, who has to be fortified with food and mescal occasionally. Generally several others stand about, and he frequently appeals to them. They express great interest and satisfaction when I repeat the term correctly. The boys of 14–16 are brightest, the women next. The mescal makes Palado ill, but he cannot refuse it.

[
SATURDAY, NOVEMBER 3, 1894
IN CAMP AT SAN FRANCISCO DE COSTA RICA.
]

Made several more photographs in the morning at the Seris rancheria, and later at the ranch; also made a number of purchases of objects exemplifying practically all the arts of the tribe save those connected with navigation and fishing. They are now accustomed to picture-taking, and offer no objection, expecting to remove garments so far as to conform approximately to island costume. The younger women are modest as to exposure of person, the older not; from which it may be inferred that they have clothed the breast for half a generation. One young girl at the ranch, evidently there for her picture, declined to remove her shirt when asked through Palado (who is her kinsman); but it was evident that the objection was largely Palado's. So she was taken dressed to show her face paint. An hour later she came back with a much more elaborate design on her face, and a supposed design in her heart not to be left out of the series of island beauties; and she consented when addressed by Sr. Alvemar-Leon in Spanish, and on receiving a mouth organ Palado himself withdrew his objections; yet it was evidently a trying ordeal for the girl.

So far as can be learned through inquiry the Seris are absolutely pure of blood, and with the possible exception of the tawny hair no contrary evidence

WJ McGee collects a Seri vocabulary from Mashém (looking into the camera). Pascual Encinas is seated at the table between McGee and Mashém. Standing (left to right): Ygnacio Lozania; Manuel Encinas, Pascual Encinas's son; Juan Lozania, a grandson of Ygnacio Lozania; Arturo Alvemar-León; and Jesús Contreras ("Mr. Griggs"). Rancho San Francisco de Costa Rica, November 2, 1894. (4277a-2)

can be seen among the people. They are of magnificent physique as a rule, and their purity of blood, after nearly three centuries of contact with white men, to say nothing of the much longer contact with red, tells of their virtue. The men marry young, apparently soon after, and sometimes before puberty; they do not pretend to virtue either before or after marriage. The girls marry still younger, often before menstruating, and are virtuous before and faithful after marriage. So says Palado, who like most civilized men, deludes himself with the fallacy that the women of the group can be virtuous when the men are not. Señor Encinas is of the opinion that lapses from virtue are strictly endogamous; he thinks no Seris woman has ever yielded to alien, and says it is impossible even to rape one—at least before death; he instances a case when half a dozen "boys" tried to rape a Seris girl and failed—she fought so desperately and persistently that they were compelled, after some hours, to release her.

The first purchase from the Seris was a comb; then a head cushion; then other articles as they were brought. The women and children became excited and brought forth all sorts of articles, so that the rancheria was soon impoverished of property, though enriched in money. In nearly every case the purchase was simple, the article being offered and the price tendered being accepted without question, though in several cases the prices were fixed by the sellers; if the purchase was not made for any reason, the article was taken away without much show of disappointment; in one case a woman asked (and received) an exceptional price for an olla because she was a widow and very poor. She was a bright woman who aided in giving vocabulary. In half the purchases the money passed through Palado's hands and sometimes through two or three hands, but it was soon sent to its proper recipient, no sign of cheating being discovered. Palado, however, wanted an occasional piece of silver for himself. The greater part of the day was spent again in taking vocabulary. Palado did better than yesterday though he was very difficult to hold toward the end of the day. He is an insignificant looking man, but is bright, and this seems to give him a certain standing among the tribe.

In evening witnessed the Paskola. There are three dancers, one taking part only occasionally. There are two bands, who alternate: The first is the string band of two pieces, violin and harp, both of native manufacture, a knife being the only instrument used; the other the drum and flute, with accompaniment of water drum, bass fiddle, and gourd rattle. The drum and flute are exactly as seen at San Ignacio. The gourd drum was not well seen, nor was the base fiddle; Mr. Dinwiddie describes both, also the gourd rattle, which is simple. The dance began at noon and will continue until 8 or 9 o'clock tomorrow. Two performers work the whole time, the performance alternating between dances, separate, and supposedly, humorous conversations (in which bystanders sometimes participate), with occasional animal dances in which all three join, the idler representing a deer, the joker a coyote, and the other remaining Paskola (?)[83]

Lewis ascertains that 8 families of Papago live at La Palma, having little farms below; and when their water fails they go to La Palma and "live," sometimes hunting in the mountains. 3 families live also at Aguaje, but how they live is unknown. There were formerly some at Tonojo,[84] but they are now at Costa Rica.

There are 53 Papagos at Costa Rica, in about 7 houses, 13 family groups. They are temporarily here; most have houses at Tonojo, where they spend most of the time; others are from various localities including Pozo Nuevo. They are largely hunters, the women making pottery in winter.[85] All are presumptively pure blood, and all Catholic, though the mantle of Catholicism is very thin and sadly tattered.

[
SUNDAY, NOVEMBER 4, 1894
COSTA RICA TO HERMOSILLO • 55 MILES.
]

In morning drove out to the cultivated portion of the ranch, which is in part of the delta of Sonora or Hermosillo river. Soil of remarkable fertility. The alita [quelite] grows in remarkable luxuriance, often 10 ft. high; said to be best of stock feed, on which horses, cattle and deer are now fattening. Returned and retraversed road to Hermosillo. The little buttes of volcanic aspect near the Perez ranch are mineral bearing, a beautiful one of copper, gold and silver being shown us. But here and at the little igneous ridge 12 mi. from Hermosillo there is almost no talus about the base. The rock mass seems to rise like a post from the plain—it is evident that the plain is built around the bases.

Señor Encinas repeats ex-consul Forbes account of the ruins on Guardian Angel Island—a stone roadway 9 miles long, a cemetery, a village of 178 stone houses, etc.[86]

The Molino Encinas (also known as Hacienda San Ignacio), about three miles from Hermosillo, November 5, 1894. W J McGee stands by the wagon. Those by the house are (from left to right) Arturo Alvemar-León; Adolfo Encinas; Pedro Encinas; Angelita Encinas, daughter of Pascual Encinas and Anita Espinosa de Encinas; Anita Espinosa de Encinas; Artemisa Encinas; Angelita Encinas, sixteen-year-old granddaughter of Pascual Encinas and Anita Espinosa de Encinas; Pascual Encinas (in black overcoat); Dolores Encinas; Julio Encinas; and Manuel Encinas. (4277b-2)

*T*he Molino Encinas, November 5, 1894. Left to right: Anita Espinosa de Encinas; Adolfo Encinas; Pedro Encinas; Artemisa Encinas; Julio Encinas (kneeling); Angelita Encinas, sixteen-year-old granddaughter of Pascual Encinas and Anita Espinosa de Encinas; Pascual Encinas; Dolores Encinas; Arturo Alvemar-León; Manuel Encinas; and Angelita Encinas. (4277b-4)

> ## MONDAY, NOV 5, 1894.
> ### IN CAMP ABOUT HERMOSILLO • 4 MI.

Called on the acting governor [Ramón Corral] and his Secretary of State, as well as the Prefect, with no special event.

> ## TUESDAY, NOV. 6, 1894.
> ### HERMOSILLO TO AGUA NUEVA. • 42 MILES.

The road ascends a plain of oblique or transverse drainage, the mountains at first having their bases buried. The plain inclines S., yet the streams flow W. or S.W. We constantly ascend, yet cross streams—or sand washes—; we are constantly approaching divides, yet from each see another uphill beyond, and hardly change our grade at the arroyo until we are going up again. At first, from some 15 mi., the plain is mostly torrential, then occasional bits of rock appear in place, and during the last half of the distance we are on essentially a base level plain. On the W. lie scattered peaks and mesas of igneous rock; on the E. the mountains are much the same as already noted, a sort of double range, the first igneous apparently, the main range beyond probably older crystallines. The boulders and pebbles along the road and in arroyos are chiefly igneous, the rocks exposed in base level plain chiefly granite. On the E. the mesa type becomes better developed as we go on, and we camp in a region of mesas; on the west at end of day the mountains look more like granites or other old crystallines, with the Sierrita looking like a limestone mass. The flora is much the same as along the lower Zanjon, with the addition of a new cactus-tree, a cross between palo verde and opoten.[87] The gray-leafed plant from which the Papago make chewing gum also abounds [the brittlebush, *Encelia farinosa*].

Camped at a tanque [water pond]. The horses come to water about sunset, and cavort and gallop about at sight of wagon and men, in charge of their stallion leaders, the mares and colts neighing much and the stallions and young mares snorting loudly. After dusk the cattle come in the lead of bellowing bulls, who engage in fierce battles lasting hours, dozens of cattle collecting to watch each and add to the turmoil and noise. Some cows too visit the remains of a bull recently killed and lament vociferously. So, the early night is hideous. Approaching camp, Lewis showed his trail sense again: "Where you thinking them cattle come from?" "What cattle?" "Them cattle that we seeing the tracks of them. I think we seeing a ranch when we getting on that hill." And sure enough, we did.

[**WEDNESDAY, NOVEMBER 7. • AGUA NUEVA TO**
NEW POZO NORIEGA • 45 MI. (BREAKDOWN AT NIGHT)]

The same succession of uphill, of divides no sooner reached than past, of washes cutting across the slopes; and the same flora. The green-leaved tree with the red berries in pods is the guaican of the Mexicans [*Guaiacum coulteri*]; the hybrid tree cactus is another opeten; and the palo verde and opeten sometimes prevail, almost to the exclusion of other forms. About the ranch Sierrita and for some miles N.W. fronting the mountain Sierrita, limestone pebbles and boulders abound, and tepetate is well developed, the earth giving out the characteristic hollow sound. The pebbles are of black limestone, weathering into polygonal ridges and furrows indicating inward structures, like that of eastern Mexico.

At Pozo Nuevo there is a stamp mill with the usual aggregation of houses and Indian huts. Most of the Indians are Yaki, but there is a Papago rancheria of half a dozen houses, with a shed attached to one. The houses are the best seen except perhaps at Pozo Verde; they are built of upright posts set in rectangular plan, the walls are opeten branches interwoven between the posts horizontally, and the door is made of split opeten poles bound with raw hide.[88] The roofs are covered with earth; that of the shed with sagebrush.[89] The woman washes on a large slab of stone in the shed; the principal fireplace is out of doors, but there are others in the houses (no smoke holes), and there is a curious cistern outside, formed in the fashion of a great olla with mortar sides and top, a large olla being set in the ground beside. Only an elderly woman and a little girl are at present at the rancheria, the others being at Costa Rica. Obtained a rawhide carrying basket, as well as photos. This is a permanent residence of 4 or 5 families, which they only leave for hunting, etc. The customs are almost identical with those of the Yaki, which are essentially Mexican; and it is probable that the blood is mixed.

A typical Tohono O'odham house at Pozo Nuevo, Sonora, November 7, 1894. Jose Lewis stands at left. (2788b)

Detail of a Tohono O'odham house showing walls and door, Pozo Nuevo, November 7, 1894. The stool with a hide seat is called an equipal or taburete, a kind of stool in use in northwest Mexico at least since the seventeenth century. (2788—e)

Jose Lewis examines a cistern in the yard of a Tohono O'odham house at Pozo Nuevo, November 7, 1894. (Mex. 109: 3694[136])

At Pozo Nuevo a stream breaks through the mountain westward, flowing off south of El Carnero,[90] probably to the Bacuachito. The road here winds around the Santa Lena [Elena] mass in which there are mines of silver, though the upper rocks are certainly lavas, like those forming most of the mountains W. of the valley and E. of it as shown in photo taken from near Sierrita; probably the silver occurs at the base of the flows. Then follows a long stretch of up hill with streams flowing toward the igneous mountains on W., relieved only by broken wagon tongue, until within two or three miles of camp, where we cross a divide of some consequence. So high have we climbed that the surface is essentially base level, the mountains in E. have blended with our plain and those in W. rise but a little way generally in rounded, scattered buttes, with one inclined mesa of considerable magnitude.

Took photographs of the hybrid opeten, the regular opeten, etc.

W J McGee (right) examines an "ocatiya tree" (Fouquieria macdougalii), apparently the plant he calls the "hybrid opeten," three or four miles south of Pozo Noriega, Sonora, November 7, 1894. (Mex. 109: 3700[142])

W J McGee stands next to a huge ocotillo (Fouquieria splendens), apparently the plant he calls the "regular opeten," about five miles north of Pozo Nuevo, November 7, 1894. (Mex. 109: 3701[143])

[**THURSDAY, NOVEMBER 8, 1894.**
IN CAMP AT POZO NORIEGA. • 2 MI.]

The ranch here is on another stream breaking through a range westward, and the range is inconspicuous; but after going a very few furlongs that interminable upgrade recommences, as on yesterday. A few photos were made, and the wagon tongue repaired.

The mountains in E. have dwindled with our rise, and hardly appear above the valley floor.

Jose Lewis examines a burro-powered flour mill, Pozo Noriega, November 8, 1894. (Mex. 109: 3704[66?])

FRIDAY, NOVEMBER 9, 1894
POZO NORIEGA TO SANTA ROSA[91] • 38 MI.

Crossing the wash, the up-grade continues, past two ranches, at which a few photos were taken (one of drawing water), and on to another, Milpias [Milpillas],[92] at which a family or two of Papago, probably from Cavorca, commonly spend part of the winter. None here now. Then on over endless slopes resembling great alluvial fans, though in reality there is but a veneer of torrential deposits over granites, various igneous rocks, with schists, jaspers, greenstones, etc., in endless confusion; the prevailing up grade continuing. A photo of this plain with Tecolote mountain in the background was taken. For on emerging from the wash it appeared that the stream cuts only the end of the first range (that traversed day before yesterday), and that another range comes in en echelon the Tecolote. This appears indeed the characteristic of the system further S., as it certainly is northward; for as we rose over apron slope after apron slope past Las Cruces (where the wash has a rugged bed of dark, almost jaspery rock) and gradually turned W. over the pass, we were looking on the W. slope of Tecolote, and another range came in just W. of the one we passed, rising into prominence northward. The rocks remain crystalline, apparently largely metamorphic with many intrusions, not much modern igneous here. Tecolote is granite-like in configuration. In the pass caliche or tepetate occurs, and about middle, in an arroyo leading S.W. limestone crops again, hard, semi-metamorphic, blue or black with an infinite number of joints or faults breaking it into irregular cuboidal fragments, showing, either naturally or brought out by weathering. It occupies quite an area, granites and granitoid schists following. On approaching Santa Rosa quartz becomes conspicuous, particularly in a great castellated mass cutting across an arroyo on N. of road. It is noteworthy that on crossing pass, the streams still flowing S., the veneer is even thinner than on E. side of range, the surface being on approximate base level; and the slopes are steeper, and the streams are surely retrogressing through the mountains.[93]

SATURDAY, NOVEMBER 10, 1894
SANTA ROSA TO CIENEGA.[94] • 27 MI.

Santa Rosa is near E. side of a broad valley analogous to that of Querobabi; the wash there drains S., but within a mile we get on a broad flat apron leading down to a wash near Cienega mountains draining N. This apron is of great extent some 20 mi. across where we crossed it (at widest part) and much longer N. & S. It is made of torrential deposits, no rock showing except in hills on N., where greenstones, etc., come down. Evidently the land-tilting is such as to handicap streams flowing N.; this has been noticed in crossing all divides cis. Hermosillo—the short down grades are relatively smooth and even, the long up grades rough and steeper, with rocks in situ.

About mid-width of the valley there are grain ranches. Near them traces of an ancient village appear conspicuously. Mounds of earth and small stones are scattered over a considerable area, arranged in tolerably definite lines; and the group, comprising not fewer than 50 mounds, is traversed by a trough evidently an acequia [irrigation ditch], in straight courses between slight angles; a part of the houses being arranged along its banks; and near the ranch house, entirely outside the modern fields, a well defined raised acequia some 15 ft. wide inside appears, with a few house mounds scattered about. This acequia looks fresher than most of the works seen but the ranchers consider it ancient, entirely prehistoric. Certainly it represents irrigation works more extensive than the present. No art work either in stone or pottery was seen in the casual inspection given the works.

Sleeping apartments in the Great American Desert." W J McGee asleep in camp at Santa Rosa, Sonora, November 10, 1894. (Mex. 109: 3711[68])

Breakfast at Santa Rosa, November 10, 1894. Jose Lewis and W J McGee (left), E. P. Cunningham (center), and C. T. Gedney (right). (Mex. 109: 3713[70])

Cienega range is crossed in N. low pass, with a stream way, also flowing N. nearly cutting through by retrogression E., showing that the western valleys have the advantage in cutting. Over the divide tepetate occurs, with abundant fragments of the black limestone. The placers here are simply in the talus, generally carried only a few feet beneath the surface, the material being so cemented by lime as to be rather difficult to break up; a few shafts are deeper. The material is dry sifted by simple machines worked by two or three men.[95] Cienega derives its water from a pool dug in the earth, with two or three wells; it is situated in an amphitheater, the low Cienega range on E. and a spur, with a high hill just S. of town, turning off on S., W., and N.W. A broad valley extends far N. and N.W., whence distant mountains rise range after range.

At Cienega proper there are two groups of Papago Indians with another at "the other town." The first group occupy three houses N.W. of town; they are peons, at work in placers, the women making pottery: six in all, a father & mother,

*D*ry-washing operation at Ciénega, Sonora, November 10, 1894. (Mex. 109: 3719[155])

two grown sons, a nearly grown girl and a little girl. Two of the houses are of wigwam pattern made of sagebrush and opeten poles, one with earthen covering, the other with debris on top—chaff of some sort, with corn husks, etc., evidently designed as a sort of substructure for an earthen covering when it became convenient to put it on. The third house is large, evenly circular, of sagebrush, with no roof. One of the women had been making pottery, and the tools of her trade were lying about. The other was making squash ready for grinding. The elder woman was combing the hair of the sleeping little one, using a yucca brush.[96] The other group, in S. part of town, is larger, though living in a half-subterranean home inherited from some unknown builder probably Yaki.[97] There are two middle aged women, with a half-grown girl and 4 or 5 smaller children. They were making pottery, being engaged in burning a kiln; the girl was washing a mantilla.[98] One of these women wore sandals; all others seen were barefoot. Here, too, the men are placer peons. The father in the other group owes $60, one of the sons (who dined with us) $50, the debt being incurred in the outfitting for the work, and the more they work the deeper the debt becomes.

7 or 8 ollas and a half dozen dishes were fired at once. A fire was burning in a shallow depression, perhaps 6 inches deep and a yard across; it was burned to embers, which were scattered, then a few fresh sticks were laid on the coals, then the ollas were placed on their sides, mouths outward, the dishes being put between and over them at random. Then fresh wood and bows were piled over all [three illegible words] and the fire rapidly extended itself to it, so that the whole was soon blazing.[99] Among the utensils used here were two pieces of stones, anvils and hammers, used by miners in breaking up ore; the anvils are 10 or 15 lb. stones, the hammers are rounded or spheroidal pieces of obdurate stone of 2 or 3 lbs. These are used by Papago for pounding meat, etc.

Lewis visited the other settlement of Cienega 2 mi. S. of the main town, finding there 6 families of Papago, all working in mines under peonage; and learning of still another group of two families, 2 mi. farther away, similarly under bondage. All of these Cienega families, except perhaps the newest comers, are of doubtful purity of blood; most speak Yaki, and intermarry freely with the Yaki; it is also probable (though not ascertained definitely) that they are more lax in morals and that Mexican and possibly American blood is thus introduced.

A Tohono O'odham woman firing a pottery kiln at Ciénega, November 10, 1894.

It should be noted that the flora over the Las Cruces–Santa Rosa pass displays no striking peculiarity; Yucca comes in, though not abundantly (Spanish bayonet [*Yucca arizonica*] and sotol[100]) and a purple cactus of the prickly pear order [*Opuntia santa-rita*]. Descending on the slope, in a cañon, several pear-like trees with small berries were observed.[101] Five cacti were Kodaked on the cis–Santa Rosa apron.

SUNDAY, NOVEMBER 11, 1894
CIENEGA TO CAVORCA. • 45 MI.

Early morning. Ciénega is in the great gold placer region. Hundreds of peons are employed in the vicinity securing gold dust. The region has no water and a so-called dry washer is used in shoveling the dirt into small wooden ripples on an inchurned board. At least 50% of the gold must be lost by this process." November 11, 1894. (Mex. 109: 3728[72])

For 25 mi. the road runs nearly W., crossing the low rim of the amphitheater and then following in general down a drainage way across a broad valley. On N., 8 mi. from Cienega, there is a great mountain mass of highly tilted clastics, of which a photo was taken. The debris indicates that all are more or less metamorphosed and cut by veins of quartz, etc., as well as dikes of greenstones. A variety of jasper rocks, greenstones, schists, quartzites, etc. appear. It is noteworthy that the range is orthogonal to strike, or nearly so. In background, farther on, there is a noble mountain, nearly white. Still farther on N. there is an irregular group, a plexus of low mountains set in no definite relation. On S., 8–20 mi. from Cienega there is another E.W. range, also of bedded clastics, trending with strike, dipping S. some 30°, the russet edges exposed and giving a rugged topography. Then the valley contracts, and there is a ranch in the neck, with a well of about 100 feet. This is Beruga,[102] where there is a family of Papago, working sporadically on ranch. They are "living Mexican." Two adults were seen, a man beyond and a woman below middle age, the man quiet and reserved, in usual Mexican dress with straw hat, barefoot, the woman in calico, also barefoot; and two or three children were also seen. The woman was more forward and talkative than the man.

Some 4 or 5 mi. beyond this ranch the rd. turns N., and remains northerly to Cavorca, all through a valley, generally sandy, sometimes silty and productive of clouds of dust, occasionally gravelly. There are several minor ranches within 8 mi. of Beruga, and in their neighborhood there are indications of ancient acequias and (probably) house mounds, all beyond the present ranch limits. A few large stones, not shaped but artificially transported, occur over the site. On S.W. the valley is boundless so far as the eye can reach; on W. there is an irregular series of mountains and buttes, with higher mountains beyond; on E. the same is true, one white mass showing regularly dipping strata throughout the mass, and there are a few outlying buttes rising sharply from valley bottom. It was not ascertained whether Cienega creek embanks S.W.; or whether it turns N. toward Magdalena sink, though the former seems rather the more probable. There is no break, however, in the valley bottom, no divide; so there must be more or less merging of the waters. Within 6 or 8 mi. of Cavorca there is on W. an expansion of the mountain system in a prominent mass much like that photographed in the morning, with nearly vertical strata showing in a group of great ribs forming a spur on E. side; the strike being apparently at almost exactly right angles to the trend of the mountain. This, with other phenomena, indicated that the mountains here are very old, measured in erosive terms—the structural effects of the original drainage are lost, and the sculpture is independent of structure. At base of this mountain there are a few bosses of lava-like rock, and 3–4 mi. S.E. of Cavorca there are one or two larger bosses of similar aspect; but no other indications of recent volcanics are seen. Beyond the Magdalena an imposing mass, much like Santa Catalina,[103] trends E.–W.; at its W. extremity and on N.W. a panorama of knobs and buttes appears, the whole probably modern igneous, judging from configuration; and a few buttes and low ridges, which may be volcanic, lie near the river; one just W. of Caborca. The latter, like the buttes toward Costa Rica, look like dwarfs—they rise abruptly from the plain as though their feet were buried. The valley is fertile, and the storm-course of the river can be seen stretching away W. for miles in a belt of green—cottonwoods, etc., shadowing ranches.[104]

[MONDAY, NOV. 12, 1894.]
CAVORCA TO PITIQUITO.[105] • DROVE 6 MI.; WALKED 5 MI.

How the mighty are fallen! Caborca has been for weeks a Mecca as a great Papago town, the Papago metropolis of Mexico![106] And there are two rancherias, one of five families at present, the other none! It is true that there is also a "temporal" a dozen miles down river, where there are half a dozen families, chiefly from Cavorca.[107] In winter there may be so many as a score of families here, though commonly some of the people are absent hunting.

Visited the chief rancheria, in which a dozen adobe houses, two lodges (A tents in form, commonly used as stables), and a few sheds, besides a coverless enclosure, were counted. Only 4 or 5 of the houses are occupied. In the first 3 women and two children abide. The water is good, taken from one of the

Papago wells, of which there are several. Two of the women were making pinole, one parching corn in a broken olla, the other grinding on the metate with flat muller in usual way.[108] The third was cleaning squash seed. They are Catholics and go to fiestas and sometimes to church, though they seldom come in contact with the priest. All children are baptized by priest, however. They never intermarry with Yaki or Mexicans. The houses are adobe, of Mexican type; fire-place the usual half-moon, no beds or table, the furniture being limited to ollas, baskets (including a large, nearly closed one), metate and muller, wooden spoons,[109] etc. A comb or brush of fibre was acquired. The women are kindly, cheerful, yet dignified, and of good presence; the dress is Mexican.

At the next house two women were making pottery, with a half-grown girl, a little girl, and an infant, the latter in cradles. The work is conducted in a lodge of mesquite bows with greasewood and other brush for roof. Photos were taken. The little girl, say ten years, had spent a year at school in Phoenix, and her hair was combed and braided.[110] She is Susann. The pottery making is noted by Mr. Dinwiddie. Briefly, the clay is kept moist in a nearly buried olla; it is taken out as needed and moulded on and in a spheroidal wooden tray (for breadmaking) with a paddle of wood curved; rings are added not in a spiral but complete, and welded by pinching and paddling; from time to time the mold is inverted in the sun to stiffen, the edge being kept moist by inverting it on a blanket, which is turned up to protect the margin; and later the molding is continued on an inverted olla. In the early stages a discoid stone may be used for molding in lieu of a paddle, particularly when initial shaping is in a broken olla. The finishing operation is wetting and painting with an ochreous paste kept (thin) in a nearly buried olla, a bit of quartz being used as a rubbing tool. (The one used by the group was presented to me.) The firing is done as at Cienega except that cow chips are used as fuel.[111] This group, despite the Mexican apparel was a striking one; the mother-in-law was rather gray, yet strong and vigorous, with a strong yet pleasing face; the daughter-in-law was a handsome woman, graceful, dignified and courteous; the little girl is strikingly handsome, with expressive eyes and winning manners; the halfgrown girl (an orphan) is handsome and intelligent looking. The group could not have been more attractive were they the kinswomen of an American gentleman. The third group comprised one adult woman, a girl of 12 or 13, a smaller boy, and two adult men and a third just grown. Soon after our arrival the men brought two watermelons for our delectation, having invited us to sit, on arrival, on the stick-rawhide chairs. Afterward an old man, stout, sedate, rubbing a bura [deer] skin, arrived. The woman was making tortillas with great skill, making them some 15 inches in diameter and of paper-like thinness.[112] She cooked them on an iron plate, i.e., a bit of sheet iron laid on the torrid furnace. These people are pure blood; the boy had sores on face suggesting scrofula or syphilis, but the history of the case indicated an acute attack of skin disease. All the men marry Papagos, all the women the same. And on pressing Luis [Lewis], it seems probable that the Papago blood even at Cienega and Hermosillo-ward is practically pure; now and then a Papago woman marries a Mexican, but in that case she is alienated from the tribe and affiliates in all respects with the Mexicans; and sometimes a Papago man cohabits with a Mexican or Yaki woman, but the relation is, so far as Luis knows, only temporary, and looked on precisely as the keeping of a mistress among ourselves. The women here were prepossessing of expression and demeanor, though not handsome; the younger men were not in any way striking, being probably the culls, the abler men being at the Temporal. The elderly man was fine looking and eminently dignified. The boy was much ashamed of his infirmity. All this group are baptized by a priest, and occasionally go to church.

Cavorca is on an immense wash at the confluence of that from Veruga with the Altar (or Magdalena); there is an old town and a new, the old having been partly invaded and threatened by floods: it is an oasis in the desert, though the old town has a deserted air. The church is typical.[113] It was photographed.

The rd. to Pitiquito crosses a low pass, an isthmus connecting the range or irregular series of mountains on S. with a curious mountain that has been attracting attention since first seen yesterday p.m. It is approximately E.W. in trend, parallel with river; at a distance top seems remarkably even; and the rocks seen from S. are black, as if basaltic. But on approaching the pass a horizontal line, like a burro trail except for the horizontality, was seen, and photos were taken. On ascending the mountain it was found to be entrenched. The great wall stretches its whole length of probably a mile, ending on E. in an inaccessible precipice; and both above and below there are short barriers, crossing salients and re-entrants in such manner as must effectually be for approach. In some cases these are widened considerably, giving flat plats a rod across, generally triangular; and in some cases they are bastioned in such manner that the plats are commanded from narrow parts of the same barrier. Altogether seven or 8 barriers are found at the most accessible point, an isthmus connecting first with a little outlying knob of trachyte and afterward forming the pass noted. The entrenchment is a rude wall of blocks up to 300 lbs., selected at random, laid with little care, no mortar being used, and the alignment, vertical and horizontal, changing with the conforma-

Southwest elevation of Mission Purísima Concepción de Nuestra Señora de Caborca, Sonora, November 12, 1894. (Mex. 109: 3743[73])

tion of the mountain. In general it is 3–6 feet high, some times higher, averaging say 1½ yds, the width being about the same. The main wall represents perhaps half the work on the S. side of the mountain.[114] The structure of the mountain is peculiar; it is a monocline of siliceous and ferruginous limestone dipping S. some 40° or 45° (morning light shows that the mountains are about N. 15 W.), giving steep cliff faces in N., steep slopes only on S. Then this rock on S. slope is partly dissolved, the lime being gone to form abundant tepetate in the valley below, and the residue of silica and iron remaining to form a black, rough, vesicular mass; sometimes an almost quartzitic laminated rock; and it is the harder phase which is commonly used for the wall, the more vesicular, slag-like phase covers the mountain side. On the N. the mountain is generally inaccessible by reason of the steep cliffs; but where climbable spurs occur the salient of talus below has an embankment across it like that on S. but at somewhat lower level—thus:

Pass and entrenched mountain from camp at Pitiquito. a = entrenchment on S., b. do. [illegible word] on N., c pass.

Some indications of work appear on several other knobs in vicinity, and the Papagos and the Mexicans tell of a wall, less prominent, on one of the mountains seen to the left above. At Hermosillo I heard of Intrenchera, or Entrenched mountain, on the rd. from Cienega to Altar[115] and the guide from Agua Nueva to Cienega described Intrenchera as much farther E., near Santa Ana. Probably both accounts are correct. At Hermosillo also we learned through ex-consul Forbes and Señor Encinas of the remarkable works on Guardian Angel island. And the Cavorca mountain explains the curious, horizontal trail seen semi-circling Santa Lena mountain just N. of Pozo Nuevo, a trail supposed to be an old burro mining trail, though exactly like Cavorca and sensibly horizontal.

In evening visited the fiesta originating with much fireworks and Japanese lantern display and dismal clanging of the bell at the church, and passing thence to the Plaza where gambling and mescal drinking were rife; men and women, the latter often with children, participating. Up to 10 o'clock Paskola had not appeared; later he came, according to Luis, and as a new feature danced on his harp making music with his feet.[116]

On Intrenchera two new trees were seen: the first is rather a shrub, with a great number of stems, 5–50, growing in a bunch; each reminds one of leather-wood in habit, save that it branches more frequently and less bifurcate, and has a great many brush-like pods that at proper season bear leaves, probably populus like; and the wood is soft, yet of great toughness:[117] The second is a cross between cedar and mesquite and palo verde, apparently. The trunk is the most robust thus far seen, 3–10 inches, soon dividing, and growing shoots; it is light-colored and the bark scales slightly like birch, otherwise it is smooth; the leaves are of mesquite form and rather abundant and bright green; there are little green or purple berries, each with a large seed; and seed and leaves give a strong and eminently agreeable (in this country) odor of cedar.[118]

[TUESDAY, NOV. 13, 1894.
PITIQUITO TO ALTAR.[119] • 18 MI.; WALKED 3 MI.]

The Papago pueblo is located on the foothill E. of Pitiquito, well beyond limits of village. There are two little houses in one group, near town, two more and a semi-enclosure on hill top 300 yds. beyond and 8 in another group 200 yds. still farther. Nearly all architectural varieties occur here; the first house seen (home of Juana Garcia with little boy and two little girls and also a young woman, 2nd. cousin) is of adobe front and sides, with stone doorway, and opeten and cajon back,[120] roofed with opeten and sagebrush covered with earth, with no shed. The next is all adobe with large shed. Near hill-top there is an unoccupied house, probably Papago, all of stone, with ventilated roof (i.e., space of a foot between wall and roof); on hill there are two houses, one, apparently incomplete, simply a shed with a bit of adobe wall on one side, the other of stone with doorway in corner; in addition there is a rude stone wall forming two sides of a square and in the angle a habitation, ill furnished. This wall merges in an irregular embankment of earth and stones enclosing a rectangle of say 150 X 200 feet, on summit of hill. Lewis is of opinion that the embankment is Papago, though it may be older. The bank is 1–4 feet high, 3–10 ft. wide, steeper on out side. In the main pueblo some houses are of sagebrush ("grass"), some of stone, some of adobe, some of combination, one chiefly of opeten. The men are nearly all drunk by reason of the fiesta of San Diego last night. The women are sober and at work. A number of photos were taken, including Juana Garcia and her two little girls. A beautiful pottery finisher was obtained from Juana. The customs are essentially Mexican. All children are baptized by priest. Marriage is first by Papago manner, afterward by priest or Judge. They consider themselves Catholics. There is a tray-maker here, but he is a Mexican with a Papago wife living in the town and not in the pueblo.

Juana Garcia and her children proved to be the family of a Papago in jail at Altar for accessory to homicide, or something similar.

The rd. cuts off another peninsula of hills, one or two of which appear to be entrenched, particularly that in the drop between Altar and the tributary from S., crossing a pass of 250 or 300 ft. from which the two valleys, Altar & Magdalena, are well seen. Magdalena valley is just a plain, over which water can seldom flow, and only a trifling wash occurs in it. It is quite broad, 20± mi., and opens S. into the Cienega valley. A half-bared butte rises a little way from the plain. The Altar is a real valley with a river in it—albeit a feeble one not half a mill-stream; the two merge nearly to Altar. The mountains are nondescript, characterless and distant, save the Cavorca range parallel with river far to N., and two noble mountains, one S. and other N.E. of Altar. Both of these trend N. & S. The valley is laid with alluvium and would be richly fertile with water. Suggestions of old acequias and furrows appear, but nothing definite.

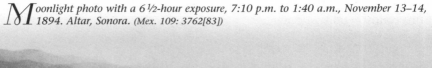

Moonlight photo with a 6 ½-hour exposure, 7:10 p.m. to 1:40 a.m., November 13–14, 1894. Altar, Sonora. (Mex. 109: 3762[83])

At Altar a Papago family of father, mother and 3 daughters reside permanently, the father farming, i.e., working for a Mexican. There are few living also at Oquitoa, 6 mi. up river.[121] It appears that there are about equal numbers of Papago at Sonoyta and Quitobac, "a good many" at either place.[122]

The mountains show no characteristics of volcanic origin, and are probably clastics. On the foot slopes and over the pass tepetate abounds.

Altar is typically Mexican notable for a rather new brick church and an abundance of palms.[123]

WEDNESDAY, NOVEMBER 14, '94.
ALTAR TO LAS PAREDONES.[124] • 28 MI.

The camp is on a spur of debris cemented by lime, through which a subcrystalline rock peeps now and then; it is on drop between Altar river and the wash from N. The valley is ordinary for several miles, rather indefinite mountains in foreground on E., with no noticeable trend, Oquitoa mountain in background being eclipsed. Then we round the end of the range N. of river, the continuation of Cavorca mt., and about 10 mi. from Altar see its rocks; they are red and purple rather shale-like metamorphics suggesting red beds, strongly tilted S.; and the range is a monocline also tilted S., russet edges on N. Then follows a wide expanse of valley, and finally, W.N.W. of Paredones, the rather imposing mass mapped as El Hornia. On E. the mountains gradually become more prominent, and E. of camp there is a notable knife-edge (apparently) crest with a near-by peak of white rock, and a less rugose mass still farther S., or a trifle N. of E. of Paredones. This group is photographed. It is probably all clastic. Directly N. lies a low, dark ridge of mass that seems to be volcanic.

Camped at a tanque, with most obliging Mexicans and many stock, the burros being fagged. The valley suggests prehistoric occupation, and a few wrought stones have been seen during the day, and Mr. Dinwiddie picked one up near camp; but nothing more. This is Sierra El Corisal [Carrizal]. The wash is Las Paredones.[125]

Mr. Gedney's[126] [illegible word] locates Intrenchera proper 7 leagues from Santa Ana, 12 " from Altar, 12 " from Cienega, and says there are fully a dozen entrenchments about it.

> ### THURSDAY, NOV. 15, 1894.
> ### PAREDONES TO SAN JOAQUIN. • 25 MI.

The upslope of the valley continues, and it remains a vast plane of torrential deposits. Over this plain there are occasional suggestions of acequias and house mounds, and a broken metate was seen, though it may be modern. The drainage soon turns S.W. into some other wash than Paredones, though it may be confluent farther S. There is, however, a great gap in mountains on S.W., through which there may be drainage. The rd. turns N.W. here, toward W. end of the low black mountains, which on approach rise into a rather striking chain of mesas and buttes of basaltic rock, outcropping in heavy faces, and 500 ft. or more high above plain—probably 1,000 in highest points. Through the puerto [door or pass], with a strong up grade we pass and the wash is large and broad; the wall on W. shows a whitish bed below the black sheets, probably tuff; and a beautiful little mesa of the table form is in center of pass. Through the pass suggestions of ancient work continue, and there are a few modern ranches.[127] In one case a metate and [illegible word] were seen together; but they were simply a boulder and pebble of suitable form, which had been used for a meal for a week by a passing traveler; and in other cases products of temporary use were seen, with no means of determining whether ancient or modern. This difficulty of discrimination in this country is immeasurably increased by the similarity in ancient and modern art. Ten miles after traversing the pass we rise on a gently undulating plain to the divide—and Boboquivera [Baboquivari] is in sight. On the left Sierra El Humo rises in bold but not rugged lines, save at N. where it is somewhat rugged; probably it is stone cov-

*R*ancho de Félix, near the divide, 45 miles north of Altar, Sonora. Volcanic mountains covered with cacti." November 15, 1894. (Mex. 109: 3770[89])

ered [or storm carved?] clastics except toward N. where there may be some volcanics, though doubtless older than those of the pass range. On W. a spur of this
volcanic range shoots up somewhat inconspicuously, and farther N. the few scattered masses of Sierra Union appear.[128] On S.E. the continuation of the pass range
stretches a score of miles as a series of low knobs and mesas of volcanic outline.

On both sides of divide many mounds 1–3 ft. high, 8–40 ft. across, approximately circular in plan, appear, commonly more pebbly than general surface; and
they may be seen in all stages of growth here as on torrential plains elsewhere here-
about. Primarily they are either doab-buttes[129] or deltas; and being once started
they increase in dimensions and coarseness of material until a limit is determined
by some condition. In addition there are many rot mounds, which grow because
selected by mesquite trees for sites, etc.

Luís says Papagos have no myth concerning rainbow—save that a semi-
lunatic claimed to have visited the end of one and cut it off to be cut up into
belts, he afterward fell into the fire and was burned to death.[130] There are cloud-
myths, according to which the clouds are four "old men," one for each point of
the compass;[131] the corn is also an "old man."[132] They have rain ceremonials in
which the people assemble for four days, two devoted to singing, with waving of
eagle feather wands, two to drinking mescal. The wands are made of the finest
and whitest feathers of the eagle and are kept only by the "doctors." Commonly
the people are called together at night, when a singer sings the rain song, the others being arranged in a circle of which he is one; the doctor waves the wand over
him, and then successively over each person in the circle, returning to the singer;
and afterward the ceremony is repeated, and the ceremony goes on through the
night, a day, and the next night, when the doctor predicts the time of rain. "Sometime it rain, sometime it not rain at all;" but the mescal drinking goes on just the
same.[133] No snakes are ever used in this or any other ceremonial, and the Papago
are much afraid of snakes. They believe that certain diseases are produced in a mysterious way by snakes, and the doctors have a ceremonial to cure them, which
consists essentially of a dance with the rattling of snake rattles, which to be effi-
cacious must have been cut from living snakes; "dead snakes no good."[134] There
is no mother-in-law taboo.[135]

[## FRIDAY, NOVEMBER 16, 1894.
SAN JOAQUIN TO LOBURIN (LA VENTANA).[136] • 30 MI.]

San Joaquin is in a new valley cut into a plain, escaping W. through a narrow gorge
and apparently ending in its own basin beyond, being tributary (said) to neither
Altar nor Sonoita. The cañon is some 250 ft. deep. On reaching the valley side, the
plain is seen to be one of the vast torrential areas of the region; it rises on the
flanks of El Humo [Smoke Mountain] in a most entrancing grass-plain. It sweeps
away E. or S.E. to the pass hills; it stretches E. & N.E. nearly as far as eye can reach,
apparently to a low plain divide; and on N. it reaches into the Baboquivari valley
and that W. of it, lapping on the flanks of the volcanic range between and its N.
continuation Sierra L'Union. In this plain the whole drainage system is incised in

the most perfect autogenic form, and thus another divide is shifted from the pass, this time E. from pass connecting El Humo with Union. Immediately N. of this basin lies its mate, somewhat smaller but otherwise like it in all respects, embanking through Union W. Then the waters flow toward the Gila, over granite plains, with a good many paloverdes, scattered mesquites, and much grass.

A few volcanic buttes rise from the valley (Baboquivari) near its S. extremity, one of them a mysterious mountain with a hole through it which must be quite near the boundary.[137] On W. a volcanic range rises boldly from the valley, dividing it in half, and this dies out and is followed by the apparently non-volcanic Union.

E. of Union, on W. slope of valley is rancheria of Miguel (called Magill by the ranchmen) with a dozen houses ranging from adobe with tin rain-spouts and board bedstands and door down to opeten and brush shelters. Miguel is a chief, and a man of means. The rancheria is vacant, most of the doors having brush piled across.[138] Picked up an olla with narrow mouth, and photographed form of a large brush house. Took a photo of Baboquivari from S.W.

[### SATURDAY, NOV. 17, 1894.
LA VENTANNA TO FRESNAL.[139] • 25 MI.]

Luis relates story of Coyote and Bear. They ventured into a partnership. They said, We will plant potatoes; all above the ground shall belong to Coyote, all below to Bear. When the crop was ripe they divided in this way. When Coyote saw he had nothing but worthless stalks he was angry. The Bear pacified him, saying: Next year we will share the other way. Now next year the Coyote wanted corn, and the Bear agreed. When the corn was ripe the Bear took all above ground and made a store [of] the corn; Coyote dug in the ground but found nothing; and he was very angry. Then they went fishing. They cut a hole in the ice (this is significant, both fishing and ice), and the Bear put his tail in the hole; When a fish seized his tail he jumped out quickly, threw the fish on the ice and caught it. Then Coyote tried; for a long time he felt no fish, and said so to the Bear, who urged him to wait a little longer, meantime his tail was frozen into the ice. Finally the Bear said the fish might have bitten without Coyote feeling, and advised him to jump. The Coyote tried to jump, but found himself fast in the ice.

There are many stories of Coyote, but in all he is "foolish," the victim of a joke.[140]

The rd. is on a torrential valley, with lateral washes but no central wash seen. The flora is as in San Lewis [Luis] with more mesquite. The cooperation of plants and animals is well displayed: A Mesquite springs; here the bird drops a cactus seed, and the cactus grows and branches and protects the mesquite, which also protects the cactus; the rat burrows in the shelter of both and fertilizes the ground and aids it to retain water of slight storms; and a mound is built in which the soil is exceptionally fertile and friable, and the cactus and mesquite (or paloverde) grow apace.[141]

Fresnal is between an outlying butte of trachyte and the range.

3–6 mi. from Ventana [Ranch] there is a Papago rancheria known as Ventana. There are three houses in one group, but generally there is only one house at a place, with a little field enclosed in a Mexico-like fence of mesquite, say 2 or 3 acres. All are vacant. Most of the houses are grass, a few opeten; the grass houses are usually circular, but one is square with rounded corners, the corner posts outside. This house has a grass door. Both door and house are photographed. A wooden spade and a needle for grass house-building were achieved. The door was barricaded. At the group of 3 houses one interior was photographed. From another house a bow was taken. A mesquite mortar and pestle under a tree near by were photographed. Another was seen quite a distance from any house. It is noteworthy that the mortars are very little worked boulders, imbedded in the ground, the cup being almost the only indication of work; and that the pestles are unwrought save the battering of the ends.

WJ McGee next to a Tohono O'odham house in a summer village identified as Ventana—probably the modern Choulic—in the Baboquivari Valley, Arizona, November 17, 1894. The structure may have been the ceremonial rain house. (2779-e)

Jose Lewis stands by a Tohono O'odham grass house, "15 miles west of Fresnal, Pima Co., Ariz." in the village "known as Ventana," November 17, 1894. "The houses in this vicinity were all deserted, as they are upon the agricultural land, and scarcity of water prevents their occupation for a prolonged period after the rainy season and the harvesting of the crops. They are surrounded by defensive guards of some sort to keep cattle and horses from devouring them and coyotes from an entrance. . . . This house is built in the shape of an ellipse by setting up a series of mesquite uprights at intervals. Uprights are selected which have a slight natural curve and are so placed that all of them curve inward around the ellipse. A rider of mesquite is firmly bound on around the top of the uprights. . . . Also there are two heavy forked posts in this circle of outside uprights placed opposite one another through the greatest length. This line of the major axis is divided into three parts by erecting two forked uprights equidistant with the ends & each other. Across these, or into the forks are laid heavy roof beams. The rafters of this particular house consisted of loosely placed split saguaro logs, resting transversely across the central supporting roof timber."

Luis tells me of a ceremonial dance, formerly quadrennial, now when there is an exceptionally abundant crop somewhat in nature of Harvest Home. It is held at Santa Rosa. For ten days the people are engaged in carrying produce of all kinds, corn, squashes, beans, etc., to a single place from all the farms; then they gather and feast all day. There are two classes, the dancers and the others. The dancers are in breech-sheets with bodies painted, wearing masks in imitation of various animals, coyote, deer, etc. The others collect in groups. The dancers pass from group to group, and at each group dance around and sing the accompanying song, they are then given presents of food, and go on to the next group. This continues all day.[142]

Lewis repeats his account of Papago-Apache wars: The Apaches are thieves, and steal from the Papago, and sometimes murder. After a time someone will organize a raid, and a war group is organized, who go into the Apache country. A battle soon occurs: If the Apache are successful, the Papago return quietly (this is seldom the case), if the Papago are successful, four men from each village are detailed to some houses and proclaim the victory, when all things are made ready for celebration on the return of the warriors. But in this the killers of Apache and the wounded take no part; both are sequestered, with one attendant, and fast for 4 days; no salt, no meat, very little food or water, with no exercise, the attendant assuming complete charge of them.[143]

[The following appears to be a list of places occupied, or said to be occupied, by Papagos in 1894.]

on Baboq
{
[San] Miguel. 12 houses, vacant.
Ventana, 4 mi. long, 25 families,
Puerta Redonda, 8 fam.
Fresnal,
Coyote [Village; Pan Tak]
[Little] Tucson
} 300 Indians

Sierrita Alvarez, 5–6 mi. N. of Lab[urin] 6 or 7 fam.
Topawa, farther W., 50 fam.
Coababi [Ko Vaya or Cababi]—N.N.W., 30 families
Horseshoe [Logan, a mining camp near Quijotoa], 300
Quijotoa, 500
Covered Well[s], W. of Q[uijotoa], 30 or 40 families
Gunsight [Schuchuli] and vicinity, 30 fam
Santa Rosa [Gu Achi] 200–300
Coverty—23 mi. from Lab[urin], in Mex 4 mi, much stock,
    30 men, say 150
Sonoita [in Sonora], say 200
Quitobac [in Sonora]
Tecolote [Chukut Kuk], permanent, 50–75
Reservoir—A good many.
Mesquite [Kui Tatk?], say 200
San Domingo [in Sonora]
Quitovackita, [in Sonora] } say 300
Cobo, 300 here and another village
San Anton[io] (Mex) Several
Gila Bend [San Lucy]
Casa Grande.

*T*he W J McGee expedition with Baboquivari Peak in the background to the east, November 17, 1894. *(Mex. 109:3790[98])*

*T*ohono O'odham cowboys at Fresnal on the west side of the Baboquivari Mountains, Arizona, ca. November 18, 1894. *(2763a)*

*J*ose Lewis, far left, and W J McGee (head showing by the chimney), talking with Tohono O'odham at the adobe house of the headman of Fresnal, Arizona, ca. November 18, 1894. *(2785e)*

*P*anoramic view of the Tohono O'odham village of Coyote Sits (Ban Dak), Arizona, ca. November 20, 1894. *(2789e)*

[The following appear to be notes McGee made on properties for sale in Sonora, all presumably by Pascual Encinas of Hermosillo.]

Bacuache; controlling interest.

(5,000 hectare ÷ 3 = 1,666 X 8 13,330) hectares. Agricultural; on Bacuache river; plenty of water; mountains, with tillable land in barranca, used for Injun corn, etc., but not much in cultivation; gold placers; few houses; no special personnel. 25± leagues from Hermosillo, same distance from coast.

Wheat store 25 stalks, 50 given to herd.

C.T. Gedney
Culiacan, Sinaloa, Mexico.[144]

La Libertad.[145] Concession.

Taxed. 2,500, 4,190 meters square, oriented diagonally. N. of S[illegible], 5 leagues, nearer coast, 5 leagues from coast, 20 leagues. W.N.W. of Hermosillo, good sands, level ground; several houses, good well, timbered, windlass; tillable, but water scant, chiefly stock; overflow of Bacuache river. Used in common with other ranchers; no men except when needed. Well—100 feet, good supply.

This and Coronado covered in recognition of services in controlling Seris Indians.

Coronado, Concession

5 leagues N. E. of Libertad, 18 leagues from Hermosillo, 11–12 leagues from coast. 5,000 hect. 8,222 X 4,270 hectares, oriented diagonally (like Libertad) agricultural land, small house, no well, new ranch, good for stock, overflow of Bacuache river.

Ranches for sale by Señor Pascual Encinas, Hermosillo, Sonora, Mexico.

San Francisco de Costa Rica.

5,000 hectares, 5,000 N.E.W., 9,391.63 N–S. with a potrero [fenced pasture] left out, 16 leagues from coast, where there is a good anchorage. About 1 sq. league in cultivation. About 1,400 cattle, 600 horses, with a great many burros. First rate wagon down on ranch with 60 or 70 vaqueros and workmen, chiefly Yaki; besides Papago and Seris. Most do task work at 3 or 4 bits per day, some at $8[00] (Mex), per day and rations; mostly in trade; Some, with all Papago and Seris do job work, mostly trade. Taxed. Includes water right to overflow. About square league under fence. Has contract for sale of all produce delivered on coast.

Santa Ana y El Molino [146]

5,000 hectares. Two sections, each 5,000 meters square, 5 leagues N.E. of Costa Rica, about 6 or 7 leagues from coast, newer than Costa Rica, about 16 l. from Hermosillo in direct line. Stock ranch, not fenced. Houses, well, good large horse windlass, brick reservoir. Overseer and vaqueros from Costa Rica look after it; a water man present. Well 120 ft., plenty water, much wood, part tillable. Taxed.

[The following is a list of names of some of the Seri Indians who were at Rancho San Francisco de Costa Rica during McGee's visit there.]

1 Jesus Aguirre
2 Juan Estorga
3 Juan Chavez
4 Francisco Aguiler [Aguillar]
5 Juana Maria
6 Josepha
7 Candelaria, d. of Juana Maria
8 Luis

[The following is a list of Papago Indians with whom McGee visited at Querobabi on October 26 and 27, 1894. It probably identifies individuals who appear in photographs taken by Dinwiddie.]

looks 35 or 40
Juan Rosara   family

looks 18 (G)
pt. of   Meriana   Aurakeras. 1st,
family

not ma. looks 16 (G)
Laura   Aurakeras 2nd
daughter. Querobabi pictures,

Pedro Flores

Chief's house—Santiago Chief.

looks 40–45
Checo Margarita—husband

looks 35–40 wife,
Lara Martine.   Two infants.

Not. m.
Francisco Martinas   large

Marcie Martinas   small

Cousin of L.M.

God child of L.M., baptised by herself.

Opodepe; one of posts.[147]

Second Expedition
Papago—S...
1895.

SECOND
EXPEDITION,
PAPAGO—SERI,
1895

W J McGee

Bur... Am. Ethnology
Washington, D

In case this book is lost the
finder is requested to forward by the
above address. Ten dollars
reward will be paid for the return

Party: W J McGee in charge; W
Johnson, topographer; J. W. Mitchell; Hugh Norris, Papago interp-
r; José Contreras, teamster; ...

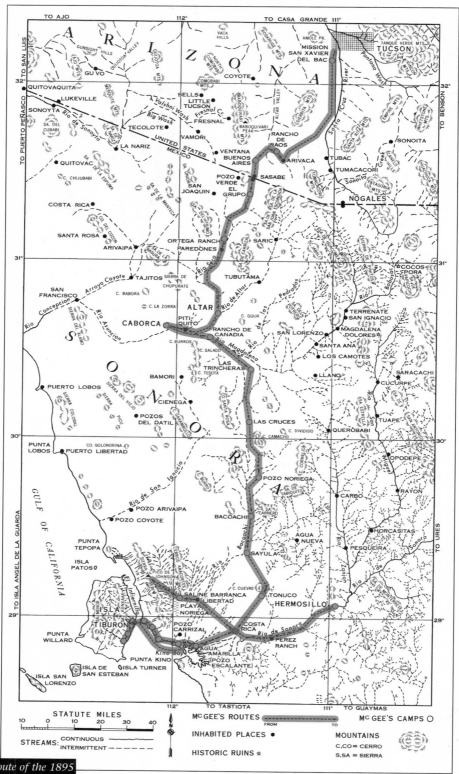

Route of the 1895 Expedition

Map by Ronald Ives

W J McGee

Bureau of American Ethnology
Washington, D.C.

Second Expedition, Papago—Seri 1895.

*In case this book is lost, finder is requested
to forward by mail to above address.
Ten dollars ($10.00) reward will be paid for the return.*

*Party: W J McGee in charge; W.D. Johnson,
topographer; J.W. Mitchell, cook; Hugh Norris,
interpreter; Jose Contreras, teamster. Six horses.*

[**OCT. 27**
LEFT WASHINGTON]

[**NOV. 3**
ARRIVED TUCSON]

[**NOV. 9**
TUCSON TO SAN XAVIER]

By reason of the exceptional rains the road up Santa Cruz valley is wet and the foliage is notably abundant and green.

[**NOV. 10.**
SAN XAVIER TO RANCHO DE RAOS[1]]

The vegetation has a much more lively and vigorous air than last year, and verdure prevails. About junction of San Xavier and Tucson roads there is a considerable ancient village with a dozen or more house mounds sprinkled with broken pottery. And at several other points similar mounds were seen. The chief note of the day relates to the extent and number of these ancient villages.[2]

[**NOV. 11**
RANCHO DE RAOS TO BUENOS AYRES.[3]]

The grade increases gradually. All day there is a strong head wind which prevents reaching Sasabe and presages rain. Mitchell photographed Baboquivari from S.E. and also the rugged granite mass on E. The house ruins continue, but are less abundant. A favorite site appears to be the low mesa on W., over which the road passes from time to time after crossing San Luis wash.[4]

San Luis wash is a vast arroyo up to 3–4 mi. or more wide, and sometimes expanding still more widely. Through a considerable distance (as indicated on map[5]) it is flanked by mesa scarps. These are notably higher and sharper on east, where they are sometimes sharp bluff lines, sometimes lines of washed salients with deep [illegible word]; height varying from say 20 to fully 200 ft. On West the sweep is straighter and lower, seldom over 10–40 ft. This relation is doubtless due to S.W. tilting. The incision of the cañon suggests increased stream-activity during a geologically modern period, say Pleistocene; but there is no means of fixing date. No indications of geologic change since human occupation began were discovered. Johnson suggests that cutting of San Luis arroyo is simple gullying, without further significance.

½ mi. north of Buenos Ayres, 100 yds east of road, lies a beautiful mortar of the eo-Papago type, with two deep incisions, parallel, 2½ or 3 in long like Rom. [numeral] II at one side of the pit, tangent thereto.

All day upper-layer, fleecy clouds have drifted lazily, sharply cut off below by the fierce lower current, which during the day moved from S.E. to S-S.W. The altitude of the cloud base was a little below the crest of Baboquivari, which occasionally was lost in the fleece, occasionally made a banner. After sunset the upper clouds dissipated and a few lower black cloud masses began to scud, and I had wagon curtains put down, beds carefully arranged, etc. The clouds thickened and darkened, and about 8 p.m., a few minutes after turning in, the rain began with increased wind. Showers occurred at intervals during night, but wind subsided.

Nov. 12
[Buenos Ayres to El Grupo.[6]]

The sun rose clear, but within a few minutes clouds already concealing the mountains thickened, and soon all the ranges and smaller buttes were lost; Baboquivari was not seen at all. By 7-30 rain was imminent, and the wagon was hurriedly made ready for rain; by 7-45 rain was falling and gradually increased from what Mitchell called a "dry" rain to an unmistakably wet one at Sasabé.[7] Then heavy showers followed, through some of which we pressed, making puddles in low places in road, but not making rills; the wind was not high, just high enough to prevent use of poncho. Toward evening the clouds lifted, and the sun set clear, though El Humo was buried. By 7-30 the clouds were mostly gone; but after midnight a heavy fog settled, wetting walls and floors, drenching wagon covers, and covering the plants with moisture. The temperature remained just above freezing.

Some stone-covered graves, one marked with a wooden cross, are on the road about a mile north of Sasabé, and are said to mark an Apache raid. Just above Sasabé there are piles and rings of stones, evidently artificial, and a huge metate, worn through and broken off, lay in the road; it has just been pried out.

The divide is about 1 mi. S. of B.A. [Buenos Aires], and at once grades increase and ant-forms appear. The secondary erosion of the alluvium is increased, though the gullies are only 3–5 feet deep, striking coarse gravel, which, like that of the entire region is chiefly angular, partly subregular, never rounded. Two-thirds of the way to Sasabé, hard rock—a light-colored igneous—begins; it continues to some distance below the boundary, where the alluvial [illegible word] coming down from the Pozo Verde mountains covers it.

At Sasabé the [Mexican customs] collector explained that he was sorry, very sorry to turn us back, but—. I there issued an ultimatum to the effect that we were going to Altar. The collector looked surprised. I offered to subsist and pay hire of a guard to Altar, but he declared his readiness to trust me to report properly. He desired us to wait until he could send a message to Nogales,[8] but I declined to wait. I then offered to pay the cost of a message to Nogales, which he accepted. So he compromised by letting the expedition go on.[9] Perhaps the end is not yet; but we went on rejoicing—through the cold rain.

The course lies across the great talus from Pozo Verde into the low hills W. of Pozo Verde arroyo; here the plain, which has been flattening and levelling, abuts sharply against the hill, the drainage apparently north. Over the hills the rd. soon passes on another vast plain, almost level smooth, sweeping down W. of Baboquivari—the plain already seen. Again there is a horseshoe, though ill defined, Baboquivari on E. scattered ranges on W., with El Humo toward toe; but generally the plain rises to the summits of the branching cross range, which look buried to the necks—yea ears. The plain is exceedingly smooth and well graveled. It extends to the divide into the little retrogressing basin at El Grupo.

Just below Sasabé ancient house mounds appear in considerable numbers, with bits of pottery, etc.

[NOV. 13]
[EL GRUPO]

No rain during night but toward morning a dense fog with an exceedingly heavy dew; for two hours after sunrise the plants were drenched.

Johnson made a map of the drainage westward through the San Joaquin gorge taking in also the parallel captured basin on N. On approaching from Sasabé, as well as on leaving San Joaquin last year, the great talus forms running down from El Humo are seen to merge with the plain stretching toward Fresnal, and the San Joaquin depression is simply cut in this slope. Johnson finds the salients of this basin lower than the general level of this old slope—probably by reason of the removal of part of the summits. It is noteworthy that the pebbles increase in size from Sasabe-ward toward El Humo.

Johnson picked up a quartz spearhead during the day, rude. Metates occur in vicinity, one having been found on site of superintendent's house in El Grupo. A house ring of loose stones is within yards of the same spot.

The change in flora in crossing divide is quite marked. Even here the flora is of Sonoran type, having come up apparently through San Joaquin gorge. The visnaga [barrel cactus, *Ferocactus* spp.] is deep [illegible word]. The ordinary chollas [*Opuntia fulgida*?] and slender-stemmed variety [*Opuntia versicolor*?] abound. There is also a very slender opuntia, bearing red berries [Christmas cactus, *Opuntia leptocaulis*], growing in shelter of mesquite and cat's claw [*Acacia greggii*], which becomes arboreal farther southward. The following were collected within a few yards of the house, all being exceptionally full in leaf, the bean-bearing small mimosa[10] was seen near by but not collected.

1— Small fleshy plant with thick light green subpinnate leaves; rare.[11]

2— Wide-branching tree, several trunks in bunch, each 1½'–3' in diameter, 5–10 ft. high, pyriform leaf-bearing paloverde; common; communal [foothill paloverde, *Cercidium microphyllum*].

3— Three-tipped mimosa; dead-looking, covered with minute bright-green leaves. Common, communal; in shrubby tufts 2–4 ft. high, stems up to 1½ in.[12]

4— Chaparral, generally leafless, now in full leaf and partly in fruit. Common, communal; stems gray, leaves bright green [desert hackberry, *Celtis pallida*?].

5— Slenderest vine-like cactus in fruit. Common, communal [*Opuntia leptocaulis*?].

6— Alkali plant. Rather rare and small; northern limit. Not communal [*Atriplex* spp.?].

7— Hill mimosa; a small underbush, communal, moderately abundant; usually almost leafless, now leafy [*Caesalpinia palmeri*?].

8— Related shrub with entire rudimentary leaves, purplish in color; rare, communal [ratany, *Krameria* spp.?].

9— Creosote bush [*Larrea tridentata*].

10— Mex. leatherwood; leafless now, broad spatulate leaf in season. Quite sappy, sap being astringent, rather bitter. On southward slopes common, not communal [*Jatropha cuneata*].

Nov. 14
EL GRUPO TO ORTEGA (FELIX) RANCHO[13]

Clear, cold, heavy frost (first of the season). Clouds nearly gone, Baboquivari being distinct.

The divide is considerably below level of old plain, the W. & S. drainage being in competition. There is evidently not a great-deal of alluvium, though the low old hills of H. [Humo] are almost buried—or cut down. Beyond divide the surface slopes rapidly and black igneous rocks soon appear, extending to Ortega. Here another wash comes in from eastward.

The flora is changing rapidly. The saguaro abides on the volcanic slopes, and one specimen of pitahaya was seen. The cats claw is more abundant than mesquite, and the pinnate-leaf paloverde appears. Following collected at Ortega ranch:

11 — Cat-claw [*Acacia greggii*]. Commonest tree except mesquite.

12 — Pinnate-leaf paloverde.[14]

13 — Ironwood, occurs in cañons [*Olneya tesota*].

Nov. 15
RANCHO DE ORTEGA TO ALTAR.

The wind roared down the converging cañons from N. all night long, and kept the same pace all day. Clear and beautiful, hardly a cloud in sight all day, sun boringly hot, but wind chill.

Noted late last night that wood-pecker note is indistinguishable from that of quail and mesquite bird.

The divide W. of rio Seco is only a little way from the wash, so that nearly all of the waste from below the cross range drains S.W. This is a cholla plain, and soon after emerging from the cañon the cina [senita cactus] begins and soon abounds. The pitahaya [organ pipe cactus] is not seen until within 5 or 6 mi. of Altar, which suggests that the specimen seen high up the cañon wall yesterday was wrongly identified. The long-thorn paloverde[15] came in soon after crossing the rio Seco.

The eastern extremity of the transverse monocline range is beset with little volcanic buttes, and igneous rocks crop in arroyo 7 mi. from Altar.

On starting out a large mortar was seen near road, but no other works of prehistoric or pre-Mexican work.

[NOV. 16]
IN CAMP AT ALTAR

Placated the Secretario de Prefectura and through him the Jefe de gerente [illegible word] fiscal during the morning, and after noon the approval of our invasion came from Sasabé.

Weather clear, hot, chilly at night; no dew.

Within memory of men now living the Apache lay in wait about Altar to steal food, etc, and none ventured out after night fall except in armed parties. There is a tradition of an Apache thrusting his arm through a window in a house occupied by a woman to steal a meal of frijoles [beans], when she quickly threw a riata [lariat] over his arm and held him until his cries brought help to her.[16]

[NOV. 17]
ALTAR TO CABORCA

On Pitiquito pass collected specimens (14) of the abundant leathery shrub called toróte [*Jatropha cuneata*], which abides all over the foothills and lower slopes (perhaps higher also), and (15) of the leathery stocky tree or bush with leaves of mesquite, trunk and branches of leatherwood, and strong odor of cedar [elephant tree, *Bursera microphylla*]. Of this neither Indian nor Mexican could give me name. The toróte is ordinarily leafless, though specimens in leaf were collected. The leaf is small, spatulate, and in pairs of tufts. The wood is largely used by the Papago Indians for basketry, after scraping thin. It has an abundant astringent and rather acrid juice. The 15 have a less abundant juice with a peculiar cedar–castor oil flavor. After the experiment of tasting, suffered a short time from a belladonna-like sensation with slight malign and irregularity of vision.

Johnson finds the Pitiquito butte entrenched with rock rings overlooking the entrenchment.

Mitchell photographed a number of plants, and tried exposures on Trinchera de Caborca.[17] Johnson completed map here.

Warm and balmy. In evening sheet lightning in mts. S.S.E.

NOV. 18.
IN CAMP AT CABORCA

The greater part of the day occupied in waiting for Dr. Jules Foucoult,[18] who owns boats in Gulf which might be used in visiting Tiburon. In vain. Saw him in evening, but his boats were out of order and his song was "Ils vont vous tuer" [They will kill you] in endless repetition with varying emphases and intonation— for such is his estimate of the Seri.

The rest of the day was spent in examinations and surveys of La Trinchera de Caborca. Besides the great rampart along S. side, there are many supplementary works especially toward extremities. The arroyos are barricaded with walls 2–6 ft. high and flat terraces above; and the spurs are terraced in similar fashion, with rectangular, circular, or irregular spaces of sufficient size for domiciles. Johnson mapped the works on this side, and also ascended to the summit, finding house rings carefully built of small blocks of stone, and finding indications that the structural shelves near crest have been artificially cleared of debris. I noticed several large blocks perched above arranged leading N. as if to be rolled over and down against invaders. Pottery was found in fragments in considerable quantity along the terraces. The ware is distinctive, finger worked without, scraped within. One decorated piece was found on the summit, where also bits of quartz and other erratic rock were picked up. No trace of permanent reservoirs or storage cists was found. No petroglyphs.

Further examination only strengthens the conviction that the works were not used for trails, and indeed that they were built by people without knowledge of usual trails—sections of the work are sometimes connected with finger-and-toe climbing between. A somewhat vague way leads down the S.W. spur toward the valley.

S.E. winds during last night, wet-looking clouds toward S.E., wind soon fell and clouds dissipated; heat followed, the evening being also warm.

NOV. 19
CABORCA TO RANCHO DE CANADIA

Clear, somewhat balmy, cloudless, hot. The plants are soft in aspect and verdure prevails.

Another spur, overlooking Pitiquito from S.E., is entrenched, and a third also. The works were seen from the valley only.

Between rancho de Ventana and rancho de Canadia stretches a vast alluvial plain, inching S.W., trenched slightly by rio Altar and a multitude of minor washes. 3 to 5 mi. from the latter the rd. traverses the finest of the prehistoric villages thus far seen. Pottery fragments abound, plain and decorated, with the scraped inside, two fragmentary pestles and a perfect muller were collected; many stone heaps, apparently survivors from cajon walls or fire-places were seen; and at least a dozen remains of cajon walls rose above the ground, in one case in a circle some 3 ft. across. The plain is now one of visual overwash, and no relief features are preserved.

Canadia	**NOV. 20 • CANADIA** [**RANCHO DE CANALIAS [CANALES?]** **TO ALAMITO (LAS TRINCHERAS).**]

Clear, cloudless, hot, a westerly breeze about our route so we journeyed in dust.

Across the broad, flat valley of Magdalena river, with mountains of nearly horizontal or tilted strata far away on both sides. Nearly half the day was spent in crossing sheet water plains. Rio Magdalena is dry, a bed of cobbles 200 yds wide up to 8 or 10 in. in diameter, generally 2½–4, with a few sand stretches.

The colonization of plants is well exemplified on both sides of Magdalena river. The flora is the same as previously noted. The leaves of mesquite and iron-wood, overgrown by reason of wet, are shrinking, and many are withering and dropping off—on many trees half the leaves are withered and white, ready to fall.

Prehistoric remains here and there, but in general our route misses them. On both sides of rio Magdalena there are a good many scattered remains of habitations, generally reduced to rude heaps of scattered stones from the cajon walls; a few bits of pestles and mullers, and some fragments of pottery are associated.

Las Trincheras promises well, as does Trincheritas close by.

There is a good deal of garambullo, the acacia? collected at El Grupo, in fruit; the ripe fruit is an orange or reddish berry the size of a pen with a moderately thick pulp of sweetish berry flavor, much liked by birds, enclosing a single large hard seed [desert hackberry, *Celtis pallida*].

[**NOV. 21**
IN CAMP AT LAS TRINCHERAS]

The butte is about 500 ft. high, ¾ mi. long, ⅜ mi. wide. It is crescentic, concave north. The northern concave side is terraced from base to summit, and the western end is nearly as well terraced. Terraces also extend around the S. side of the main body, which is western cusp; and on E. side of this cusp toward the lower cusps. The first terrace is just above level of plain, the highest near crest. In general terraces consist of a wall of stone laid neatly without mortar 2–15 ft. high, and glacis of smaller rubble with a veneer of fine rock debris 10–40 ft. wide. Many house rings occur on the glacis, or attached to terrace walls. Character and distribution shown in Johnson's map and in photos. Toward summit rock carvings occur in considerable numbers. Some of the forms are as follows, others are shown in photographs:

Most of the carvings are so far obliterated by age as to be illegible. A fine Aztec-looking design was photographed near the summit looking W., and near it an Aztec-looking frieze. The above designs are less interesting. It is noteworthy that some of the designs (like 5 above) are much fresher in appearance than others.

Particularly at lower levels the terraces abound in potsherds, generally less than an inch across, all of the same class of ware, like that indicated at Caborca and intervening villages. Broken metates and mullers also abound. A terrace-wall

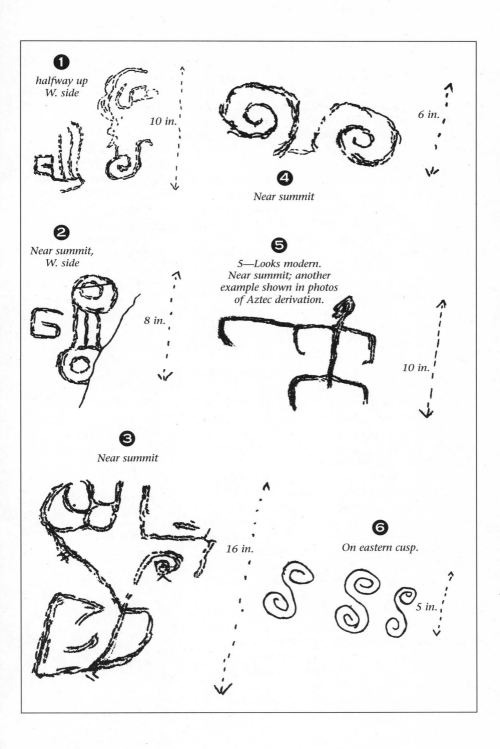

1 halfway up W. side

10 in.

4 Near summit

6 in.

2 Near summit, W. side

8 in.

5 5—Looks modern. Near summit; another example shown in photos of Aztec derivation.

10 in.

3 Near summit

16 in.

6 On eastern cusp.

5 in.

stone was observed to have been used as a metate, and a mortar in the rock of the hill was seen near by; also a broad pavement of flat-lying rock worn as if by reciprocal grinding over a surface of some square feet. The rock of the butte is a trachyte (?), sometimes fluent or ropy in structure, sometimes dense, sometimes jointed, or on the whole quite variable; on W. slope and sometimes elsewhere it is a breccia or brecciated tuff.

The neighboring buttes are artificialized, but to less degree. A small one on S. has a few house rings, and its summit is built out into a buttement or rim with a narrow terrace inside. Broken metates and mullers found here also.

Between E. and middle spur of Trinchera there are two enclosures, one nearly circular, 15 ft. across, one rounded rectangular about 40 × 20 ft. outside, walls 3–4 ft. thick. The entrance is protected thus: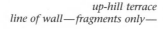

Within it a pottery button and a large piece of broken metate were found, as well as a large number of potsherds and spawls.

Pits ½–1¼ in. deep and 1½–2½ in. across, like shallow mortarlets are not uncommon toward summit.

Clouds drifted from S.E. with threat of rain until about 2:30 when the wind veered to S.W. and clouds were dissipated. A little after sunset fleecy, high clouds obscured part of the sky, but soon disappeared.

Nov. 22
In camp at Las Trincheras.

There are two enclosures well down the concave slope to N. on main butte. The western one is as follows noted by Johnson:

Two wall rocks in place are in part worn smooth on top, one photographed; Norris says they are for pounding meat. The smooth pavement on W. side of butte was photographed, and pronounced by Norris to have been used for rubbing face paint. A mortar in situ (photographed) was said by him to have been used for grinding mesquite beans. His explanation of the terraces is that "There was a war, and then the walls were built." Among the articles found were broken grinders, mortars, hammer stones, etc., with one football.[19] There are vast quantities of spalls from water worn pebbles of hard tough rocks, most commonly greenstones, more rarely quartz, etc. Many fragments of marine shells also were found. The most abundant material is potsherds which occur in thousands—the ground is literally sprinkled with them and with the spalls of erratic pebbles—they might be collected by bushels.

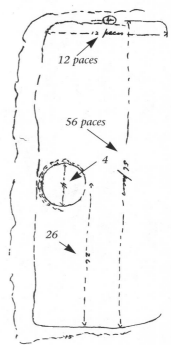

up-hill terrace
line of wall—fragments only—

On the summit and at other points the stones have small pits, already noted; Norris says they are for the game with [illegible word] beans.[20]

Proceeded to the small butte—Trincherita. It is some 250 ft. high—Johnson thinks 200 or less. It is entrenched or terraced on W., E., and in part on S. as shown on map (made on 23rd). The art products are like those of Trincheras in all respects save that here much pottery is decorated, while none of that on larger mound was seen thus painted. Shell was also very abundant, and rock carvings also. The following is an example:

many others were photographed and sketched by Mitchell. Near the summit smoothed stones, in place, were found, including one large one evidently a metate. Pits also are found.

All day there was a high S.S.W. wind with clouds scudding, so that it was difficult to photograph. At night the appearance grew worse, and all was made ready for rain.

Nov. 24
In camp at Trincheras

Rain began about 8:30, and continued to shower with passing clouds all night, the wind weakening meantime. The fall was apparently ¾ in. during the night. Morning brought diminished showers, but they continued till noon, and at intervals later, aggregating perhaps ¼ in. more at camp. Wind S.S.W. and gusty, at other times on little butte a still wind with rain and a few small hailstones.

Johnson mapped smaller butte. Some fine inscriptions were seen, some being quite old and Aztecan. These are so far weathered away as to be indecipherable—only faint lines can be seen collectively, but none can be followed individually. Most of the carvings are undoubtedly new, and they appear to cover a long period—some being quite fresh, others are in grading continuity, the Aztecan specimens nearly weathered out. Painted pottery, shell carved in rings and otherwise, an entire aquatic shell, and a broken capstone-like piece of red granite

WJ McGee examines petroglyphs on the "little trinchera" at Las Trincheras, Sonora, November 22, 1895.

which Norris cannot identify, were picked up. Many worn stones were seen. It is probable that some of these meat-stones or paint stones are modern. The works here look less defensive than some of those on Trinchera.

By vertical angles Trinchera is found to be something over 600 ft. above the plain on N.W.—about 650, 612, and 588 on three trials. An acequia skirts its northern base but becomes lost toward N.E.

After sunset sky cleared, and rain entirely ceased, wind remaining S.S.W.

[Nov. 24
In camp at Las Trincheras]

Before midnight rain recommenced, and as much fell as last night continuing until morning. About 8 a.m. the wind veered to N.W. and rain ceased, save for a few trifling gusts. Temperature fell—uncomfortably cold even by campfire.

[Nov. 25
Alamito to Las Cruces[21]]

A heavy frost with ¼ in. ice on exposed water; clear, northerly breezes. Temperature fell during the day, probably with increasing altitude; cold at night.

Nearly all day spent in crossing a vast alluvial plain, stretching thru the lower transverse ranges and rising above the level of their summits. The wash at 11-o'clock butte was nearly as large as Magdalena river, and remained large for miles. The valley represents a horseshoe-toe like that E. of El Grupo, but the bounding mountains are more nearly buried or cut down. The divide is within 5 mi. of Las Cruces.

At 11 o'clock Johnson occupied a butte on right, which he found entrenched and platformed, pottery of the usual type abounding. Then for miles through the well-grassed valley house remains with bits of similar pottery were noted in passing. This valley is now unoccupied save by antelope.[22]

The vegetation shows the effect of frost. No noteworthy observations, except the abundance of grass in the long valley and the appearance of great groves of okatillo [*Fouquieria splendens*] as the divide is approached. A few ant forms after crossing the divide, but the grass too luxuriant to make them stand out. The crater-building ants are small reddish brown; the grass-crater ants are small black; the furrows with small drying girds are large red ants, of which a part are large-head.[23]

Las Cruces is an abandoned hacienda of considerable significance. The house one-story except the round-tower which was two or 3, great tanques, horsepower, stonewalls, a bridge of which pieces remain, etc.

[Nov. 26
Las Cruces to Pozo Noriega]

Night cold, moderating toward morning; slight frost. High,—light clouds, no wind. Fair all day, light southerly breezes, light high clouds slightly veiling the sun, warmer.

The route is an old one, made noteworthy chiefly by Johnson's mapping and collateral studies. In morning he went to outlying butte near Las Cruces, and found it entrenched and coroneted. The chief work is a wall, vertical inside and 4–6 ft. high, carefully laid, sloping and irregularly piled up outside, with a gateway, thus forming coronet; but the walls below are almost equally conspicuous.

Pottery of the usual type abounds. It is seen from the summit that the divide has migrated northward a considerable distance; and south of this the surface is generally of spheroid rocks swept clean or covered with a trifling veneer of disintegrated, but not decomposed debris. It is only toward the center of the valley that alluvium is found in any quantity. Most of the rocks are igneous or greatly metamorphosed; but a few blocks of limestone were seen.

The small mimosa–scrub mesquite abounds, generally devoid of leaves but often covered with pods, over the rocky slopes and in small draws therein; and a larger mimosa with a much larger pod was seen near the crest S. of Las Cruces; not collected.[24] A maguey [*Agave* spp.] was seen somewhat further S. The effect of frost was not noticed much below Las Cruces, though the acacia is shedding leaves, still green, in profusion. Mesquite is quite large in the Noriega arroyo for several miles. At the settlements here the vultures[25] are semi-domesticated, and abundant.

Johnson went up on the hills at the N. of the river and at margin of plain found a couple of arrowheads which Norris pronounces Seri. They are, with a single exception (at El Grupo) the first arrowheads seen by any of this party, tho careful search has been made, especially at Las Trincheras.

Nov. 27
IN CAMP AT POZO NORIEGA

Last evening drifting clouds, light and high, with a circle about the moon; temperature much more moderate. This morning a light frost, warmer soon, with clear sky; temperature hot in sun, chilly in shade, without a coat.

Johnson made a station nearby, and a sketch station later. The first (signal peak) is in the low range extending toward Pozo Nuevo and Hermosillo. He describes it as a symmetrical crest, and El Carnero and Sierrita falling in line with it. The rocks are quite metamorphosed, granitic, or rather gneissic, with abundant quartz in veins and crystals. He recognized an old planative surface coinciding with the great valleys, the modern sculpture being wholly independent of the structure.

Spent the day talking with Norris, trying to gain an insight into the Papago organization. Success meager. The Papago like the plants of their region seem to have risen above specific characters to general habits in which they are allied to other peoples, especially the more advanced, of the world.

Nov. 28
POZO NORIEGA TO BACUACHI

Night warmer, moderate dew, no frost. A few light clouds evening, none morning, light airs, clear, warm.

The entire way was down, generally in channel of Agua de Chino. In the lower part of the range water flows in the gorge; it is then dry to a granitic subrange midway to Bacuachi, where water rises, and where Agua del Sangre enters, said to be from a spring a short distance off. This water lasts only a mile or two, when the channel is dry to Casa Vieja, where abundant water rather suddenly arises and continues to Bacuachi, where it all ends. This stream was a surprise, by reason of its length and strength. Between Casa Vieja and Bacuachi the gorge is deeply cut in volcanic breccia, and is often picturesque; toward Pozo Noriega it is sometimes cut through great masses of granite, and is almost as scenic. The rocks are granite in the first range followed by beds of tuff, etc., and granite again midway with the breccia and a few dark lavas thence forward. The last 7 mi. is a damp, dark passage through rocks over a bed of sand saturated with the wandering waters of a score of rivulets into which the water divides. The wandering of the waters over this narrow belt illustrates the flow of sheet water: At first it tends to form rivulets, but so soon as channels are cut the flow increases, when a heavier load is taken on, and this handicaps the stream, so that the final tendency is to equalize the flow.[26] In Agua de Chino the bottom is permeable sand, and perfect equalization is attained only within it, so here most of the water goes, only a small portion rippling over the surface in ever shifting rivulets.

The flora is rather rich. The guiacore [guayacán, *Guaicum coulteri*] was seen first at the midway point; the leather-cedar [*Bursera microphylla*] in tree size nearer Pozo Noriega in the great cliffs of granite; the San Juanito [*Jacquinia macrocarpa*] at camp. Below Casa Vieja two new trees were seen—a broad-leafed rich green tree with white trunk and roots growing on the cliff faces and sending roots down to water clinging to the rocks in curious fashion,[27] and a wide-branching white-trunk tree 8–20 ft. high which may be the tree okatillo [*Fouquieria macdougalii*]. The guiacore is quite a tree with wahoo-like seed, abundant rich green leaves hugging stem, thornless; the San Juanito is still larger,—thornless save for a few sharp thorns at the tip of each narrow, rather bright green leaf; its foliage being abundant, and its acorn-like or nut-like fruit being edible—a cupless acorn, with thick shell, enclosing a mass of pulp and several brown seeds, edible when fresh.

Plenty in

[**NOV. 29**]
[BACUACHI TO SAYULA]

Clear, warm, balmy, growing hot. Little dew, not a cloud.
Plants collected at Bacuachi:

16 — Guiacore, twigs and fruit. Common at rather low levels.
17 — San Juanito, twigs and fruit, common at moderate levels.
18 — The Sonora Sage, abundant along all arroyos at all altitudes; sometimes 12 ft. high.[28]
19 — Fly-bush; a fleshy-woody shrub growing in exceedingly dense masses, fragrant, thornless, loved by birds and flies; twigs in flower and berry; gray green small leaves.[29]

Toward Sayula the leather-cedar [*Bursera microphylla*] comes down to the plain about the bases of buttes, and abounds in great trees, one sometimes bearing a half dozen branches divaricating at ground each 4–10 in. thick, the whole standing 12–18 ft. high. There comes in also a related tree or shrub, with much smaller stems and more slender habit generally, with a delicate fern-like leaf and a berry much like the larger. Its skin is red or red-brown instead of yellow or gray, as in larger [red elephant tree, *Bursera hindsiana*]. There is a small bushy shrub with lanceolate leaves and a peculiar berry, which greens the landscape—the lance-leaf [*Sapium biloculare*]. The toróté [*Jatropha cuneata*] also abounds, and is partly in leaf, partly in peculiar condition of occasional extremities of stems, which may mean fruiting, or injury by insects, or both. The collections at Sayula are—

20— Lance-leaf.
21— Little cedar.
22— Toróté.

The leather-cedar drops a gum freely. The alkali plant of previous pages is Canalía, Mex. It is used as a tea for some disorder. It tastes and smells of rosin. It shoots a slender stem above the leafy portion to flower and fruit [brittlebush, *Encelia farinosa*?]. For this is one of the characteristics of the region—to get flowers and fruits high.

Johnson notes the abundance and beautiful coloration, and especially the variegation, of small birds.

For five or six mi. the road goes on down arroyo, then passes over some miles of of [*sic*] plain on W., then approaches the narrowed arroyo at Sayula. No water in river here: a well. Little stock, so good grass.

We are in Seriland. Yesterday guide Ramon,[30] within five miles of Pozo Noriega, pointed out a Seri? footprint in the sand, and stuck closer than a brother to the wagon the rest of the day; today our guide is Mr. Griggs, so-called because merry as a grig, who has a Seri arrow wound in his breast and another on his wrist;[31] says that two prospectors have been killed within 15 days,[32] and that the Papago Indians of the Encinas and neighboring ranches have been detailed by the state to live along the coast and check advance of the hostiles. He also confirms the press accounts of the depredations last autumn.[33] He says the Seri shoot as well with arrows as white men with guns, that they are swifter than dogs, and their teeth are more to be feared than those of dogs. But the Seri have withdrawn farther from here than from Pozo Noriega, and have not robbed Bacuachi for many years.

A few light, high clouds; warm, pleasant evening, bright moon, light airs.

NOV. 30
SAYULA TO TONUCO

A few red-tinted clouds at sunrise; air sharp, no dew, light airs. Fleecy clouds hang over Seri mts. José shoots a coyote before sunrise, and Mr. Griggs skins him. By the way it appears that Mr. Griggs first name is Jesus.

The Mexican name of the little cedar is toróté [*Bursera hindsiana*], and it is used as medicine. The leather cedar is torote blanco [*Bursera microphylla*], and the torote of Pitiquito is torotito [*Jatropha cuneata*]. The lance leaf (called yerba) is poisonous, used for poisoning arrows, and its stems are used for arrows.[34] Photographed torote, torote blanco, and torotito, as well as Canalia, the rosin plant, which is also medicinal. One of the characteristics of the plants is aromatic or pungent odors and flowers; the party collected a lot of mint-like plant called orégon, to be used for flavoring as an improvement on pepper [oregano, *Lippia palmeri*]. It is also used as a preservative for meat.

Two-thirds of the way is a well and small cemented tank forming the pueblocito of San Jose. Here is a family of Papago, parents, young man and 10–12 yr. old girl. On being asked if they would have a watermelon, having none themselves, they deliberated and then declined on the ground that we were traveling and would need it worse than they.

Collected also bara-prieta (black whip), a short almost vine-like shrub with pyriform leaves so arranged as to face in pairs; and except in the wet they fold together. The fruit is a bean in a broad, thin pod, red-purple, two beans or one, hard and woody, lying loose.[35] In addition a twig of chaparral (accin?) bearing thin zebra-striped acorn-squashes (*Cucurbita* spp.). Another accin has a translucent juicy, sweet mistletoe-like berry.[36]

At Tonuco found a fine portable metate (kai't-tou-i-ku't, grinder for saguaro seeds), which was preserved. A few miles from Sayula passed a low butte on S.W., and at its foot saw a small camping circle of stones, was surprised to find no clear indication of prehistoric occupation, no valley house mounds, pottery, no entrenchments.

DEC. 1
TONUCO TO COSTA RICA

Clear, warm, not a cloud evening or morning; the clouds are gone from Seri mts. Johnson awoke camp by shooting a coyote from bed with his six-shooter. Jesus Griggs skins him. Here as elsewhere along the route Mexicans are shocked to learn that we are en route to Tiburon, and coax José [Contreras, the teamster] not to go, they have made him pretty nervous. The Papago family at San José looked on the trip as a matter of course and never thought of dissuading Norris. The Mexican [illegible word] a gringo [three illegible words] a few gringos more or less in the long run.

The route winds among low granite peaks and ridges rising almost sharply from the plain. By the way, yesterday's route was over planed granite most of the way from San José to Rancho de Tonuco, though Sierra de Tonuca is in part, at least, limestone. A few limestone ledges also were noted, but generally the limestone forms sierras no less imposing, indeed more imposing, than granite or other rocks. So it would appear that degradation here is not a function of chemic work. On the whole, it would seem that in this region of equable temperatures and scant vegetation disintegration proceeds slowly; and that the flowing waters of the rare streams find little to do in mountains, and only push along the debris on the plains.[37]

A little way from camp Johnson found a bit of shell on an ill-defined site; nothing else artificial was found that was not modern; but a bit of Seri pottery on the butte.

[DEC. 2
IN CAMP AT COSTA RICA.]

Clear, warm, a faint haze, a few light clouds occasionally.

Afternoon Mitchell with José and Papago guide went to Hermosillo for interpreter, etc.

The elderly Papago seen at San José is chief of the tribe here and hereabouts; name Manuel. There are about 7 families here, one or two at Bacuachi, or rather near Sayula, the one at San José, a few at Hermosillo, and a few below Hermosillo near river; nothing learned about Papagos S. of Hermosillo.

Mitchell goes to Hermosillo afternoon.

[DEC. 3
IN CAMP AT COSTA RICA.]

Airs, hazy growing into clouds; in morning red-tinted horizontal bands of cloud in W., extending most way around horizon; sun more or less obscure; moderate dew in morning. Toward noon wind rose to moderate breeze, S.W., and S. Seri mt. was cut off except at summit by dust cloud, Tiburon being entirely concealed. Toward night sun generally lost in light clouds, with threat of rain. Probably raining up the slope; moon veiled in light clouds.

[DEC. 4
IN CAMP AT COSTA RICA.]

No rain, no dew; clouds obscuring sun at sunrise, lifting slightly, later, veiling sun; variable airs, a S.W. moderate breeze at altitudes.

Spent afternoon in collecting information from Papago old man, hard of hearing, defective of vision; recorded in Introduction.[38]

Mitchell returned from Hermosillo at sunset with Thompson, as interpreter.[39]

The Papago are rather afraid to visit the island, but so far as I can gather their chief objection is one of principle—the Seri have occupied Tiburon from time immemorial, it belongs to them, and they are justified in repeling [sic] invasion.

[DEC. 5
IN CAMP AT COSTA RICA.]

Clear, warm, no dew light airs, few light fluffy clouds and faint cloud bands in evening.

Spent the day in arranging details. Two Papago employed to visit Seri mountains, which they do not object to, because this is the mainland.

[DEC. 6
COSTA RICA TO SALINE BARRANCA.[40]]

Light clouds in morning (no dew), growing heavier as day progressed until sun was veiled, and sometimes half the sky overcast; light airs, with S.W. winds at cloud level.

Santa Ana [ranch] is on the delta of streams coming down from Tonuca sierra and neighboring ranges, probably including the drainage from the eastern and southern slopes of Sierrita. It is a great, mud plain, partaking in less degree of the characteristics of the Sonora delta at Costa Rica, mesquite large and luxuriant, flora generally strong, etc. Most of the way from Costa Rica is over sand, not drifting ("milpias"),[41] abounding in cholla and other cacti. Beyond Santa Ana the delta character grades into broad sheetwater belts and saline-looking playa-form flats, scantly clothed with low herbage [*Atriplex* spp.], just enough to color the landscape. Mesquite belts and zones of light sand, sometimes windblown, intervene. Libertad [abandoned ranch] is on a long dune, surrounded by sheetwater surfaces from Bacuachi river. The flora is scant, but includes okatillo, torotito, etc., apparently transported from the mountains. W. of Libertad the sheetwater flats continue for some 5 mi., and then give place to sand flats. The sand is more or less windblown, light, often burrowed by squirrels, and the vegetation scanty, and, of course, bushy. Before reaching the barranca great sand banks and dunes were encountered.

Over the plains, with increasing abundance beyond Libertad, bits of shell and pottery of Seri type were found, and a mortar or two were seen. Two thirds of the way from Libertad to the barranca a cracked but practically entire olla, of Seri ware and the usual bottom form but with wide neck and ornamented border, was found half embedded in the sand. It was collected.[42] The shell is of such abundance as to suggest that it is in situ.

[DEC. 7
SALINE BARRANCA TO SERI MOUNTAIN]

The barranca is a canalform tinaja[43] perhaps half a mile long, 20–40 ft. wide, and up to 4 ft. deep at least; the water is quite brackish. It is cut in a great arroyo bottom, itself cut in beds of sand; and all about lie dunes and drifts of fine, light sand. Below, toward S., this arroyo quickly becomes a vast playa of whitish, or brownish encrusted earth—the Seri absent.

Clear, warm, seldom a cloud to be seen; moderate dew.

After a stretch of sand, the way lies along a broad plain of sedentary sand abounding in cacti, other forms of vegetation being quite subordinate. The prevailing form is a new variety of saguaro, a woodstumped, wide-branching monster of a dozen or score of branches, and often with twice as many branchlets—this cactus being more abundant so far as individuals are concerned than in any region heretofore seen, and much more abundant as to trunks. The main trunk is nearly solid, a slight pith only; the lower branches also are nearly solid; and it is only toward the top that the ribs are well differentiated. It is noteworthy that in this region of cacti the aim of the giant is not to branch high, but to branch low and often and follow the desert habit of spreading—of increasing land tenure through air holding. The roots are large, but not so large as of trees, the 2-foot stump has one or two six-inch roots near surface, and the 3-foot specimen may have a root nearly a foot thick with smaller branches; but there appear not [blank] be many low roots. Still, the plant appears never to be uprooted by winds, and it is possible roots are larger than appears.[44] The pitahaya [organ pipe cactus] and cina [senita] also abound, but are especially noteworthy, and appear dwarfed in comparison with the larger cactus. Cholla also abounds, and okatillo is quite abundant. Mesquite, toróte blanco, creosote, paloverde, etc, with a variety of acacias and other shrubs form a relatively inconspicuous feature. Still higher the slope becomes rocky and the vegetation assumes the usual torrential-slope character.

The mountains are of red rocks, igneous in part, though there is in many cases a structure suggesting bedding.

Traces of Seri are found everywhere. Shell is abundant, and after getting in the gorge a good trail was struck—excreta suggest that they have been here inside 3–4 days, great quantities of pottery appear. Water is promised at the arroyo, which proved to be a Seri fortress and well—dry. Many terraces like those of Trinchera, sometimes with house circles, were found, but not studied in detail. About the well many bones of fowl, fish, turtle, deer, etc. were found, as well as bits of turtle shell, a meat pounding (metate like) stone, a bit of bent sheet metal, and slightly used mulling stones. Miguel and Anton, Papago guards,[45] display great independence and courage in following the fresh trail.

Started to climb the peak[46] with Johnson, Mitchell, and the two Papago, but the debility of malaria knocked me out; set out to return with Anton, when a call from Miguel in Papago announced that one of the gringos was dead, and a later call that he was mucho malo [very sick]; started to rejoin party, sending Anton in advance, when he returned with a note announcing that Johnson was faint but better, and going on to spend the night on the mountain. Anton returned to camp with me.[47]

DEC. 8
SALINE BARRANCA TO [STAYED IN CAMP]

Clear, warm, light dew, a few fluffy clouds, light or stiff breeze from N.W. which began last evening. Fine mirage effect on playa.

José brings in a fine mulling stone and many fragments of Seri pottery.

Thompson (of Maine) is a genius; witness the following conversation with Mitchell en route:

M.—Mr. Thompson, what is that cactus called?

T.—That cactus there? Oh, that is the apple cactus. D'ye see, my friend, that it is all covered with little apples? That's why it's the apple cactus. Come to look at them things that are more like pears. It's the pear cactus, that's what it is. (Pause) The Mexicans call them tunas.[48]

M.—Are they of any use?

T.—What; them cactuses? Yes, they are that. They're jist splendid for pies. Ye can make a fine pie out of them things, and if there's any one thing I know when I see it, it's a good pie; not but what it looks like boastin', but I had ought to know good pies, don't ye think so yourself; with makin' butter and things?

M.—Do they use the stems or the fruit?

T.—When ye make pies? The fruit; of course; them little pears you see hangin' all over it. They're jist like pears, too; the only difference is that one's sweet and the other's sour. So, you see, my friend, the one first rate for pies.

M.—How do you get the spines off the tunas?

T.—Jist throw them on the ground m'fren', and pretty soon they all fall off; (pause) at least I should think that would be the best way to get them off.

M.—What preparation does the fruit require in making pies?

T.—Them cactus pears? I can't tell ye that, though I'm ready to do anything in my power for an American tha's the right kind, don't ye understand. I never made a pie out of them. (pause) I never saw a pie made out of them; but it stands to reason that ye can make good pies out of them for as I told ye, m'fren', a little while ago, they're jist like pears, the only difference is that one's sweet and the other's sour; ye can see from the wagon that they look like pears, only smaller; and a good pie is mighty fine eatin'. I dunno what they're like inside. They're good for stock feed too; make the milk rich; these darn Mexicans don't go much on milk but if they did they'd make a fortune. They make lots of cheese. Ye may know the cows eat them because ye never even see a steer in this country that don't have two or three of them stickin' to his jaw. Jist see them under that cholla over there! By George; there's half a bushel, or maybe three pecks, right there! My, if ye could only get stock to eat them things this would soon be a rich country! Say, m'fren', what d'ye think a New Yorker would say if he saw a cow with a dozen of them things stickin' to her jaw, hey? Think he'd kill her to save her, wouldn't he, hey? They get them pokin' their heads under them chollas tryin' to find a stray blade of grass; and it's mighty poor pickin' them cows get here, m'fren', and the stems too; for there's not a blame thing in the world in this country for them to eat but them little yalla weeds the Mexicans call grass darn 'em, don't ye understan' m'fren'. They get fat on it, too, not what ye'd call fat, but it's fat for this country; they can run like deers, too; an' if ye'd believe it m'fren' they go <u>six</u> <u>weeks</u> without water 'long when them cactuses is ripe, an' get <u>fat</u> as wethers, too, don't ye understan', so't they can't move faster'n a blame ol' sheep on a hot day, like, m'fren.

Toward noon the wind rose, and increased until late in afternoon, weakening toward sunset and nearly dying sometime after nightfall. It raised great quantities of fine sand which filled the air, completely concealing the playa and desert adjacent, and sometimes eclipsing the mountains. From N.N.W. or N.W. Sky clear.

Lay in camp all day, and until half an hour after dark waiting for the return of the party, Anton having been dispatched with water and food with 4th watch. They came in reporting success, but nearly exhausted, especially Mitchell. Johnson brings specimens of rock (reddish igneous) from peak, and reports shooting at one of herd of 4 bighorns[49] with Miguel's rifle.

DEC. 9
SALINE BARRANCA TO COSTA RICA

The eastern side of the arroyo-like trough in which playa lies proves to be a great bank or dune 50 or 100 feet high parallel to playa, and apparently formed by sanddrift from it. The playa is little below level of plain, thus:

Plain   *Dune*   *Playa*   *Dune*   *Plain*

Barranca

The western dune is the lower, and no exposures were seen; the eastern one is often if not generally cut into steep faces flanked by taluses, so that structure is revealed; it is observably weathered sand, lying horizontal, [illegible word] so far as seen, probably wholly wind laid. Evidently this embankment is moving eastward before the wind. Marine shells in abundance and variety over the plain, but possibly or probably all Seri-borne. No ancient beaches or other indications of sea occupancy. Suspicion that playa is below tide, and basin analogous to Mojave desert, formed by Sonoran delta increases.

Cloudless, light northerly breeze, no dew, warm.

Near Libertad rancho Andres picked up the skull of a Seri Indian who attacked him while digging well there, and who he shot. Preserved it.[50]

The party to Seri mountain included Johnson, Mitchell, Thompson, José, Andres, and Anton and Miguel, Papago. The first night was divided into four watches, viz., Mitchell & Thompson to 12; Andres & Anton, 12–2; McGee 2–4; José & Miguel, 4–breakfast. The second night Johnson, Mitchell & Miguel were in mountain, 500 ft. from summit, without coats, and slept little; in camp watches were, Thompson to 11; Andres 11–1:30; McGee 1:30–4; José 4–breakfast, Anton rising with him and setting out for mountain at daybreak. The third night all were in camp, and watches were as before, the climbers all sleeping.

[**DEC. 10**
IN CAMP AT COSTA RICA]

Clear, warm, no dew; camp in casa, so all Americans wheezy in consequence of organic dust. Light northerly airs.

Johnson & Norris making boat; Mitchell with José to Hermosillo for interpreter and American volunteers, etc.

[**DEC. 11**
DITTO, DITTO.]

[**DEC. 12**
DITTO]

Ditto, except slight dew, noticed because I slept out in a herder wagon instead of in casa; and that I took a hand in boat building.

Mitchell returns with Samuel C. Millard[51] as interpreter. "The doctor," who has been deluding Señor Encinas with false promises, declines to come; M.M. Rice of Minas Prietas[52] who has applied for a position also fails; and another American, promised by the doctor is not to be found.

[**DEC. 13**
IN CAMP AT COSTA RICA]

Clear, warm, light dew, a few fleecy clouds now and then, light airs.

All hands boatbuilding, including Chemali, the Señor's carpenter, who was chiefly occupied, however, in fitting water-blocks to the wagon designed to transport boat to coast.

[**DEC. 14**[53]
COSTA RICA TO AGUA AMARILLO.[54]]

Clear in early morning with light dew, rather warm night. Soon after sunrise clouds began to drift in from gulf, with light breeze, sky being half overcast. About 9 o'clock much threat of rain; at 11 Seri mountains came in view and soon after the island, and it appeared that the darkest cloud was merely a heavy fogbank. Soon after sky cleared, but a low fog bank lay in valley between Seri mts. and Tiburon until well toward evening. Light airs, promises fair.

Set out just after sunrise, 15 men and 20 horses with the sloop *Anita*,[55] flat bottom and sides, bottom sloped up for 2 ft. at prow, 17 ft. long; 4'8" beam, 1'6" deep, with sail abt. 6 X 9 ft., scull rudder and 8 paddles. I rode in on 4-horse light wagon, with José Contreras, driver, and Mr. Millard; Johnson in saddle attending boat wagon; Mitchell in saddle miscellaneous; Señor Andres and Don Ignacio in saddles giving trail; Norris in boat, with Anton (Papago) who led his horses; Miguel, José Maria, Anton Ortiz, Anton Castillo[56] and Mariana in saddles; and Rupuelto [Ruperto Alvarez, a part-Yaqui Indian] driving six horses to boat wagon.

The flora changes slowly at first, but as we get into playas and saline flats with intervening dunes and banks of sand, it changes rapidly and completely, hardly anything but mesquite, saguaro, and okatillo remaining. A characteristic is fleshiness of leaves; a stout bush with whitish barkless stems, thick and vigorous, has leaves about 1¼ X ⅝ X ¹⁄₁₆ in. or more, in habit resembling nopal leaves, with saline and unpleasant taste [*Maytenus phyllanthroides*].

After reaching flats all doubt as to indigenous character of shells disappears; they are in thousands, indeed in tons, sometimes paving the way for rocks, pectens, murexes, oysters, nerites [?], etc. in great quantities.[57] Remains of turtle also abound, possibly transported. The largest was a nearly entire shell, 18 X 24 inches, with dermal coating still adhering.

Bura [mule deer] tracks and coyote sign abundant; few small birds, not many jack rabbitts [*sic*].

About midday began to find bits of Seri pottery, which increased in abundance, some half ollas being seen. A modern shell with a cotton string attached to a bush nearby were picked up by Mitchell. During afternoon tracks of barefoot men with widespread toes, undoubtedly Seri, were frequently seen, some days or weeks old. At A—A— [Agua Amarillo] found fresh sign, apparently but a few hours old, and tracks were identified by Papago as those of Palado, with some doubt. Andres, Ignacio, and the six Papago with Millard set out to follow their trail and return at dark.

On the little hill overlooking the shallow well (Mexican?) stretch remains of Seri rancheria. The house forms [two illegible words separated by a comma] being of okatillo stems, 4½ ft. and less in height, 5 ft. and less wide; the best preserved has 4 bows, say 3 ft. apart, making house 9 or 10 ft. long. The bows are connected at sides with horizontal stems. Most of the houses are much smaller. There are 6 or 7, all told. There are also two brush piles, each marked by an upright stick, which Norris thinks are granaries. Postponed investigation until return. Norris and other picked up broken mortar, point shells, bits of pottery including a handled and painted piece as well as a piece perforated, two or three stone arrow heads[58] and a partly made metal arrowhead (all collected), with a whittled stick, a basket repaired with sealskin,[59] etc.

Andres et al returned before sunset with a lot of clams, having struck the mudflats, but no Seri Indians.

Found a copper arrowpoint and pebble mortar (collected) later.

3 watches: 1, to 12-30, Mitchell & Rupuelto; 2, to 3, José Maria & Norris; 3, to 6, José & Miguel.

DEC. 15
[AGUA AMARILLO TO GULFO DE CORTEZ [

At abt. 9 p.m. fog drifted in and veiled stars. sometimes partly, sometimes completely, when a fine mist wet everything. Lasted all night, and sun was only a faint spot until reached coast at 10.

The way is an alternation of dunes and flats alkaline, with shells abundant and growing newer and more fragile. Half an hour before reaching coast boom of surf was heard, and we pushed up the final sand bank slowly. Boat team broke down; put in Johnson's [illegible] as high wheeler, and leaders from our wagon ahead, and the 8 horses hauled the *Anita* up; in a few minutes all hands were caulking.

Saguaro (the Seri form) [*Pachycereus pringlei*] and okatillo extend on sandbanks almost to coast. Meantime all shrubbery fails except fleshy-leaved stuff, the bush seen yesterday, parsley-like creepers, and a variety of others being club-shape or otherwise thick pulpy foliage. They seem to be fog-plants, all.

On caulking the boat, in which Johnson led and Mitchell, Millard and Rupuelto did nobly, and Norris and Jose well, it was found rather late for sending the stock back to Costa Rica; and since I was also apprehensive about ordering stock away before boat was launched, I decided to camp. So Johnson, Mitchell, Millard, Andres, Anton & I went over to Alcatraz island. This is simply an igneous butte caught in the gulf; it has a long apron of debris on N. & N.E., but elsewhere is cut by the tide. It is exceedingly steep, either rock or talus. A hook juts out eastward from apron, an[d] on this a large flock of pelicans sat. Approaching within some 75 yds. Mitchell and Millard opened fire with winchesters, continuing the fusillade after the birds rose; about a dozen shots were fired, and two birds brought down, one on land, and one on the wing. Anton fired against the sun at a single incautious pelican, but failed to bring him down. Johnson shot two or three gulls and Mitchell a curlew on island.[60]

*W*J McGee, right, writes in notebook while others caulk the bottom of the sloop Anita for the trip to Tiburón Island, December 15, 1895. (N-6784)

Afternoon clear; light variable airs with fog and some clouds toward Tiburon. All day surf was strong, and pushing off and landing were not easy and resulted in wetting all concerned.[61] It did me much good to see Anton get aboard, since it was a precedent.

Retiring from the island we touched at a Seri rancheria a mile or so up the shore. It was of okatillo houses as at Agua Amarillo, still partly covered with sticks, with a bit of metate and mealing stone (collected) lying about, as well as turtle shells, bones, etc. Several older houses were about. None occupied apparently within a fortnight. Near shore a ruined balsa was seen, and close by a much older and decayed one.

In evening clouds gathered occasionally, veiling the stars; and during night a stiff southerly breeze blew an hour or two, followed by a light N.W. one. As darkness fell the breakers were seen to be phosphorescent; brilliant bluish white flashes shot along the combers, and [illegible word] dots of light remained on the sand, and all night the sea thundered.

DEC. 16
ALCATRAZ TO GRANITE COVE.

Morning fair, little dew; light breezes, some drying owing to feeble airs. Heavy surf.

Organized watch. Night from 8 p.m.; to 6 a.m. in four watches of 2½ hrs; 1st watch, Johnson, Captain, Norris and Anton Ortiz; 2nd, Millard, Captain, with Don Ignacio and Anton Castilla [Castillo]; 3rd—self, with Anton & Miguel; 4th, Mitchell, Captain, with Andres & Mariana.

Sent José, Norris, and José Maria back with stock, giving explicit instructions as to return and camping. Norris went back because ill;[62] he exchanged with Rupuelto, who is an admirable substitute.

Fearing defection, decided to walk with several Indians up the shore to the Seri landing, said to be less than 3 leagues by Andres and Ignacio; took Ignacio, Miguel, Mariana, and Anton Ortiz. We got the boat off in surf at cost of wetting all hands and the entire outfit. Within 10 miles Anton Castilla was sea-sick, and Anton soon followed, and both were dead weight all day. Rupuelto was soon after taken, but stuck to his paddle, and so, later, Millard. Mitchell kept up by effort; Johnson was not, of course, affected. Occasionally sail was set, but in general *Anita* crept under paddle; and she is not fast.

About 1½ mi. above Alcatraz camp found a huge shell mound.[63] It is a prominent landmark as seen from Alcatraz island and elsewhere. It is say 75 ft. high. The chief mound is 40 × 50 ft. at summit and slopes steeply to sea, gently in other directions—indeed it and others of the series are cut by the advancing coast. Others, covering an area of over an acre, are nearly as high, sometimes rising in sharp cones, sometimes flat topped. All are built almost entirely of clam shells, of which nearly all are separated. There are very few other shells, and these various. Mixed with shell at summit and also at depths are bits of pottery and pebbles showing slight wear. The pottery appears to be Seri; so pronounced by Ignacio and Papago without hesitation. The pebbles are also just such as Seri use—smoothed shore pebbles, slightly worn, the best was brought along. It is noteworthy that the shore has pushed quite a way, at least, into the mounds; also that no clam flats now occur near by, though the playa in rear is cut off only by sand banks; finally that the shells appear quite fresh; and are not associated with turtle shells and bones, which abound about Seri rancherias.

Soon after found rancherias Seri, commonly old, more or less filled with drifted sand; for the sand lies in deep sand dunes, often 20 ft. long, 8 or 10 ft. wide, and 4–8 ft. high. In one case the house was transformed into a dune. Just at foot of peak next to Kino pt.[64] a fresh one was found, used apparently within 3 days; a muller still stained was carried away. At Kino pt. struck fresh trail, apparently today's, recognized at once by Papago as "Palado," and we followed it most of the afternoon. At one time there were 5 tracks: and I noted that though barefoot they walked over sharp-pointed [rocks?] quite as freely as sand, when both were side by side. The behavior of the waterfowl indicates that the narrow range is less than 50 yds, probably not more than 100 ft.

From camp to Kino pt. the beach is sand, with wind-blown sand inland; the first short point below, which hardly interrupts the curve of the bay, is opposite a butte of igneous rock within 100 yds. of water's edge, and only separated by a narrow belt of storm-washed sand; and the base of the butte had been storm-washed quite recently. Here the nearest rancheria occurs; it is partly formed of driftwood, including a palm trunk. Horse bones are among the debris of rancheria. Thence to Kino pt. there is a beautiful beach rising up to a flat bench with a higher and less regular shelf above, behind which the surface is generally lower thus:

These lines are practically straight. Near Kino pt. the inner beach dies out, and great storms must break over. The interior is a gently sloping torrential apron of the type usual in this region. Kino pt. is of dark igneous rock washed by the waves into sea cliffs with the usual tidal beach. At base on N. granite begins and continues generally for some miles. It is frequently veined, and is promising for prospecting. It is overlain sometimes by unconsolidated torrential deposits, sometimes by conglomerates, either ferruginous or siliceous (or calcareous), sometimes by both—the conglomerates being often more resistant than granite, forming protective caps. The granitic coast is rugged, with jutting points and coves and boulder beaches affording no landing.

Seeing that *Anita* was laboring, I proceeded slowly, resting at intervals, though Ignacio and Indians appeared to become tired. At two o'clock we were beyond Kino pt., having crossed isthmus; and fearing that *Anita* might not round the point I ascended the point, keeping in sight of my party, to look for her. To my satisfaction she was near and at 2:40 disappeared behind the knob. Thence forward pushed on, resting at intervals, but gaining on *Anita*, looking for possible landings and following the Seri trail. A few landings were made out, one around second point, and another at Granite cove. Here I did not stop, but pushed on, skirting across isthmus of next point. On divide I halted to sight *Anita*, but it was then too dark for me to make her out certainly, though Indians saw her. While in doubt, and looking forward to ascertain the chances for landing beyond the point, heard a shot from boat, which I had Mariana answer with two. I then returned hurriedly to Granite cove, the only possibility for safe beaching (*Anita* was past the last preceding landing), and on reaching it fired 3 shots westward from my big express, to make a decisive shore signal; and soon as Indians came up, had a fire built on one of the walls of the cove. In half an hour, in full darkness, *Anita* appeared; I ran out knee-deep, caught the rope thrown by Johnson, and the boat was with difficulty beached and unloaded. Then, with much effort, often tipping her on edge, the tired men got her up to what appeared to be above tide, and camp was made in the narrow cove which even to inner wall was strewn with drift. A storm here would have been fatal. Johnson was tired, Mitchell at point of collapse, Millard little better besides having a foot punctured by two nails, and Rupuelto and two Indians limp as rags, Anton Castillo being especially forlorn and helpless. I administered medicines all around, and Johnson got up bravely. Indians chose a cavern for resting place, some put their beds on cove-drift, but I chose the granite floor, laying a few boulders to prevent slipping down the slope; and it was an [illegible]. The sicker men were relieved from guard duty, and the watchers were, 1, Johnson and Rupuelto, 2, Millard and Ignacio, 3, self and Miguel; 4 Mitchell, Andres and Mariana. The medicine chest was wet, as well as other things, and I opened it before the fire today. On turning in, I imprudently turned it over to Johnson, asking him to let it dry to the end of his watch, then close it. He was zealous, put it too near the fire so that corks of liquids started, and when he turned in they caught and prevented closing, so he laid it on its side; with the result that all the ammonium, half the [opium?], and some of the laudanum were passed out to mix with sea water in drenching the absorbent cotton and bandages, and to get among the tablet triturates. Johnson's watch stopped, so he did not call Millard until about midnight, and at 12-30 I was surprised to have him awaken me to say that something must be done with the boat; she was caught by the 15 ft. tide and was rubbing on the rocks. Fortunately the swell was greatly reduced, and the water outside nearly still; so Johnson, Millard and I pushed her off, anchored her astern with a sack full of rocks and snubbed her nose in shore with a long lead rope, and let her ride. I watched her until 4-30. Then, the tide being well out, I cast off the lead rope, held her between rocks with paddle until tide ran out farther, and finally pulled her in as far as possible on the sand, tied her fast, drew up the anchor line, and left her nearly dry on the beach; and at 4-30 called Mitchell and turned in until 6. But the swash of the surf was in my ears, the burning brine was in my eyes, and the vile smell of the sewage of the ages filled my nostrils, and sleep was slow in coming and fitful in its stay.

DEC. 17
GRANITE COVE TO SAN MIGUEL.[65]

Clouds and a red sunrise; variable airs, with surprisingly low sea. Half the day clouds were about, drifting N.E., often veiling sun. Breezes southerly and variable all day until about 3-30, when the wind veered to N. and stiffened to a moderate gale, under which clouds blew away. This continued all night.

Launched easily about 7-30, men feeling better; Johnson, Mitchell, Millard, Andres, Rupuelto, Miguel and Mariana in *Anita*. Don Ignacio, Anton, Anton Castilla, Anton Ortiz, and I afoot. We rounded the first point and skirted the bay to a minor point, where the boat pushed in to suggest that we embark; and for the first time the entire party were aboard *Anita*. She drew about 9 inches when tried in smooth water. Soon a breeze sprang up and the sail was used, and we got on fairly until about one o'clock and halfway out the point; then a choppy swell came up, and I had the course laid just out of the trough until we approached shore; where I with my party of the morning scrambled out through the surf, awkwardly enough. I led, jumping into knee deep water; Anton Ortiz followed, carrying his sandals, waiting until he had but three inches of water, his trousers being rolled to the knee; then came Anton, cheerfully but shiveringly, and Anton Castilla was still more hesitant; finally dignified Don Ignacio came slowly around the sail to the prow and looked sorrowfully at the surf; I had called and gestured to the rest with success, but as the boat was already backing—the *Anita* party supposing we were all off,—I saw this would not do for the old man; so I rushed out, and as he stood with legs apart bracing himself on corner of boat and holding to mast with right hand I came up behind, put my head between his legs, caught him on my shoulders and carried him off; Anton ventures rushing up and holding him on. The old man seemed hardly surprised, and his dignity did not forsake him an instant; as I set him down he turned about and raised his gorgeous sombrero, and said, "Muchas gracia, Señor," just as he did on laying down his coffee-cup at mess. We then walked to the point. I went at once over to the lagoon, and found it to be saline, and separated from the gulf only by the low ridge of sand. Half a mile down the point we found a camp fire with Seri tracks, the fire in a half buried log, still hot; beside it a fresh turtle shell, penetrated apparently by an arrow and a fire drill. So the trail is literally hot. A little further along one of the Indians picked up a cane 8 ft. long with cross-stick at end, apparently used for drawing the turtle ashore. Thence on to the point we found occasional tracks. There an old house site (part of frame-poles standing) with a few sticks, and near by a flat stone, slightly concave on one side, evidently transported and used as a metate. On the dunes inside the point we found old rancheria sites with many shells, bits of Seri pottery, etc., including bones and teeth of horse. Soon after our arrival the *Anita* arrived, having been tracked halfway after the wind changed. There was so stiff a breeze and so strong a tide-rip that it was impracticable to cross, and we beached her on the lee side of the terminal spit without difficulty and with little wet; then we unloaded, tipped her to spill the bilge, and for the first time picked her up and carried her above tide reach. Things were wet only from below, and the gale dried them out. All in good spirits, and an early supper did something toward keeping up this condition. In my speech this evening I relieved the four American captains of watch for the night, partly as an expression of confidence, and with good effect all around; and I turned in early, after greasing my boots, sheltered from the tireless yet tiresome sound of the sea by a dune, and slept—*how* I slept.

Granite continues from the cove to the root of the point. In general it is planed smoothly and mantled with torrential aprons, sometimes cemented at base; but now and then a butte rises from it, and the planed surface, and sticks up above to torrential-plane surface. The coast line is simply a section through the torrential plains normal to the district, which the coastline invaded; and the section is exactly what I had pictured.

[
DEC. 18.
IN CAMP AT SAN MIGUEL PT.
]

Turned out at sunrise to see fair sky with a few scudding clouds, the gale continuing. A few white-caps appear, and I consider dividing the party, but fearing an increase in wind decide not to do so; for if half were over we might be kept apart for another night. Sure enough the gale stiffened and we soon had white caps in abundance. The delay is a thorn in my flesh, but the gale dries everything and alleviates the misery.

Later the gale stiffens and sand drifts freely. Afternoon Mitchell accompanies me back along the sand point to the alleged site of rancherias. Sure enough we found 4 or 5 house forms scattered along the beach, two together at one point, but all old and devoid of special interest. Illustrations appear of the use of pebbles and flat boulders, picked up and abandoned after use, for domestic purposes.

Returned to find my bed covered with drifted sand, and the gale stiffer than ever. The wind fell slightly about sunset, and rose again. Johnson and Millard brought in a few little clams, and the former a case of muscular neuralgia in head and shoulders; and while one [one or two illegible words] relieved him, it made him petulant and capricious.

[
DEC. 19
SAN MIGUEL POINT TO THIRSTY CAMP.
]

The watch last night was 1, Johnson and Anton Ortiz; 2, Millard and Anton Castilla; 3, McGee & Anton; 4, Mitchell and Mariana. During my watch I chanced to remember that a little water was left in the large canteen when I last noticed, and I looked for it and on picking it up heard the delicious swish of water within; there was only a moderate drink, and I swallowed it. Next morning Mitchell missed it, and I confessed—stopping thereby his denunciations. For our water was out, there was only enough to make one pot of coffee two-thirds full. I dispensed half a cup to each, having left a spoonful, mostly grounds, for myself—but this was atonement for my theft of the night before.

The gale still continued, and during night and morning I formulated a plan for sending 8 of the party, 4 by boat and 4 on foot, back to Agua Amarillo to fill the casks. The plan was stated in detail in a speech, but was not very well received, all the party, especially Johnson and Andres being anxious to get over the little infierno.[66] Andres with two Indians and myself were to stay in camp, living on canned tomatoes mixed with pinole, and drinking eau de Panguis.[67] But at the last moment, after the boat was at the water's edge, Johnson again appealed for permission to try a crossing, and if he found it favorable to return and take part of the party, returning for the remainder. Worn out with solicitation I foolishly yielded. He soon got *Anita* underway, and though I was afraid he made too much leeway, was confident of success. So when he returned, only a little way down the beach, I had all the party but Andres, Anton, and Anton Castilla get aboard, taking precaution only to carry two cans of tomatoes and two bottles of mineral water. At first we seemed to do well, then not so well; and after two hours' battling with huge rollers and occasional white caps, which *Anita* rode surprisingly well, I noted that our leeway was at least twice or thrice our headway, and that we were simply drifting down the coast. I took a paddle and gave one to Mariana, whereby our leeway was reduced to something like the headway; and after 4 hours sailing, Johnson decided to have down the sail and paddle in. This soon brought us to a beach of boulders, 3 in. to 3 ft. in diameter, on which we could not land nor track. So Johnson, Mitchell and I went hip deep into the swell (I had previously carried a rope ashore to try tracking), and pulled and pushed *Anita* up the rocky beach half a mile or more; I carried old Don Ignacio out, wading ashore and walking alongside. Then we unloaded and lunched on tomato and pinole; and Johnson and Mitchell set out to return to San Miguel point.

W J McGee

Bureau of American Ethnology
Washington, D.C.

Second Expedition, Papago—Seri 1895.

*In case this book is lost, finder is requested
to forward by mail to above address;
ten dollars ($10.00) reward will be paid.*

2nd book.

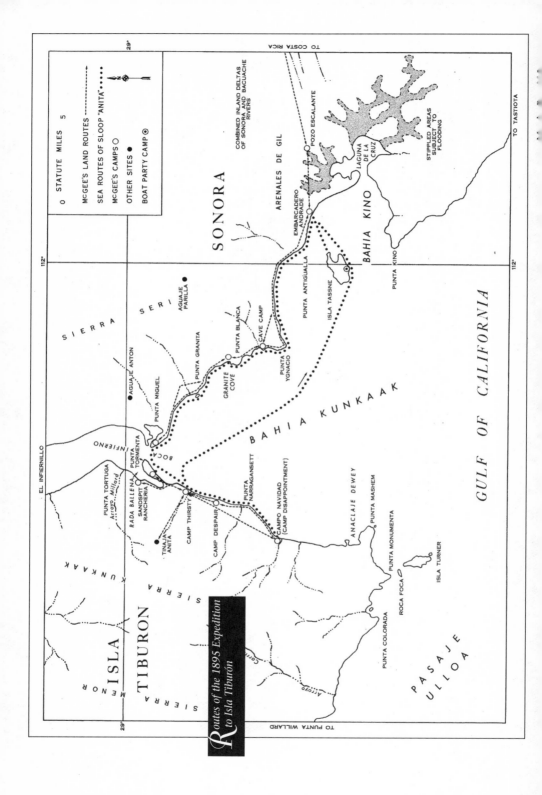

Routes of the 1895 Expedition to Isla Tiburón

[DEC. 19—CONTINUED.]

Leaving Mariana and Anton Ortiz in camp, Millard, Don Ignacio, Rupuelto, Miguel and I set out to hunt for water. Toward the "yellow spot," past it we plodded, and on up to canyon following a fresh Seri trail; past the place where Don Ignacio had once found water in the sand, and on until darkness began to fall and Don Ignacio began to be discouraged; at last, look up the deep barranca from a little knob, I saw it and against an abrupt mountain wall in a narrow gateway; and just below the gateway I made out in the dusk a most welcome spot of verdure. On we went, and at last reached a little patch of canes (a carrisalito) with water slipping over the rocks and lodged in nooks and potholes.[68] How we drank! Then, hastily filling a bucket, two canteens, a gourd bottle, the coffee pot, we set out for camp. Darkness soon fell; we pushed on by the 3-day crescent moon, hurrying to get in before it was gone. All were tired; yet through arroyos, against and around thorny brambles, playing into squirrel [rock squirrel, *Spermophilus variegatus grammurus?*] tunnels on the smoothest plains, and always crouching over jagged lava pebbles we went, Rupuelto now in the lead with Miguel a close second; all were ready to drop save those two fates clearly outlined in the faint moonlight who seemed tireless. At 9-15, just as the moon set, we found camp—a difficult task, as seen from the interior the coast is all alike. The two foolish Indians were asleep, but we soon had them up and some coffee on, and Millard fried some bacon; and we fared sumptuously. Then we turned in; Millard shared his meagre blankets with me—for my bed and all baggage were on the other side.

The gale abated, though the wind was still strong. Mariana and Anton Ortiz watched until midnight; then Miguel and Rupuelto until 3, when they called Don Ignacio, and at 4-30 Millard and I came on.

How we slept! The thin bed provided by Millard was the softest couch I ever lay! Millard's shoes were worn through; outsole, insole, sock and skin on one foot, nearly as much on the other; but all pain was lost in the [one or two illegible words] of sleep following complete physical exhaustion.

[DEC. 20.
IN CAMP AT CAMP THIRSTY.]

Moderate northerly wind, clear, cool; during day wind abated, and a few clouds came.

Leaving Millard and Miguel in camp, we set out for water, carrying all available utensils, bottles, etc., making in all about 7½ gallons; it is about 5 hours' trip. I studied the carrisalito, and considered the possibility of poisoning; also took special pains to guard against ambush. Odd how the Papago would bunch in the deepest gorge if left to themselves!

No sign of *Anita*. I bitterly deplore the change of plan. In response to inquiries and suggestions of disaster, I say that Johnson, finding himself unable to make a good landing, has probably gone to Agua Amarillo, in which case he cannot get up before tomorrow evening or next morning. They are only half reassured.

The flora is much like that of mainland. Mesquite is not abundant, but cat claw and smaller thorny brambles are fairly abundant, so that walking is not easy. The thorny paloverde [*Koeberlinia spinosa*]—i.e., the thorn-tipped-twig form—is rather abundant. Along the mountain sides and barrancas, and even down the arroyos midway to coast, paloblanco [*Acacia willardiana*] occurs, waving its light trees gracefully in the breeze. Saguaro occurs rarely; also cina and pitahaya, only a few specimens of each being seen. Fouquieria [ocotillo] is also quite rare. Two or three specimens of visnaga [barrel cacti, *Ferocactus wislizeni*] were seen, but not until after water was found.[69] The dearth of cacti is surprising. Why? Perhaps frequency of rain, which relatively promotes other vegetation. The fauna is also apparently much like that of the mainland. The most noteworthy feature is the burrows, tunnels, paths, of the squirrels [probably rock squirrels, *Spermophilus variegatus grammurus*]. But as usual, none are to be seen. Coyote [*Canis latrans*] tracks are abundant, and so are signs of deer [mule deer, *Odocoileus hemionus*] or sheep,[70] and rabbits [antelope jack rabbit, *Lepus alleni*].

The rocks are wholly volcanic, a few solid, some with great and small nodules and aggregations of quartzitic material, partly tuffaceous, often [illegible word]; the whole taking on a curious topography on which arroyos head abruptly against sheer mountain-sides. The torrential deposits rise in great aprons on the slopes, and extend to the strait save where sand spits are built beyond.

Somewhat cloudy at night, with threat of fog or rain; wind light, westerly and southerly.

1st. watch, McGee; 2 Miguel and Rupuelto; 3 Don Ignacio and Anton Ortiz; 4, Millard and Mariana.

Millard proves an excellent cook, not only technically but as a harmonizer. Again shared Millard's blankets with unspeakable comfort.

[**DEC. 21**
IN CAMP AT CAMP THIRSTY.]

Cloudy, light S.W. winds; threat of rain all day.

Millard (who had insoled his shoe with canvas), Miguel, Anton Ortiz, Miguel and I set out, leaving Don Ignacio and Rupuelto in camp. We went up the coast to the sand spit opposite San Miguel point, where we found a rather old Seri rancheria, at root of spit.[71] Millard and I went out to point, and exchanged shots with Andres' party, proving that they were there and *Anita* was not. We vainly sought the spit for balsas, but found many small articles of which some were collected. Saw another rancheria half a mile northward, on shore. Then proceeded to carrisalito for water, having brought utensils. The Indians are gloomy. I tell them they cannot expect now to see *Anita* before night or next morning; but my own anxiety many times exceeds theirs—for I have myself and them to look after, and also realize that I am responsible for an unpardonable error in allowing the wishes of the party to override my judgement. Secretly I test wood for rafts, and find that paloblanco promises to be excellent; also one of the objects in coming up the coast was to look for good drift timbers; saw only a palm log 16 or 18 ft. long, 6 in. thick.

Looked for other water; an old trail leads up the next gorge to right of carrizalito, but it seemed useless to follow it; no water signs appeared in other gorges.

Reached camp just before sunset. The first question was whether boat had been seen; but no sign had been observed by men in camp. Millard uttered the opinion that he had long harbored—that *Anita* would never be seen again. The rest of the party were quite despondent. I explained that we had several days flour and beans, plenty of water by carrying with one day's supply ahead, a little coffee, etc., and abundant clams and oysters at sand spit, with game in mountains; that we should probably find balsas at the upper rancheria, and that if not I could easily construct a raft; and I laughed away their fears—but mine would not down. I slept none that night.

Watch, 1, Anton Ortiz & Mariana, 2, Miguel and Rupuelto, 3, Don Ignacio, 4. Millard. A light drizzle half the night and more, enough to moisten clothing and rust guns but not enough to catch. Light southwesterly airs.

[DEC. 22
CAMP THIRSTY TO SANDSPIT RANCHERIA.]

Cloudy in morning, air damp; soon clearing; with light airs, followed by northerly wind with clouds about Seri mt.

Packed up stuff in good season, and carried it 4 mi. up the shore to new camp, leaving two barrels for another trip; then Millard and I went up to the nearer rancheria, sending the four Indians back for the barrels and also to look for a pole seen by Don Ignacio on the way up, leaving the old man in camp. We found fresh tracks, made during the night, and warm ashes in the houses; but no trace of balsas. Returning, we found the Indians not yet in, and the old man and I went after them, leaving Millard digging clams near camp. We met them duly with the barrels and a round pine stick six or 7 in. in diameter, with most of the bark off, new, evidently a telegraph pole or something of the kind thrown up on the beach. I had meantime noticed a palm trunk 6–8 inches thick and 16 or 18 ft. long, and now examined it, finding it pretty strong. As the Indians went up with their load, the old man and I took up the palm log; but soon finding the small end too heavy for him, we laid it down to leave for another trip by the Indians. After a hundred steps it occurred to me that I might carry it alone, and returning I did so—the mile and a half to camp. Then Millard put on coffee, and the four Indians went up to look further for balsas, soon returning. After lunch we set out for the hills to get poles for the raft. It was designed to have the pine and palm poles for side pieces, the latter reinforced by a paloblanco trunk; the barrels for end pieces, the poles being notched to fit the chine (we had a hatchet), and the outer ends to be joined by ropes drawn with toggles. Cross pieces were then to be lashed on top, those against the barrels being lashed thereto; the center cross-piece being a stout pine plank 8 ft. long found on the beach, which was designed to act as a double outrigger. Palo blanco stringers were to be lashed under, and a floor made of palo blanco branches interlaced and used as withes. To make the necessary rope (we had none), Don Ignacio was set to cutting up mess bags, etc., and twisting them into ropes; the toggle ropes were to be made from Johnson's canvas plane table cover; and my shirt and Millard's overalls were allotted for lesser ropes. The old man began his work, and the rest started for the hills four miles away where paloblanco grows. The Indians were apathetic and dull and I was some distance in the lead when we reached the first hill; I had stopped and was selecting suitable trees, when a call from Millard, who with the Indians were then within a few yards, attracted me; the Indians were looking seaward, but all at once turned toward me, their stolid faces beaming, their dull eyes glistening, even Millard being radiant. It was unnecessary for them to say that 3-days overdue *Anita* was in sight. I asked them whether they were certain the boat was square sailed; they thought it was; and I observed that there was then no need for poles; even if the *Ani*— was half a day late, she was better than a raft; and all the way down the Indians were close on my heels. Reaching the coast I scanned the boat and boatmen; two, three, four, yes five; and after a time, Andres and Anton paddling forward, then Mitchell's dark garments; then Anton Castillo on one side and Johnson on the other, paddling—all there.

I selected the best part of the beach for landing, and *Anita* came in amid much rejoicing. The first inquiry by Mitchell was for water—the Indians did not wait to inquire and Johnson kept busy with the boat—and I assured him that we had plenty to drink but not a drop to waste—its cost was exactly equal to that of the fresh champagne in case lots.

Duly Johnson and Mitchell reported a terrible trip. They were washed down the bay past red bank, past grey point, past 1st black point, and finally past 2nd black point on which they strove desperately to catch, the sea being so high as to wash over the sides every few minutes, threatening to swamp the craft, and necessitating constant baling [sic]. They then strove to make wagon camp, but failed, and at last barely succeeded in reaching the last point on Alcatraz island after midnight, where they were just able to beach the boat in a spot formed by the tide for a few minutes only. They and their beds were drenched, and their entire supply of food was two bottles of water and a can of tomatoes. Next morning they found *Anita* packed full of sand, and it took six hours hard work to empty her and get her afloat; then they had an exceedingly hard pull tracking waist deep over rocks, to get around the eastern point, where she had to be baled [sic] out; and just as they got started, they saw José drive up to Wagon camp. They paddled across, despoiled the land party of water and food and sent them back to the ranch for five days more, then to return prepared to wait another five days. Then they made a mile or two up the coast before night and rested. The third day they paddled and pushed or pulled waist deep to Granite cove, and again camped and proceeding in the same way they reached San Miguel point by 2 o'clock. Here they stopped only long enough to land, and pushed off. Johnson forgot his rifle, lying on the sand.

Andres and his two Antons had consumed the Eau de Panguis and [one or two illegible words], but not all the tomatoes and had faithfully stood by camp in ignorance of movements of rest of party except as indicated by occasional exchange of shots (they had fired a good many during the morning) puzzling them as to what it meant. They had been so fortunate as to find some visnaga, of which they had eaten two or three. They were quite thirsty; but some bags of food had been sent up from wagon for Andres, Rupuelto, and the Indians; so the camp that night was a cheerful one; a dozen crabs added zest to supper.

The new rancheria is about half or ¾ mi. N. of root of sand spit. There are about a dozen houses, all formed with bows and strips of okatillo and covered chiefly with shrubbery with turtle shells at bottom. Nearly all have meat stones, simply flat boulders worn above, and hammer stones, lying beside fire places, the fireplace being nothing more than the spot selected for building fire. No olla sherds were seen. A few other articles lay about, chiefly shell cups, with a few spits, a harpoon shaft, etc. There are two or three extremely large whale vertebrae in the village, one out in the open, another in the wall of a house; they may have been used as seats, but there was little indication of it. Beyond the rancheria the skeleton of a whale [probably the gray whale, *Eschrichtius robustus*] was found; jaws 15 or 16 ft. long; other bones proportionately large. 16 of the vertebrae were carefully set on end in a straight line as if to serve as seats for a council. One or two nearly complete and usable ollas were seen.

DEC. 23
IN CAMP AT SANDSPIT RANCHERIA.

Clear, light variable winds generally northerly, clouds about Seri peak.

The watch last night was 1, McGee, Anton Ortiz; 2, Millard, Rupuelto; 3, Andres, Miguel; 4, Ignacio, Mariana; Johnson and Mitchell being relieved.

The last water was used for breakfast coffee, and entire party except Don Ignacio and Millard set out for water, the Indians carrying a cask, and all other utensils being taken; Mitchell tagged along half an hour behind; Johnson also was late in starting, but soon overtook. These men will have to be born again before freely visiting an Indian country. Some coffee was made at the Tinaja, and I collected some plants: a, The large white bark tree with large, fleshy palmate leaves, having a small fig-like fruit, the same as seen sending roots so far to water at Bacuachi [the cliff fig, *Ficus petiolaris*]; b, paloblanco; c carrizal [*Arundo donax*]; d, a large mimosa (manta), with light gray bark [*Lysiloma microphyllum*]. Johnson and Mitchell were authorized to return a little in advance; through misunderstanding the Indians filled cask only about two thirds full; but they trotted along with it so briskly, changing men every two or 3 hundred yards, that Andres and I could hardly keep up; they nearly overtook J. and M.

*I*ndians of McGee expedition carrying a cask of water, Tiburón Island, December 23, 1895.

S C. Millard stands guard on Tiburón Island at Sandspit ranchería, opposite San Miguel Point on the Sonoran mainland, ca. December 23, 1895. (N-6780)

After lunch took Mitchell to make photos of new rancheria and he also made a few about camp.[72] We found a huge scorpion [possibly *Hadrurus* spp.], which we collected, and he took a Kangaroo rat.[73] Millard came in with a bag of oysters, nearly half a bushel; he failed to find clams or crabs. I arranged with him to cook for party until our return to Costa Rica; Mitchell treats the Indians ill.

After a long discussion with Don Ignacio and Andres concerning water and routes, decide to go next to the Carrizal.[74] Beans are exhausted, and jerked meat low.

Watch, 1 Johnson, 2 Mitchell; 3, McGee, 4, Millard & Don Ignacio.

DEC. 24
SANDSPIT RANCHERIA TO CAMP DISAPPOINTMENT.[75]

Clear, northeasterly breeze, changing to northwesterly; light dew.

Cached collections. Carried Gal-*Anita* down to beach, and put her off with Johnson, Mitchell, Andres, Rupuelto, and Mariana; the rest on foot, down the coast. The boat at first made good time, almost outrunning land party. Find old rancherias at intervals, and toward spot marked on Hydrographic map[76] find extensive sites marked by shells, pottery, and worn rocks. Find also fairly recent rancheria[77] of half dozen houses of usual type except that cane is used largely in construction. Turtle shells, fish bones, shells in great variety, the usual rude stones, etc. abound. Collected a few shells used as paint cups, etc. Went down the coast faster than *Anita,* now harassed by off shore winds and compelled to take down sail; when within plain sight of [south] end of island, held another interview with Don Ignacio, who pointed out the vacant spot to the Carrizal, and indicated clearly the route to be taken but instructing that it was farther than we had come today, i.e., 12 or 15 miles—"cinco leguas o menas" [five leagues or less]. It is therefore evident we cannot make the Carrizal, and we turn back to stop *Anita.* We meet here before sunset, and make camp. The beach is rocky, and we have hard work carrying the vessel above tide. I have walked today with out trousers and have a thorn in one heel, which I leave to be extracted in morning; Johnson crushes his fingers by having boat laid down on them. Seri trails and old sites are all about, but no fresh tracks.

Watches, 1 Johnson & Antone Ortiz, 2, Mitchell, Anton Castilla; 3, McGee & Miguel; 4, Millard & Mariana.

DEC. 25
IN CAMP AT CAMP DISAPPOINTMENT

Clear, northerly gale too stiff to warrant putting off. Johnson makes a [surveying] station.

There is enough water for breakfast with a trifle over for canteens; so I set out with Millard, and the six Indians to Carrizalito [Tinaja Anita] for water, while Johnson, Mitchell and Andres strike a trail leading away from large rancheria to see whether it runs to water; Don Ignacio in camp. We make over 15 miles to water in 5 hours 20 minutes, rest and eat a few minutes, and set out with about 9 or 10 gallons of water. The Indians' sandals are practically gone, and the jagged spawls cut their feet, leaving a trail of blood, yet they complain little; Millard wears light tewas,[78] and his feet are bruised; my own heavy soles are nearly worn out, and the sharp rocks are plainly felt. It is a terrible journey, but we get in about 9 o'clock and coffee and bread are soon made. We have been on or crossing Seri trails and old camps all day, and find that the large rancheria got water from Carrizalito, at any rate during dry seasons; making a carry of 12 miles.

Johnson reports a highly successful day so far as topography is concerned; he has seen all the island not previously seen. This relieves the absolute necessity of climbing the high peak.[79]

Watch, 1 Johnson; 2 Mitchell; 3, Andres & Anton; 4, Ignacio & Rupuelto.

The watch was so arranged as to relieve so far as possible the men who were the hardest worked. Took stock of shoes: My insoles would be worn through in another day's walk over the jagged volcanics of Tiburon, the outsoles being practically gone; Johnson's shoes are gaping at many points, the outsoles gone, the insoles through in places, and are tied on with strips of manta and reinforced with canvas; Mitchell's hunting boots are a little better than mine as to soles, worse as to uppers. Millard's shoes are entirely gone and thrown away, and his tewas need repairs, and soles are practically gone; Andres has light cowhide shoes with single thickness of leather for soles, and they are worn so thin that on rocks he limps with both feet; Don Ignacio has been patching old tewas with canvas for some days, and might almost as well be barefoot; Rupuelto has the remnants of a pair of cowhide shoes tied to his feet with strips of cloth and canvas; Anton Castilla has a pair of shoes in addition to his worn out sandals, Mariana's sandals are thin and cracked but whole; all the rest are worn through at soles and heels, and practically useless.

I have noticed today that my system is coming up to the state of prompt physical responsiveness; the heavy rifle no longer galls the shoulder, and the dozen blisters of today's march are less painful than the ones of a week ago.

It has been a sorry Xmas.

DEC. 26
CAMP DISAPPOINTMENT TO CAMP DESPAIR.

Clear, light wind at first from N. with variable airs about sunrise, then stiffening from N. and N.W.

Party slow in collecting; it was after sunrise before we carried *Anita* down over rocks and launched her. I took stock of food: Water for today and breakfast tomorrow, provided no coffee is made; milk, last used this morning; canned butter, so strong that we have only lately got down to eating it, a little left; corn meal, last used this morning; flour, enough for one day, rice, a small quantity; bacon, plenty; coffee, enough for two or three days.

Johnson, Mitchell, Andres, Rupuelto, Mariana, Miguel and Anton Ortiz in boat; rest on foot. We push up the coast slowly. The feature of the coast is the great abundance of Seri signs: Nearly all along the coast shell heaps, bits of pottery, worn stones, etc. are found; old rancherias and house sites occur in every mile; and their trails are scattered over the entire surface. At one point, found defective arrow, and at another old, mealer [muller?] with pit in one side.

About one o'clock, having cut off a point and stopped, heard a shot, and sent the two Antons back to see whether we were needed. They did not return and by and by *Anita* hove in sight, from which we inferred that they had gone aboard to paddle round the point. She seemed to be crossing the bay, so Millard, Don Ignacio and I pushed on along the beach nearly a mile to another point. Here we saw that *Anita* was bearing inshore; and at the same time I concluded, from study of the water, that she could not round the next point without swamping; so I started back, calling M. & I. to follow, to have her land on the sand beach of the bay rather than run on the rocks of the point. I found her beached, and the party ashore and around a fire when I came in sight. On reaching them, Johnson explained that the men had to rest and eat, they were fatigued with continuous paddling, tracking and baling [*sic*], and all but swamped more than once. So after a short stop I had the boat tracked up to the end of the sand beach, near the rocky caps below purple butte, and here met them with a fire made by Ignacio. We beached *Anita*, unloaded, carried her up above tide, and turned her over for Johnson to recaulk. It was before sunset, but the party were too fatigued to even gather wood without repeated urging and example. I, too, was more nearly exhausted than before though the total distance actually made was not more than 4 or 5 miles, or say halfway (probably less) to sandspit.

No coffee for supper, the supply of water being, in Millard's opinion, inadequate.

Collected here specimens of the little shrub or bush that grows in clusters all over the lowland part of the island [*Frankenia palmeri*, called *saladito* in Spanish]; also of the thick-leaved bush that grows along the coast and runs some miles inland, similar to that seen at Agua Amarilla, and probably the same as the trees on the sandspit on which Millard found thousands of oysters. Along the coast it makes a thick mat of low bushes and leaves, often set by the wind in the form of drifts [*Maytenus phyllanthoides*, called *mangle dulce* in Spanish]. There is occasionally a San Juanito similarly shaped, smaller and narrower leaved than at Bacuachi, very close like box, with smaller and very hard fruit [*Jacquinia macrocarpa*].

Breakfast consisted of bread with butter and bacon and coffee plain, all and like; supper, bread & bacon, with half a cup of coffee.

The watch was announced by Millard in a sing song way as I fixed it: Primero cuarto [first quarter], Sr. Johnson y Anton Ortiz; segundo cuarto [second quarter], Rupuelto y Anton Castillo; tercero cuarto [third quarter] El Sr. [McGee] solo [alone] (faint murmur of approval "solo" on part of Indians); cuatro cuarto [fourth quarter], yo y Miguel [I and Miguel]. And so it was.

It is evident that peak trip must be abandoned; and thus the camp is [illegible word or words].

DEC. 27
CAMP DESPAIR TO SANDSPIT PT.

Astir by daybreak, breakfast over some time before sunrise. Millard undertook to make a stew of jerked beef with bacon, but indiscreetly put in a little salt water instead of adding fat; the stew is so salt[y] that it can be worried down only with difficulty. There is also a little bread; and two cans of tomatoes are served in cups in lieu of coffee or water. Then Johnson, Mitchell, Millard, Andres, Rupuelto, Miguel & Anton Ortiz are put off, and the rest of us set out for carrizalito.

The way is hard for bruised and enervated feet, and I put old Don Ignacio with his thin soles in the lead. By 11-30 we are at the tinaja. Four times I drain the quart cup; this was my limit past trip. This is my sixth visit; Mariana has been here five times; no other more than four. We make a pot of coffee, but have no solid food. This morning I have a little water in my canteen; half spent in a half pint flask and give to Millard to meet emergency in the boat; the other half we divide midway of our trip. I drinking last, Anton declining and yet he drinks more than the rest always at the tinaja. The trip today occupied 3½ hours steady going. Hitherto there has been difficulty in getting the Indians to drink enough at the tinaja; but today there is no difficulty today: Each drinks two or three quarts before his pint of coffee, and another after. I estimate that we drink fully six gallons; and we are soon underway with about 12 gallons in 18 vessels—the heaviest load yet except when we had ten men and a barrel. I carry the 6-qt. and 3-qt. canteens; besides my heavy leather coat (slung) with pockets full of books and papers, the heaviest arms in the party, and several pounds of silver in my belt. We rest twice; but our pace is slow and dogged—a jaded horse does not shy, and fagged men forget fear. So we bunch; we should be easy game for the Seri did they appear—but they do not.

We repassed the large cairn near one of the outlying buttes today; it is fully 15 ft. across and 5 ft. high, nearly circular, flat-topped, around a torote blanco tree. It is much larger than the cairns at sand-spit rancheria.[80]

Returned to the rancheria at 2-30, just in time to see boat laboring along by rock tracking over rocky shoals laid bare by gale and low tide for 200 yds. I at once go down with the large canteen, and arrange with Johnson to push on toward pt. Then I take Don I's bottles (2 qts, 2 liters) and we go on to end of rocky beach, half a mile or more from rancheria. There we put water aboard, and I set out with Mariana and A. Castillo for my cache and some turtle shells. I also collect a number of other things, some 300 lbs. in all. My share is a mountain, of about 100 lbs. We tail out to end of spit, finding a gale and heavy sea, with party in camp, just before sunset. We carry *Anita* far up the beach as the sun goes down. All clear this evening, and all are cheerful despite a hard day's work. Mitchell shot a shark which we have for supper,[81] with a little bread, plenty of bacon, and coffee. The Indians refuse to eat the shark, and so does Millard; so later the other three Americans have another course of shark.

Watch, 1 Johnson, 2 Mitchell, 3 Andres, 4 Don Ignacio.

The gale is high; sand is drifting as I turn in. The surf rams against the point and ripples in the little bay—ram, ram, ram, with an undertone of ripple, ripple, ripple, like wavelets on waves.

DEC. 28
SANDSPIT POINT TO COSTA RICA

At dawn up for breakfast of hominy mixed with the remnants of the sea salt stew and shark, which the Indians were thus compelled to eat. With coffee, and the last bit of bread it is not so bad a breakfast.

Everything drenched, though the sky is cloudless—a temporary fog toward morning did it: The gale is slightly abated and the sea lower than last night. We get *Anita* down in the little bight in lee of the tide-belt hook at tip of the spit, and half loaded. I have been watching sea carefully; at sunrise on the mountain tops there were no white caps; now, ¾ hour later, there are hundreds. I ponder leaving while the stuff is carried down. Finally I decide not to put off—not only is the sea bad, but it is getting worse rapidly; and the wind rises with the sun. Disappointment everywhere, disgust in the minds of most of the party—but their lives are in my keeping, and Johnson is bold to recklessness.

I intend to decide at 10 o'clock whether to go after water or cross El Infiernillo; but at that hour the white caps are subsiding and the wind abating, so that I wait another half hour. Then the sanddrift on San Miguel point is also greatly reduced, and I decide to cross. When I call to Johnson that I am now ready to go over, he jumps with alacrity as do the Mexicans and Indians; only Mitchell continues shooting at a hawk [possibly *Buteo jamaicensis,* the red-tailed hawk]. In a few minutes the load is in, and the men quickly follow—and we bid farewell to Tiburon. The swell is heavy enough for me, and frequently comes to the guards, but as there are abroad no white caps the water does not come in. The wind is nearly gone by the time we anchor, and the tide-current gives little trouble. Landing on San Miguel point, Johnson picks up his rifle which has lain between high and low tide all the time of our stay on the island. Then I set out on foot, Johnson and others tracking *Anita*. After a time Johnson joins me, leaving Mitchell in charge of boat, and we proceed to the balsa seen by him on the way up. She is a beauty, only slightly marred at one end.[82] The boat arrives, we carry the balsa down, eat a cupful of hominy, and then I set out with three canteens for the wagon camp on Kino bay, intending to return with water and food in time for breakfast. Already I have walked from San Miguel point, and besides my feet are wet by leaking through the worn soles of my hunting boots; but knowing that I have a long walk before me, I keep moving. For a mile or two I follow the beach, then thinking the Seri must have a trail inland, I set out in light in search for it. Sure enough, I find a fine trail cutting across the granite ranges. On the beach, I remove my trousers and hang my canteens snugly, one slung, one tied to belt behind, one carried in left hand. My leather coat and trousers are attached across right ft. shoulder. When I find trail, I am surprised to find fresh tracks—the freshest I have seen, the sand not yet sun parched. Other signs indicate that the trail is not 2 hrs, probably not over an hour old; 3 persons. And I am alone. I reflect that they will not ambush me by day when they can just as well dog me until night; so I push on. It is my plan to get to Black point before daylight ends, and I increase the pace. Beyond the granite ranges the Seri trail turns off toward the interior, probably the little carrizal mentioned by Andres, and thence to Agua Amarilla. So I work on along the coast, aiming to get across the apron inside Black point before dark; soon I find it desirable to get inland, and in doing so I fall into the deep arroyos running down to the coast, and in them get two or three bad falls, which do not, fortunately injure rifle or canteens. A reason for the falls is the sunset debility; for the sun is nearly down. Crossing the granite spur next to black point (up which granite extends a little way only), I have an attack of giddiness, which a sip of water alleviates, then I push on, and strike the beach just below Black point before the moon has begun to cast shadows. Thence the dismal dirge of the surf jars on and on, and I am a machine of measured rate mechanically beating time on the sands and incidentally progressing toward my goal at a rapid pace. I remember the Seri, but the tide is well out and I don't seriously apprehend descent over the 50-yd. slope of the beach. With little difficulty the seven miles of beach are done, and an unnatural object fixes attention at the dune margin—it is the wagon. I ascend the slope, but see no trace of our light covered vehicle; no fire; no guards; no horses. I fire a shot from my heavy express, but there is only silence. So I look for a trail, which I soon find, with tracks of many animals, leading toward Agua Amarillo; this I take, and pace through the alternating sand dunes and saline flats, counting the chances that I shall have to plod on to Costa Rica; and they seem alarmingly good. I stumble through the last dune, and push over the playa, anxiously looking for light, fire, stock, guards—in vain. I go up to the well; the ground is still wet where the horses were watered; and a little way off I see the faint glow of dying embers; I fire another shot at a great saguesa [*Pachycereus pringlei*], and the echoes knock back from the dunes like mountain-top thunder, while the exploded bullet, touching the side of the cactus, whistles windily with each of its dozen shreds. All else is the dead silence of the desert. I put on trousers and coat, which I need in the chill, gusty, N.W. breeze arisen about sunset, hang up the two larger canteens, and set out for Costa Rica. The sand is deep, but with my lightened load I get on fairly. It is a few minutes before eleven at the well, and I have several hours of moonlight. I note again the trail of many animals, and follow it closely. Five miles, and I am out of the high dunes and playas and in continuous light sand; four or five more, and the windblown sands give place to alluvial silts; and here I can leave the road with advantage, save that I plunge into the squirrel tunnels at intervals. The attacks of giddiness become frequent, and are less completely relieved by sips of water, which is now growing scanty—I conclude they are due to hunger, and blame myself for not carrying a slice of raw bacon—then at thought of bacon my imagination runs back to the strip of bacon rind with which I rubbed my rifle before crossing the strait, and I deplore my shortsight in throwing it away; and thence for an hour that wasted bacon rind is a horrid nightmare. I am aroused by startling a flock of deer, and observe that I am in the grass belt which circumscribes the ranch; and I push on—no longer walking, but stumbling over the slippery dust kept astir by the fitful gusts. The moon sinks, and weird shadows annoy and delay me; then it sets, and I am more comfortable. But I remember that if the Seri are dogging me, it is here that they will attack, in the comparative dark of the starlight and when they think I am exhausted and indifferent; and my wandering brain rages against them for putting me thus to the torture before killing me. My misery is alleviated only by the relief from the beating of the surf. Will daylight *never* come; will the ranch *never* appear; sunrise is coming up. The cattle trails are now definite, and the dust is terrible. Then the east lightens feebly, and slowly brightens. I stagger on, more easily now in the growing light. At last the ranch chimney looms, and 20 minutes before sunrise I walk into the court. No one is in sight, all doors closed. I rap at Andres' door, but that instant the old major domo [foreman] appears in another part of the yard staring as if at a ghost. I approach him and he calls up Juan, in whose house José is sleeping; and in ten minutes all the people of the ranch are about me, and four parties are preparing coffee. Fifty-two miles (by Johnson's map) over terrible walking, the last 17 hours without sitting down. I have had some hard tramps before, but this is the hardest.

The horses are in the potrero [fenced pasture], and it is sometime before they can be brought in; then we are ready to set out with food and water.

DEC. 29
COSTA RICA TO CAVE CAMP

José with teams and Norris and José (Papago) with stock, and I in wagon, get off about midforenoon, after eating again; we have good supplies of food. The Papago wives were prompt in getting up food, the Mexicans, when told that there were neither food nor water for their party, murmured "What a pity," without thought of effort to relieve the strain; but I purchased all I could, and then Rupuelto's wife and later Mrs. Andres came to the front; so we finally had enough. I laid in a few bottles of mescal, a dollar's worth of cigarettes, and another dollar's worth of panoche [dark candy made from unrefined sugar]; for I had tasted some panoche, and lo! it was panoche and not bacon rind that I craved.

It was a dreary pull through the sand, and I counted the steps. About 3-30 we reached the well, finding my canteens untouched, watered the stock and filled canteens and demi johns; then we pushed on toward the coast: Halfway and José caught a glimpse of a figure, which proved to be that of Mariana; he brought me a note from Johnson announcing that party were [stranded?] far up the coast, and that he had sent Indians to Agua Amarillo. Mariana had come by way of wagon camp; and as he came in the other Indians were seen striking directly for the well. José intercepted them; and then food, a sip of mescal, and a bunch of cigarettes and a cup of panoche for each made them happy. Then Norris, José (Papago) and I set out for cave camp, just before sunset, horseback, with four canteens and a stock of food. We started directly across the country but found too many bushes, chollas, and squirrel holes for the waning light, and then followed the beach to black point. Then we cut off spurs and headed arroyos about to destination. I knew approximately from Johnson's note and Mariana's description where camp was located, and looked for fire, but in vain. Approaching the point I fired two shots, but there was no response; and we then crossed another granite spur, and came down beyond the next point, where again I looked for fire and fired a shot vainly. I then sent the Indians back on the trail (assuming that the party had got off earlier in the evening), while I went down and followed the beach. Over the rocks I climbed nearly half an hour, when rising a low ledge, I saw *Anita* before me with no other sign of life. At once I fired two shots (the signal that I wanted the Indians), in the hope of catching the horsemen before they crossed the second spur; when from beneath my very feet rose Don Ignacio and the voices of others. It was one o'clock, but all were awake from thirst or the craving for tobacco; they had overhauled my grip and the medicine chest the evening before and had drunk with inutterable joy, not only the fine whisky, but even the camphored brandy and blackberry diarrhea mixture, but failed to find the hoped for tobacco. The fire was down to a flickering flame over a few embers; concealed by the overhanging cliff, in sea cut caves, were the beds of the party, and they heard no sound save the swash and bellow of the surf. Johnson, Andres, and Ignacio rose; Johnson went up on the talus slope above to [cut?] the Indians; and coffee was soon on. Mitchell drank, ate cheese and panoche, and smoked without rising, while Millard drank and smoked only. I found my covers and blankets wet and filled with sand, but crept in; I had been active, most of the time at exceedingly hard work, for forty three hours; I had for some hours been experiencing curious defects of vision, akin to those of delirium tremens; and I had dropped asleep while reaching for a bit of bacon stuck between the teeth with a toothpick, and found the toothpick still there when I was called at day break.

I have had hard sieges of work; but that 43 hours, including about 23 hours walking—7 hours in wagon, and 9 hours in the saddle, is my best record.

The wind continued all day; clear, cold.

DEC. 30
CAVE CAMP TO AGUA AMARILLO

Clear, northwesterly breeze, with moderate surf; white caps in the offing.

Pushed *Anita* off and loaded her without much difficulty; then Johnson, Mitchell and Millard set off in her, towing the balsa. Andres, Ignacio and I were in the saddle, Norris and José walking along the beach. The boat sailed well before the wind, keeping up with the land party. I found the trail and set the pace nearly to the gray ridge above Black point, when I saw that it was desirable to get the men over from Agua Amarilla to help get *Anita* out as soon as we sight her, so I sent Andres across, to bring all men and horses. Then Don Ignacio and I rode down to beach above Black pt. to spell the pedestrians. Thence we alternated, the boat keeping pace with us; and at last gaining; so a little above shell heap, where Don Ig. and I took the horses for the last time, I trotted down to be at the landing. Reaching the wagon I stopped in time to beach and hold prow, while Johnson held stern with paddle, and Mitchell and Millard around the end. Here I had opportunity to examine my feet; and in addition to extensive scalding, found on one foot 10 and on left 14 blisters and abrasions.

Half an hour later Andres and Indians came in from the well, and *Anita* was carried up and put on the wagon, the balsa being loaded on top; and José (Papago) was sent on my horse after José and the light wagon. The boat team got stuck, and our leaders were put on, with men at the wheels; and after dark we reached Agua Amarillo. Coming out, we scorned the water here; but coming in we found it delicious. Yet Johnson and I are plagued with boils. My nails chipped after my walk.

DEC. 31
AGUA AMARILLA TO COSTA RICA.

Clear, chilly, northwesterly wind; no dew.

Excavated grave at old rancheria overlooking Agua Amarillo. Externally the grave is a heap of brambles with an upright stick in center, to which is tied a cross stick. Below the brambles there is a layer of cholla stems and buds, covering a slight elliptical elevation, say 5 ft. long, 3 ft. wide. Put down a cross trench 8 in. wide, to a depth of about 2 ft., the earth being rearranged and mixed with turtle bones, etc. Here found a turtle shell, right side up, through which I worked; it was covered with sacaton [some species of grass], of which also there was a layer just below ground level. Beneath shell the sand was rather loose, and I soon found him and then was able to feel a skull. So the excavation was enlarged.[83]

Body (adult female) lay on left side, doubled with knees near chin, hands before face, fronting N.W., costume, a coyote (?) for skirt and cloth shirt, with shell beads about neck; black beads apparently attached to dress. Water olla and flat dish with shells, etc., suggesting food, in front of fire; many small articles, dolls, arrowpoint, toy ollas, awls and needles, fetishes, etc. etc., about back of head, perhaps laid on neck or shoulders; over these baskets inverted; over this the first turtle shell, another being over the hips and feet. Most of skeleton in excellent condition, some skin and tendon preserved, some small bones entirely absent; all collected.[84] Another grave nearby was examined superficially; coyotes have invaded it, and human bones are scattered all over the surface.

Got off about eleven o'clock, soon overtaking the boat wagon. Two Indians had been sent in evening to explain the delay of a day and give assurance that all was right, on catching wagon we find that Andres had gone forward to send out fresh animals for this wagon. Rupuelto, Anton, and José (Papago) were left with the boat, rather disconsolate, though assured that they would not be deserted; we took up old Don Ignacio, whom I had detailed to take care of the balsa, and went in, Mitchell and Norris and Mariana in saddle, Johnson, Millard, Ignacio, José and I in the wagon; Johnson laid up with diarrhea. Abruptly after sunset we rolled into the ranch, and fared sumptuously on the feast of fat things provided by Angelita. We had met the fresh animals, including a number of mules, an hour or two after leaving the boat wagon, in guard of a crowd of boys, including a son of Don Ig., who returned along side us; and an hour after we arrived the wagon came in.

[JANY 1, 1896
IN CAMP AT COSTA RICA.]

Clear, nearly calm, no dew, somewhat cold.

Johnson down with cholera microbe, unable to lift head, damning the curious Mexicans and Indians who come to stare at and commiserate him. We had intended to get away, but this changed plans; so all day I was engaged in packing specimens, etc. Made a provisional settlement with our late soldiers, not having sufficient cash to pay any in full. There is rejoicing in Costa Rica on our return to safety.

[JANY 2.
COSTA RICA TO HERMOSILLO.]

Clear, warm, no dew, light airs.

Drove in to Hermosillo without event save the visiting with Thompson and M.M. Rice, out as a rest cure, at Perez Ranch. Thompson came back in the wagon with us. Rice driving in T.'s little cart and getting lost on the way. Mitchell pushed on ahead, tiring out his horse and getting in half an hour before us. Johnson shot a fine coyote with my express—beautiful shooting, first time when he stopped for an instant, second as he ran and leaped on three legs. Learned from Thompson that there has been much apprehension in Hermosillo, Guaymas, Nogales and elsewhere over our prolonged stay, with telegrams of inquiry from California, etc. So it is necessary to wire safe return, though too late to do so this evening.

> ## JANY 3.
> ## IN CAMP AT HERMOSILLO MOLINO DEL ENCINAS

Clear, somewhat cold, no dew or light airs; toward evening sky overcast with irregular clouds.

Occupied in official calls, etc. during forenoon; failed to find governor and prefect. Had Calusio[85] detailed to talk with me at the Molino's during afternoon; he is a man of good intelligence and force, though now old and partly deaf, and with very little knowledge of the Seri. He remembers giving a long-bearded man who had been sick ([John R.] Bartlett) a vocabulary in 1852, 3 or 4 [it was 1851], meantime which, his knowledge is sadly defective.

> ## JANY 4
> ## IN CAMP AT HERMOSILLO AND EN ROUTE

Occupied in clearing up business, etc., and taking train for Nogales.

Put Johnson in charge, Mitchell photographer with Millard and he to cook, Norris interpreter, and José care horses. They return to Costa Rica, box balsa etc., then go to Sierrita, Pozo Nuevo, Pozo Noriega, Las Cruces, Cienega, Caborca, Sonoita, Quijotoa, and San Xavier, Johnson covering former route map.[86]

> ## JAN'Y 3, 1896.
> ## NOTES FROM FERNANDO CALLACIO (KOLOSIO), SERI
> ## INTERPRETER AT HERMOSILLO

Formerly there was a gentile organization, which is now lost. All civilized when he was young. He does not remember clans, and thinks they were not recognized when he was young.[87] He then resided in Pueblo Seri.

Seri chiefs[88] are chosen in council, and choice is ratified by government. Chief is permitted to have 3 or 4 wives, and has subchiefs. Theft is punished by death, at dictum of chief. In case of killing, penalty is death by relatives; chief has nothing to do with this. If chief orders killing or kills, penalty is the same; the lower chief was killed about a year ago; might makes right. The chieftaincy goes to shrewdest, cruelest man in tribe. The chieftaincy covers entire tribe, and chief has representatives in each rancheria; but his word is not law except by approval. They quarrel continually.

Seri Indian informant "El General" Fernando Kolusio (or Calusio) and a "Mexican companion" at the Molino Encinas near Hermosillo, Sonora, January 3, 1896. (4271)

Councils are held for selection of chief, seldom for other purposes, and seldom do more than 10 or 15 assemble.

There are no feasts except the puberty and wedding feasts.[89] The first is betrothal feast. The youth makes presents to relatives of maid, until their consent to match is obtained; then he sleeps near maid until she yields, when marriage is celebrated. Often the youth supports family of maid for some months. Selection is by a young man, or his parents or male relatives; when her parents consent, he sleeps near maid one to eight nights, when if she does not consent arrangement is declared off—man goes away. Chief has 3 or 4 wives; others not more than 2. Each has so many as he can support. Never intermarry with other tribes; are absolutely virtuous with respect to each other. In case of wedding feast, parents of both parties furnishing; music is a gourd in water used as a drum, to which all dance.[90]

No midwife; as pains come on, woman goes off alone, and comes in with child; in case of difficult labor, woman dies. Dr. [W. J.] Lyons knows of a woman who went into the bushes alone, and at end of 7 days came in with child. No celebration of birth, no baptism. The more civilized sprinkle child and apply name; others do nothing. In olden times, children were named after birds and animals; now Spanish names are applied.[91] Children much loved; never killed or abused.

In case of death of a child mother cries loudly before sunrise, at the grave or elsewhere, for 8 to 15 days; painting face black, not cutting hair. In case of death of adult all family cry twice per day, sunrise and sunset, at grave, for 15 days.

Burial is either under ground in sitting position, all belongings buried with body; in trees, which is most common; or under brush or stones. Sometimes put them in caves.

Generally mourning is conducted by a teacher, who is paid to teach crying; at other times they awaken in the night, clap hands, throw up sand, and cry. No change in costume when mourning.[92]

Men and women proud of hair, which is never cut. Once the Seri were ordered by Prefect to have hair cut; but when it was attempted, they all escaped to Tiburon.

Thinks there are not more than 30 warriors; has little idea as to number of women and children. For 20 years he has not been in contact with Seri.

They adore different animals and objects; many believe the pelican to be sacred and powerful; others worship the arrow. Those who believe in pelican allege that he has a musical song, which is his adorable characteristic.

In '70 he was authorized to bring Seri here and educate them; he brought them here and established school, when measles broke out, some died, and the rest ran away.

They have no myths.[93]

In case of sickness, they breathe or blow on the painful part, shouting at the same time, and believe the flesh opens and the pain comes out. They have medicine men who treat disorders; they are chiefs, or equivalent thereto.[94]

Calusio was very small when he left the tribe; he is now old, somewhat deaf, and has nearly forgotten the language. It is my judgement that his information is practically worthless except where corroborated. So the inquiry is not continued.

Appendix A

Papago Vocabulary from Jose Lewis

The following is a selected portion of a Papago vocabulary collected by McGee from interpreter Jose Lewis, elsewhere identified as Jose Lewis Brennan, at San Xavier, Arizona, on November 24–25, 1894. McGee transcribed it before their departure on that year's expedition, writing the entries on a Smithsonian Institution printed vocabulary schedule. It is catalogued as manuscript no. 659 in the National Anthropological Archives, Washington, D.C. Portions not included here, partly because McGee's handwriting cannot be accurately deciphered, relate to kinship terms, political positions, and supernatural beings.

The "moons" of the O'odham year, alluded to by Lewis, are enumerated and named in Lumholtz (1912: 76) and Underhill (1939: 124–25).

yard (measure) . . . ot's (whispered prolongingly) . . . This is measured from tip of nose to hand, with some excluded, as in measuring cloth. No longer measure, distances simply being indicated are good. In journeys distance is reckoned by days, half days being reckoned.

The year is an indefinite period; summers, rainy seasons (sahuaro?), seasons, etc., are, however, counted. Days and moons also are reckoned, though it is not known how many days to moon or moons to year. Morning, noon, evening, etc. also are recognized.

Standards of value . . . No standards whatever; barter was carried on solely on individual estimates.

center . . . u+'-ta, when speaker is in center; su+'-ta^{up}, when speaker is out of middle. There is no down. Center is regarded as one of six directions.

Cousins sometimes marry. The distinctions soon end, the terms of [illegible] relationship being employed to the [illegible].

APPENDIX B

PAPAGO VOCABULARY AND INTERVIEW NOTES

*T*he following are selected portions of a standard Smithsonian Institution vocabulary schedule completed by McGee based on his interviews in November and December 1895 with Papago interpreter Hugh Norris of San Xavier, Arizona. The manuscript is part of no. 795, National Anthropological Archives, Washington, D.C. More recent summaries of Hia Ced O'odham (Sand Papago) and Tohono O'odham (Papago) burial customs are in Anderson (1986) and Anderson, Bell, and Stewart (1982).

My wife . . . niä-nyik. . . . A second wife (in polygamy) would be called: hü-ma-niä-nyik = other wife.

Child without known father; must be killed by mother or grandmother: pi-o-o+k

Family . . . te̱'-ki'

Head of family . . . ta̱-ä+k' . . . always man, save in case of his death; then wife is head, called te̱-gu+k.

Gens . . . u-na-djo-ne. . . . Examples: the three groups of houses at Fresnal; upper Fresnal; Poso Verde; Miguel's rancheria; etc.

Council of gens . . . u-hu-ma'p-ai . . . sometimes exists.

Chief of gens . . . tu-ku-tcik . . . usually oldest man in group

Gentile council-house . . . tu-ku-u-tcik-i . . . usually chief's house.

War chief . . . tcu-tcun-na-tcu-kit-tca. . . . None now. Chief Miguel (cul-a-ma' tce̱ = Asking) was the last war chief.

Council of chiefs of gentes . . . gu-u-gut u-hu-ma'-pai. . . . Example, the chiefs of three Fresnal villages and that of upper Fresnal. Jose Juan is head chief over the four groups (his Papago name is Sa-ve-nyo' = smells like anus).

Murder . . . mua' . . . punished by death at hands of relations only. . . . Murder is committed only in intoxication, and the vengeance is continuous.

Theft . . . stu-u+s-ku̱m. . . . No penalty except restoration at command of chief.

Mortuary Customs. . . . Bury body in ground usually. Formerly the custom was to build a little house of stone on a mountain, each village having its mountain. House built of loose stones, long and narrow, a sort of cist; posts and beams of wood were used, and a roof of stone. Women and children buried the same way. Body buried before sunset if death occurs in morning; if he dies in afternoon, body kept till next day. Favorite horse killed on mountain; saddle destroyed; also gun or bow & arrows. Body dressed in best clothes, other clothing placed outside the cist. General property goes to family. Relatives take body to resting place, and there is no ceremony, but commonly men and women gather at place of death; they believe that if they do not go to see the dead, they will themselves be neglected at death, and they gather to look on the face of the dead. In old times the house was destroyed. No professional mourners, but nearest kindred mourn. Widow cuts hair off to neck; no paint, no sack cloth, no scarifying.

Headache . . . mo's-ko'-ok ⎤
Toothache . . . ta-tam's-ko-ok ⎦ Cure—Go to medicine man (ma+-ke) who would smoke tobacco and blow

smoke on head or tooth; if unsuccessful, and patient is willing to pay more, ma+-ke would go to patient's lodge with rattles, etc., and make magic, finally taking out the [illegible] in his mouth in the form of a worm, etc.

A cut . . . ü'-hi-kwu-tcu̱. . . . A bad cut is washed with soap and water or creosote infusion, and a concoction of creosote blooms is applied, after which wound is bound up.

Medicine lodge . . . ma+-kai-ki'. . . . Residence of medicine man; no special lodge.

*T*he following notes by McGee were made December 4, 1895, at Rancho San Francisco de Costa Rica, Sonora, Mexico, based on his interview with an elderly Papago man. The manuscript is part of no. 795, National Anthropological Archives, Washington, D.C.

The information here can be compared with that presented by Underhill (1939) concerning many of the same topics. For a more up-to-date discussion of O'odham leadership and governance, see Kroeber and Fontana (1986: 53–55).

Á'-â-si'-tu' (Sifting), or Juan, talks: He resides at Visnaga, not far from Hermosillo; he is here to visit his grandchildren, including several of the men on Rancho de San Francisco de Costa Rica. The four groups are like those of Arizona. He belongs to Á+ko-li'-kune. His chief is Ta'+o-vo-lo (not known [illegible word]), or Tá-o-la (Spanish), of San Jose, whose dominion extends over Sayula rancheria of three families, the Visnaga rancheria, and the Costa Rica rancheria. He is chief by inheritance through father and grandfather; he has been chief long time. His power extends to settlement of dispute in all his rancherias; subject to Senor Pascual, the chief controls the place of residence of his clan, who are related, having same totem, Eagle. Relationship paternal. Chief has no control over marriage, which rests in parents; divorce unknown here. Formerly meetings were held about once per year at which chief set forth law. Now meetings less regular but held occasionally; about a year ago, which A. attended; all people of clan attended. Chief said: 1. must not steal; 2. must be kind and forebearing when living together; 3. must hunt, and get skins and meat to make living; 4. tell children these things soon as they can understand. No feast, simply a congregation in response to command of chief; only men attend. There is no religious teaching, here or at other times. All people of this clan Catholic. Have no fetishes. Were—The people seen at Poso Nueva last year belong to this clan, and are now gone from there. Marriage generally in clan, but extra-clan marriage (exogamy) permissible. Querobabi rancheria belong to same clan, and to same chief; there is old man there, Santiago, and two sons-in-law, but younger men are now at Cienega, leaving old man alone. They have no feasts or ceremonials here. There is one man here who has married a Yaki, but no other cases of exogamy are known; no children in this family. The annual meeting lasts all night, and the men smoke. In case of murder have the murderer goes to Arizona, Sacaton, and lives with the Pima; if he did not escape relations of victim would kill him. Crime to kill woman, even wife, and unfaithful is equal to crime of killing man. Infidelity of wife punished by beating; infidelity of husband equally criminal, but not generally punished, not even by [illegible]; chief has no power. No medicine men here; Santiago compounds herbs, but does not follow primitive practices. Norris, who is of Coyote totem, is treated exactly as if Eagle, and all other men are treated about the same. All children baptized, generally without priest, by primitive ceremonial, which was not described. Marriage not by priest, and no ceremonial. Arranged by parents, who appoint a night, when boy and girl are couched together, and this constitutes marriage. No puberty ceremonial for boys; when girl passes menstrual period first there is a dance with singing, at which men and women who desire join; neither seems to play no part; announcement may be made by "any man." No birth ceremonial. Only women attend birth, father sent away. No couvade. In Eagle totem, when eagle is killed, killer fasts (eating single dish without salt) for 8 days, when there is a feast; details forgotten. No colors or directions known.[1]

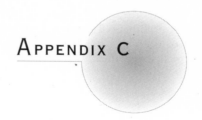

Appendix C

Marine Flooding of the Sonora-Bacuache Delta Area

Ronald L. Ives[2]

In both his diaries and his published reports, W J McGee opines, on the basis of scanty but valid evidence, that parts of the Sonora-Bacuache delta area suffered one or more marine invasions in comparatively recent times, geologically speaking.

Subsequent fieldwork by several investigators shows that McGee's working hypothesis is entirely sound, and that many parts of the now-arid inland delta of the combined Sonora and Bacuache Rivers were submerged several times during the Pleistocene.

These marine invasions are evidenced not only by the large deposits of shells in the delta area, but by "stair-step" sequences of abandoned shorelines on Tiburón Island and adjacent parts of the mainland. One of these shorelines, that nominally twenty-five feet above mean sea level, can be found at many places of both shores of the Gulf of California, and also on the Pacific coast at least as far north as Santa Barbara, California.

In the Sonoran area, this shoreline is characterized by very extensive deposits of clam shells, with *Chione cancellata* dominant in many places, as at Puerto Peñasco, Sonora. This is probably the youngest of the shorelines, and was formed after man came to North America, as is evidenced by the presence of shell mounds and middens along it. On the basis of physiographic evidence, which is in close accord with climatic data, this shoreline is not more than twelve thousand years old, nor younger than four thousand years. Narrowing of these temporal limits by radiocarbon dating is much to be desired.

There are at least two higher, and presumably older, shorelines in the Tiburón area. These have not yet been correlated with other shorelines in adjacent areas, although some sort of correlation is to be expected.

At the time of this writing, December 1961, inundation of large areas inland of Laguna de la Cruz by the high seas that produced the "twenty-five-foot" shoreline is conclusively shown by much physiographic and conchological evidence. Only details of this marine invasion remain to be worked out. Presently available evidence strongly suggests, but does not conclusively demonstrate, another marine invasion, possibly during early Wisconsin time, which extended up the Sonora-Bacuache delta plain to Playa Noriega and nearly to San Francisco de Costa Rica. One or more intermediate high sea levels are suggested by short sectors of old shoreline on Tiburón Island and the seaward side of the Sierra Seri. A great deal of intensive fieldwork is needed to evaluate this scattered and not entirely conclusive evidence.

APPENDIX D

WORKS BY W J McGEE

*I*tems marked with an asterisk are based in whole or in part on McGee's 1894 and 1895 field trips.

1878a On an Anatomical Peculiarity by Which Crania of the Mound Builders May Be Distinguished from Those of the Modern Indians. *American Journal of Science,* 3d series, 16 (96): 458–61.

1878b On the Artificial Mounds in Northeastern Iowa, and the Evidence of the Employment of a Unit of Measurement in Their Erection. *American Journal of Science,* 3d series, 16 (9): 272–78.

1878c On the Relative Positions of the Forest Bed and Associated Drift Formations in Northeastern Iowa. *American Journal of Science,* 3d series, 15 (89): 339–41.

1879a Notes on the Surface Geology of a Part of the Mississippi Valley. *Geological Magazine* (London) 6: 353–61, 412–20, 528.

1879b On the Complete Series of Superficial Formations in Northeastern Iowa. *Proceedings of the American Association for the Advancement of Science* (Salem, Mass.) 27: 198–231.

1879c On the Superposition of Glacial Drift upon Residuary Clays. *American Journal of Science,* 3d series, 18 (106): 301–3.

1880a A Contribution to Dr. Croll's Theory of Secular Change in Terrestrial Climate. *Proceedings of the Iowa Academy of Sciences* 1 (part 1, 1875–80): 24.

1880b The "Laterite" of the Indian Peninsula. *Geological Magazine* (London) 7: 310–13.

1880c On Some Iowa Kames and Aasar (abstract). *Proceedings of the Iowa Academy of Sciences* 1 (part 1, 1875–1880): 19, 25.

1881a A Contribution to Croll's Theory of Secular Climate Changes. *American Journal of Science,* 3d series, 22 (132): 437–43.

1881b A Contribution to Croll's Theory of Secular Climate Changes (abstract). *Proceedings of the American Association for the Advancement of Science* 30: 175–76.

1881c The Geology of Iowa Soils. *Transactions of the Iowa State Horticultural Society* 5: 101–5.

1881d On Local Subsidence Produced by an Ice-Sheet. *American Journal of Science,* 3d series, 22 (13): 368–69.

1881e On Maximum Synchronous Glaciation. *Proceedings of the American Association for the Advancement of Science* 29: 447–509.

1881f On Maximum Synchronous Glaciation (abstract). *Science: A Weekly Record of Scientific Progress,* edited by John Michels, vol. 2, 566–67. New York.

1881g On Some Elements in Orthographic Displacement. *American Journal of Science,* 3d series, 21 (124): 276–78.

1881h On the Thickness of the Ice Sheet at Any Latitude. *American Journal of Science,* 3d series, 22 (130): 264–67.

1881i Review of "Illustrations of the Earth's Surface; Glaciers," by Nathaniel S. Shaler and W. M. Davis. *Science: A Weekly Record of Scientific Progress,* edited by John Michels, vol. 2, 581–84. New York.

1882a Evaporation and Eccentricity, Co-factors in Glacial Periods, a Discussion. *American Journal of Science,* 3d series, 23: 61–62.

1882b Modifications proposées dans la nomenclature géologique. *Compte Rendu, International Geological Congress,* 2d session, 1881, pp. 620–22. Bologne: Fava et Garagnani.

1882c The Relations of Geology and Agriculture. *Transactions of the Iowa State Horticultural Society* 16: 227–40.

1883a Note on Jointed Structure. *American Journal of Science,* 3d series, 25 (146): 152–53.

1883b The Geological Distribution of Forests. *Popular Science Monthly* 24 (November): 115.

1883c "On the Cause of Glacial Period," by Searles V. Wood. An abstract. *American Journal of Science,* 3d series, 26 (153): 244.

1883d On Glacial Canyons (abstract). *Proceedings of the American Association for the Advancement of Science* 32: 238.

1883e On Glacial Canyons (précis of abstract). *Science* 2 (31): 315–16.

1883f On the Origin and Hade of Normal Faults. *American Journal of Science,* 3d series, 26 (154): 294–98.

1883g On the Present Status of the Eccentricity Theory of Glacial Climate. *American Journal of Science,* 3d series, 26 (152): 113–20.

1883h Report on Geology and Soils. *Transactions of the Iowa State Horticultural Society* 17: 270–80.

1883i Subterranean Forest in District of Columbia. *Science* 2 (43): 724.

1884a Iowa Building Stones. In *Tenth Census of the United States,* vol. 10, *Report on the Building Stones of the United States and Statistics of the Quarry Industry for 1880,* compiled by George W. Hawes, 256–65. Washington, D.C.: Government Printing Office.

1884b *The Relations of Geology and Agriculture.* Revised. 18 pp. Washington, D.C.

1885a Administrative Report of the Assistant Geologist. In *Annual Report of the United States Geological Survey,* vol. 5, 34–41, Plate 2. Washington, D.C.: Government Printing Office.

1885b Administrative Report of the Geologist. In *Annual Report of the United States Geological Survey,* vol. 6, 25–32. Washington, D.C.: Government Printing Office.

1885c Methods of Geologic Cartography in Use by the United States Geological Survey. In *Compte Rendu, International Geological Congress,* 221–40. Berlin.

1885d On the Meridional Deflection of Ice-Streams. *American Journal of Science,* 3d series, 29 (173): 386–92.

1885e Peculiar Ice-Forms. *Nature* 31 (804): 480–81.

1885f   *A Proposed History of American State [Geological] Surveys.* 4 pp. Washington, D.C.

1885g   The Terraces of the Potomac Valley. *Bulletin of the Philosophical Society of Washington* 8: 24.

1886a   "Geologic Formations of Washington, D.C. and Vicinity," by Smith Townsend, M.D. An abstract. *American Journal of Science,* 3d series, 31 (186) 473–74.

1886b   Methodes de cartographie géologique employees par l'United States Geological Survey. *Annuaire Géologique Universel,* 2me parte, App, 3–27. Dagincourt.

1886c   Some Features of the Recent Earthquake. *Science* 8 (190): 271–75.

1886d   Topography of Chesapeake Bay (abstract). *American Journal of Science,* 3d series, 32 (190): 323.

1887a   On Finding a Spear Head from the Quaternary Beds of Nevada. *Nature* 35 (907): 476.

1887b   *Ovibos Caviforms* from the Loess of Iowa. *American Journal of Science,* 3d series, 34 (201): 217–20.

1888a   Administrative Report of the Geologist-in-Charge, Potomac Division of Geology. In *Annual Report of the United States Geological Survey,* vol. 7, 104–11. Washington, D.C.: Government Printing Office.

1888b   The Classification of Geographic Forms by Genesis. *National Geographic Magazine* 1 (1): 27–36.

1888c   The Columbia Formation. *Proceedings of the American Association for the Advancement of Science* 36: 221–22.

1888d   The Geology of the Head of Chesapeake Bay. In *Annual Report of the United States Geological Survey,* vol. 7, 537–646, maps. Washington, D.C.: Government Printing Office.

1888e   Notes on the Geology of Macon County, Missouri. *Transactions of the Academy of Sciences of St. Louis* 5: 305–36.

1888f   Paleolithic Man in America: His Antiquity and Environment. *Popular Science Monthly* 34 (November): 20–36.

1888g   Some Definitions in Dynamical Geology. *Geological Magazine* (London), 3d series, 5: 489–95.

1888h   Some Peculiarities of the Superficial Deposits of Northeast Iowa. *American Geologist* 2 (2): 137–38.

1888i   Three Formations of Middle Atlantic Slope. *American Journal of Science,* 3d series, 35 (206): 120–43; (208): 328–30; (209): 367–88; (210): 448–66.

1889a   Administrative Report of the Geologist-in-Charge, Potomac Division of Geology. In *Annual Report of the United States Geological Survey,* vol. 8, part 1, 166–73. Washington, D.C.: Government Printing Office.

1889b   Administrative Report of the Geologist-in-Charge, Potomac Division of Geology. In *Annual Report of the United States Geological Survey,* vol. 9, 102–10. Washington, D.C.: Government Printing Office.

1889c   An American Geologic Society. *Science* 13 (309): 8–9.

1889d   Carte Géologique des États-Unis d'Amérique, donnant las distribution actuellement connue des Groupes Géologiques. In *Une mission viticole en Amérique,* plate 9. Paris.

1889e   The Geologic Antecedents of Man in the Potomac Valley. *American Anthropologist,* old series, 2 (3): 227–34.

1889f   An Obsidian Implement from Pleistocene Deposits in Nevada. *American Anthropologist,* old series, 2 (4): 301–12.

1889g   Topographic Types of Northeastern Iowa (abstract). *American Naturalist* 23 (273): 808.

1889h   The World's Supply of Fuel. *The Forum* 7: 553–66.

1890a   Administrative Report of the Geologist-in-Charge of the Potomac Division. In *Annual Report of the United States Geological Survey*, vol. 10, part 1, 148–58. Washington, D.C.: Government Printing Office.

1890b   Discussion of a Paper by Joseph B. Tyrrell, "Post-Tertiary Deposits of Manitoba and the Adjoining Territories of Northwestern Canada." *Bulletin of the Geological Society of America* 1 (April 17): 409.

1890c   Discussion of Paper by Thomas C. Chamberlain, "Some Additional Evidences Bearing on the Interval between the Glacial Epochs." *Bulletin of the Geological Society of America* 1 (April 24): 474–75, 480.

1890d   Encroachments of the Sea. *The Forum* 9: 437–49.

1890e   Geology for 1887 and 1888. In *Annual Report of the Smithsonian Institution for 1888*, part 1, 217–60. Washington, D.C.: Government Printing Office.

1890f   Introduction to Robert Hay, "A Geological Reconnaissance of Southeastern Kansas." *Bulletin of the United States Geological Survey* 57: 11–14.

1890g   Iowa. In *An American Geological Railway Guide*, 2d ed., edited by James R. Macfarlane, 232–45. New York: D. Appleton and Co.

1890h   Remarks on Certain Peculiarities of Drainage in the Southeastern United States. *Bulletin of the Geological Society of America* 1: 448–49.

1890i   Remarks on the Formations Comprised under the Name of "Orange Sane" and Relation of Certain Loams and Gravels in Vicinity of Vicksburg. *Bulletin of the Geological Society of America* 1: 474–75.

1890j   Remarks on the Pressure of Rock Gas, Especially in Indiana. *Bulletin of the Geological Society of America* 1 (March 1): 96–97.

1890k   Some Principles of Evidence Relating to the Antiquity of Man. *Proceedings of the American Association for the Advancement of Science* 38: 333.

1890l   The Southern Extension of the Appomattox Formation. *American Journal of Science*, 3d series, 40 (235): 15–41.

1890m   The Southern Extension of the Appomattox Foundation (abstract). *American Geologist* 5 (2): 120.

1890n   The Southern Extension of the Appomattox Foundation (abstract). *American Naturalist* 24 (278): 209.

1890o   Topographic Types of Northeastern Iowa (abstract). *Proceedings of the American Association for the Advancement of Science* 38: 248–49.

1891a   Administrative Report of the Geologist-in-Charge, Potomac Division. In *Annual Report of the United States Geological Survey*, vol. 11, part 1: 65–70. Washington, D.C.: Government Printing Office.

1891b   The Appomattox Formation in the Mississippi Embayment (abstract). *Bulletin of the Geological Society of America* 2 (January 3): 2–6.

1891c   Classification of Pleistocene Formations and Land Forms, a Discussion (abstract). *American Geologist* 8 (4): 248.

1891d   The Columbia Formation in the Mississippi Embayment (abstract). *Proceedings of the American Association for the Advancement of Science* 39: 244–45.

1891e   The Flood Plains of Rivers. *The Forum* 11: 221–34.

1891f   The Lafayette Formation. In *Annual Report of the United States Geological Survey*, vol. 12, part 1: 353–521, maps. Washington, D.C.: Government Printing Office.

1891g   Neocene and Pleistocene Continent Movements (abstract). *American Geologist* 8 (4): 234–35.

1891h   The Pleistocene History of Northeastern Iowa. In *Annual Report of the United States Geological Survey for 1890*, part 1, 189–577. Washington, D.C.: Government Printing Office.

1891i   Rock Gas and Related Bitumens. In *Annual Report of the United States Geological Survey*, vol. 11, part 1, 589–616. Washington, D.C.: Government Printing Office.

1891j   Some Principles of Evidence Relating to the Antiquity of Man. *American Antiquarian* 13: 69.

1892a   Administrative Report of the Geologist-in-Charge, Potomac Division. In *Annual Report of the United States Geological Survey*, vol. 12, part 1, 70–77. Washington, D.C.: Government Printing Office.

1892b   Administrative Report of the Geologist-in-Charge, Potomac Division. In *Annual Report of the United States Geological Survey*, vol. 13, part 1, 103–13. Washington, D.C.: Government Printing Office.

1892c   The Areal Work of the United States Geological Survey (abstract). *American Geologist* 10 (6): 377–79.

1892d   Comparative Chronology. *American Anthropologist,* old series, 5 (4): 327–44.

1892e   Comparative Chronology (abstract). *Proceedings of the American Association for the Advancement of Science* 41: 283–84.

1892f   Distribution of the Lafayette Formation (abstract). *American Geologist* 10 (4): 223–24.

1892g   The Field of Geology and Its Promise for the Future. *Bulletin of the Minnesota Academy of Natural Sciences* 3: 191–206.

1892h   Geological Map of the United States and Canada. In *Longman's New School Atlas*. New York: Longman's and Co.

1892i   Glacial Phenomena. Discussion of a Paper by C. H. Hitchcock, "Studies of the Corm Valley Glacier." *Bulletin of the Geological Society of America* 4 (December 27): 5–7.

1892j   The Gulf of Mexico As a Measure of Istocacy. *American Journal of Science,* 3d series, 44 (261): 177–92.

1892k   The Gulf of Mexico As a Measure of Istocacy (abstract). *American Geologist* 9 (3): 217.

1892l   The Gulf of Mexico As a Measure of Istocacy (abstract). *Bulletin of the Geological Society of America* 3 (9): 501–4.

1892m   Man and the Glacial Period: A Letter to the Editor. *Science* 20 (513): 317.

1892n   Neocene and Pleistocene Continent Movements (abstract). *Proceedings of the American Association for the Advancement of Science* 40: 253–54.

1892o   Pleistocene Geography (abstract). *American Geologist* 10 (4): 223.

1892p   Reports of the Delegates to the Congrès Géologique International. *American Anthropologist,* old series, 5: 45–48.

1892q   The Southern Old Fields (abstract). *Proceedings of the American Association for the Advancement of Science* 40: 417.

1893a   Administrative Report of the Geologist-in-Charge, Potomac Division. In *Annual Report of the United States Geological Survey*, vol. 14, part 1, 210–44. Washington, D.C.: Government Printing Office.

1893b   Anthropology at the Madison Meeting. *American Anthropologist,* old series, 6 (4): 435–48.

1893c   The Antiquity of Man in America (abstract). *American Geologist* 12 (3): 174–76.

1893d   Areal Work of the United States Geological Survey. *Transactions of the American Institute of Mining Engineers* 21: 608–17.

1893e   Correlation of Clastic Rocks, a Discussion. *Compte Rendu, International Geological Congress,* 5th session, 160–66. Washington, D.C.: Government Printing Office.

1893f   Discussion of a Paper by F. P. Gulliver, "Ice-sheet on Newtonville Sand Plain." *American Geologist* 12 (3): 177.

1893g   Discussion of a Paper by Frank Leverett, "Changes of Drainage in Rock River Basin in Illinois." *American Geologist* 12 (3): 180.

1893h   Discussion of a Paper by G. Frederick Wright, "Extra Morainic Drift in New Jersey." *Bulletin of the Geological Society of America* 5 (7): 17–18.

1893i   Discussion of a Paper by Joseph W. Spencer, "Terrestrial Submergence Southeast of the American Continent." *Bulletin of the Geological Society of America* 5 (7): 21–22.

1893j   Discussion of a Paper by Joseph W. Spencer, "Terrestrial Submergence Southeast of the American Continent." *American Geologist* 12 (3): 168.

1893k   Discussion of a Paper by N. H. Darton, "Cenozoic History of Eastern Virginia and Maryland." *Bulletin of the Geological Society of America* 5 (7): 24.

1893l   Discussion of a Paper by Rollin D. Salisbury, "Distinct Glacial Epochs and the Criteria for Their Recognition." *American Geologist* 11 (3): 173.

1893m   A Fossil Earthquake (abstract). *Bulletin of the Geological Society of America* 4 (September 23): 411–14.

1893n   Genetic Classification of Pleistocene Deposits. *Compte Rendu, International Geological Congress,* 5th session, 65–66, 198–207. Washington, D.C.: Government Printing Office.

1893o   A Geological Palimpsest. *The Literary Northwest* 2: 274–76.

1893p   Geologic Map of the United States. In *Johnson's Universal Cyclopedia,* rev. ed., edited by C. Kendall Adams and others, vol. 3, 728–31. New York: Alvin J. Johnson Co.

1893q   Graphic Comparison of Post-Columbia and Post-Lafayette Erosion (abstract). *American Geologist* 12 (3): 180.

1893r   Man and the Glacial Period. *American Anthropologist,* old series, 6 (1): 85–95.

1893s   Note on "The Age of the Earth." *Science* 21 (540): 309–10.

1893t   The Pleistocene History of Northeastern Iowa (abstract). *American Geologist* 11 (3): 178–79.

1893u   The Prairies. Itinerary from Kansas City, Missouri, to Chicago, Illinois. *Compte Rendu, International Geological Congress,* 5th session, 449–52. Washington, D.C.: Government Printing Office.

1893v   *Review Extraordinary of "Man and the Glacial Period," by a Member of the United States Geological Survey, with Annotations and Remarks Thereon by Judge C. C. Baldwin, LL.D.* 22 pp. Cleveland.

1894a   The Antiquity of Our Indians. *Epitome* 1: 1.

1894b   The Citizen. *American Anthropologist,* old series, 7 (4): 352–57.

1894c   Discussion of a Paper by Warren Upham, "The Succession of Pleistocene Formations in the Mississippi and Nelson River Basins." *Bulletin of the Geological Society of America* 5 (January 18): 100.

1894d *The Earth, the Home of Man.* Special Papers of the Anthropological Society of Washington, no. 2. Washington, D.C.: W. F. Roberts.

1894e The Extension of Uniformitarism to Deformation. *Bulletin of the Geological Society of America* 6 (December 14): 55–70.

1894f The Extension of Uniformitarism to Deformation (abstract). *American Geologist* 14 (3): 199–200.

1894g Glacial Cañons. *Journal of Geology* 2 (May/June): 350–64.

1894h Graphic Comparison of Post-Columbia and Post-Lafayette Erosion (abstract). *Proceedings of the American Association for the Advancement of Science* 42: 179.

1894i The Potable Waters of the Eastern United States. In *Annual Report of the United States Geological Survey,* vol. 14, part 2, 1–47, figs. 4–5. Washington, D.C.: Government Printing Office.

1894j Preface to John G. Pollard, "The Pamunkey Indians of Virginia." *Bulletin of the Bureau of American Ethnology,* no. 17, 5–6. Washington, D.C.: Government Printing Office.

1894k Prefatory note to Cyrus Thomas, "The Maya Year." *Bulletin of the Bureau of American Ethnology,* no. 18, 5–13. Washington, D.C.: Government Printing Office.

1894l *Preliminary Geologic Map of New York.* Six sheets, scale 1:316,800. Washington, D.C.: Government Printing Office, under authority of the Legislature of the State of New York, Albany.

1894m Reconnaissance Map of the United States Showing the Distribution of the Geological Systems So Far As Is Known, 1893. In *Annual Report of the United States Geological Survey,* vol. 14, part 2, plate 2. Washington, D.C.: Government Printing Office.

*1895a The Beginnings of Agriculture. *American Anthropologist,* old series, 8 (4): 350–75.

1895b Canyons of the Colorado: Review of a Book by J. W. Powell. *Science,* new series, 2: 593–97.

1895c A Catalogue of Scientific Literature. *Science,* new series, 1 (13): 353–55.

1895d James C. Pilling. *Science,* new series, 2: 150.

1895e James Constantine Pilling. *American Anthropologist,* old series, 8 (4): 407–9.

1895f A Miniature Extinct Volcano (abstract). *Proceedings of the American Association for the Advancement of Science* 43: 225–26.

1895g Obituary of Robert Henry Lamborn. *American Anthropologist,* old series, 8 (2): 175–76.

1895h Reconnaissance Map of the United States, a Letter to the Editor. *American Geologist* 16 (2): 113–14.

*1895i Remarks on the Geology of Arizona and Sonora (abstract). *Science,* new series, 1 (3): 59.

1895j Some Principles of Nomenclature. *American Anthropologist,* old series, 8 (3): 279–86.

*1895k The Topographic Development of Sonora (abstract). *Science,* new series, 1 (20): 558–59.

1896a Anthropology at Buffalo. *American Anthropologist,* old series, 9 (9): 315–20.

*1896b The Beginning of Marriage. *American Anthropologist,* old series, 9 (11): 371–83.

*1896c Expedition to Papagueria and Seriland. *American Anthropologist,* old series, 9 (3): 93–98.

*1896d Expedition to Seriland. *Science,* new series, 3 (66): 493–505.

1896e Explorations by the Bureau of American Ethnology in 1895. *National Geographic Magazine,* 7 (2): 77–80.

1896f   The Formation of Arkose (abstract). *Science,* new series, 4 (104): 962–63.

1896g   Geographic History of the Piedmont Plateau. *National Geographic Magazine* 7 (8): 261–65.

1896h   The Geologic Map of the State of New York (abstract). *Science,* new series, 3 (68): 418.

1896i   Honors to James Hall at Buffalo. *Science,* new series, 4 (98): 700–6.

*1896j   The Relation of Institutions to Environment. In *Annual Report of the Smithsonian Institution for 1895,* 701–11. Washington, D.C.: Government Printing Office.

1896k   Review of Franklin H. Giddings, "The Principles of Sociology: An Analysis of the Phenomena of Association and of Social Organization." *American Anthropologist,* old series, 10 (1): 19–24.

1896l   Review of William H. Holmes, "Archaeological Studies among the Ancient Cities of Mexico." *American Anthropologist,* old series, 9 (4): 137–40.

*1896m Sheetflood Erosion (abstract). *American Geologist* 18 (4): 228–29.

*1896n Sheetflood Erosion (notice). *Science,* new series, 4 (90): 385.

1896o   Two Erosion Epochs. Another Suggestion. *Science,* new series, 3 (74): 796–99.

*1897a   The Beginning of Zooculture. *American Anthropologist,* old series, 10 (7): 215–30.

1897b   Brief Sketch of James Owen Dorsey. In *Annual Report of the Bureau of American Ethnology,* vol. 15, 207. Washington, D.C.: Government Printing Office.

1897c   Hatcher's Work in Patagonia. *National Geographic Magazine* 8 (11): 319–22.

1897d   In Memoriam. Kate Field, 1840–1896. *Records of the Columbia Historical Society* 1: 171–76.

1897e   International Amenities of Detroit and Toronto. *Science,* new series, 6 (141): 380–82.

1897f   Letter of the Acting Director of the Bureau of American Ethnology to the Secretary of the Interior Suggesting an Examination of Casa Grande with a View of Its Further Protection; August 28, 1895. In *Annual Report of the Bureau of American Ethnology,* vol. 15, 344–47. Washington, D.C.: Government Printing Office.

1897g   The Mississippi Bed-Lands. *The Forester* 3: 7.

1897h   The Present Condition of the Muskwaki Indians (abstract by J. H. McCormick). *Science,* new series, 5 (128): 928.

1897i   Primitive Rope-Making in Mexico. *American Anthropologist,* old series, 10 (4): 114–19.

1897j   Review of Frederick L. Hoffman, "Race Traits and Tendencies of the American Negro." *Science,* new series, 5 (106): 65–68.

1897k   The Science of Humanity. *American Anthropologist,* old series, 10 (8): 241–71.

1897l   The Science of Humanity. *Science,* new series, 6 (142): 413–33.

*1897m Sheetflood Erosion. *Bulletin of the Geological Society of America* 8 (February 13): x, 87–112, plates 10–13.

*1897n Sheetflood Erosion (abstract). *Science,* new series, 5 (123): 722.

1897o   The Siouan Indians. A Preliminary Sketch. In *Annual Report of the Bureau of American Ethnology,* vol. 15, 153–204. Washington, D.C.: Government Printing Office.

1898a   American Geographic Education. *National Geographic Magazine* 9 (7): 305–7.

1898b   Anthropology at Ithaca. *American Anthropologist,* old series, 11 (1): 15–22.

1898c   The Course of Human Development. *Forum* 26: 56–65.

1898d   Fifty Years of American Science. *Atlantic Monthly* 82: 307–20.

1898e   Geographic Development of the District of Columbia. *National Geographic Magazine* 9 (7): 317–23.

1898f   Geographic Work of the Bureau of American Ethnology. *National Geographic Magazine* 9 (3): 98–100.

1898g   The Geospheres. *National Geographic Magazine* 9 (10): 435–47.

1898h   The Growth of the United States. *National Geographic Magazine* 9 (9): 377–86.

1898i   The Modern Mississippi Problem. *National Geographic Magazine* 9 (1): 24–27.

1898j   A Muskwaki Bowl. *American Anthropologist,* old series, 11 (3): 88–91.

1898k   Ojibwa Feather Symbolism. *American Anthropologist,* old series, 11 (6): 177–80.

1898l   Our National Seminary of Learning. *Harper's Monthly* 96: 633–39.

1898m   Papagueria. *National Geographic Magazine* 9 (8): 345–71.

*1898n   Piratical Acculturation. *American Anthropologist,* old series, 11 (8): 243–49.

1898o   Ponka Feather Symbolism. *American Anthropologist,* old series, 11 (5): 156–59.

1898p   Review of Daniel G. Brinton, "Maria Candelaria. An Historic Drama from American Aboriginal Life"; Countess di Brazzá, "An American Idyl" [*sic*, Idyll]; and Clifford Howard, "Sex Worship. An Exposition of the Phallic Origin of Religion." *American Anthropologist,* old series, 11 (1): 24–27.

1898q   Review of Leopold Schenk, "Determination of Sex." *American Anthropologist,* old series, 11 (8): 252–53.

1898r   The Science of Humanity. *Proceedings of the American Association for the Advancement of Science* 46: 293–324.

*1898s   *The Seri Indians.* Annual Report of the Bureau of American Ethnology, vol. 17, part 1. Washington, D.C.: Government Printing Office.

*1898t   Thirst in the Desert. *Atlantic Monthly* 81: 483–88.

*1898u   Thirst in the Desert (abstract). *Globus* (Braunschweig) 74: 66.

1899a   The Beginning of Mathematics. *American Anthropologist,* new series, 1 (4): 646–74.

1899b   Daniel G. Brinton. *Science,* new series, 10 (242): 193–96.

1899c   The Foundation of Science: The Relation between the Novum Organum and Powell's "Truth and Error, or the Science of Intellection." *Forum* 27: 168–78.

1899d   International Catalogue of Scientific Literature: Anthropology. *Science,* new series, 10 (237): 48–50.

1899e   National Growth and National Character. *National Geographic Magazine* 10 (6): 185–206.

1899f   The Pre-Lafayette Base Level (abstract). *Proceedings of the American Association for the Advancement of Science* 48: 227.

1899g   The Pre-Lafayette Base Level (abstract). *Science,* new series, 10 (249): 489.

1899h   Professor O. C. Marsh (obituary). *National Geographic Magazine* 10 (5): 181–82.

1899i   Review of Dean C. Worcester, "The Philippine Islands and Their People." *American Anthropologist,* new series, 1 (1): 171–73.

1899j   Review of Ernest Seton Thompson, "Wild Animals I Have Known." *American Anthropologist,* new series, 1 (2): 376–77.

1899k   Review of Ernst Haeckel, "The Last Link. Our Present Knowledge of the Descent of Man." *American Anthropologist,* new series, 1 (3): 569–70.

1899l   Review of Frank Russell, "Explorations in the Far North." *American Anthropologist,* new series, 1 (3): 568.

1899m Review of Franz Boas, "The Mythology of the Bella Coola Indians." *American Anthropologist,* new series, 1 (3): 562–63.

1899n Review of J. W. Powell, "Truth and Error or the Science of Intellection." *American Anthropologist,* new series, 1 (1): 184–85.

1899o Review of Karl Groos, "The Play of Animals." *American Anthropologist,* new series, 1 (2): 363–75.

1899p Review of Robert T. Hill, "Cuba and Porto Rico and Other Islands of the West Indies. Their Topography, Climate, Flora, Products, Industries, Cities, People, Political Conditions, etc." *American Anthropologist,* new series, 1 (1): 178–81.

1899q Review of Rodolfo Lenz, "Critica de la Langue Auca del Señor Raul de la Grasserie," and "Kritik der Langue Auca des Herrn Dr. jur Raoul de la Grasserie." *American Anthropologist,* new series, 1 (3): 564–65.

1899r   Review of Stewart Culin, "Chess and Playing-Cards." *American Anthropologist,* new series, 1 (3): 565–68.

1899s   Review of William W. Seymour, "The Cross in Tradition, History, and Art." *American Anthropologist,* new series, 1 (2): 379–80.

1899t   The Trend of Human Progress. *American Anthropologist,* new series, 1 (3): 401–47.

1899u   Work of the Bureau of American Ethnology. In *Verhandlung des 7th International Geological Congress.* Berlin.

1900a   Callosities on Horses' Legs. *Science,* new series, 12 (292): 194.

1900b   Cardinal Principles of Science. *Proceedings of the Washington Academy of Science* 2 (March 14): 1–12.

*1900c The Gulf of California As an Evidence of Marine Erosion (abstract). *Science,* new series, 11 (272): 429.

1900d   In Memoriam. Frank Hamilton Cushing. Remarks by W J McGee. *American Anthropologist,* new series, 2 (2): 354–56.

1900e   The Lessons of Galveston. *National Geographic Magazine* 11 (10): 377–83.

1900f   Occurrence of the Pensauken Formation (abstract). *Proceedings of the American Association for the Advancement of Science* (Easton, Pa.) 49: 187.

1900g   Occurrence of the Pensauken Formation (abstract). *Science,* new series, 12 (313): 990–91.

1900h   Primitive Numbers. In *Annual Report of the Bureau of American Ethnology,* vol. 19, part 2, 821–51. Washington, D.C.: Government Printing Office.

1900i   Superstructure of Science. *Forum* 29: 171–82.

1901a   An American Senate of Science. *Science,* new series, 14 (347): 277–80.

1901b   Asia, the Cradle of Humanity. *National Geographic Magazine* 12 (8): 281–90.

1901c   Asia, the Cradle of Humanity. *Scientific American Supplement* 52 (1346): 21576–78.

1901d   Current Questions in Anthropology (abstract). *Science,* new series, 14 (365): 996–97.

1901e   George Mercer Dawson. *American Anthropologist,* new series, 3 (1): 159–63.

1901f   Ice Caves and Frozen Wells. *National Geographic Magazine* 12 (12): 433–34.

1901g   *Incomplete List of Scientific Writings and Maps, by W J McGee, 1878–1900.* 8 pp. Proof, prepared for use of John W. Powell.

1901h Man's Place in Nature. *American Anthropologist,* new series, 3 (1): 1–13.

1901i Man's Place in Nature. *Science,* new series, 13 (325): 453–60.

1901j The Old Yuma Trail. *National Geographic Magazine* 12 (3): 103–7; (4): 129–43.

1901k Proposed Appalachian Forest Reserve. *The World's Work* 8: 1372–85.

1901l Review of Henry Wood, "The Symphony of Life." *American Anthropologist,* new series, 3 (4): 759.

*1901m The Seri Indians. *National Geographic Magazine* 12 (7): 278–80.

1901n The Washington Memorial Institution. *Science,* new series, 14 (342): 111.

*1901o The Wildest Tribe in North America: Seriland and the Seri. *Land of Sunshine* 14: 364, 463.

1901p Work of the Bureau of American Ethnology. *National Geographic Magazine* 12 (10): 369–72.

1902a The Antillean Volcanoes. *Popular Science Monthly* 61 (July): 272–81.

1902b Dr. Bell's Survey in Baffinland. *National Geographic Magazine* 13 (3): 113.

1902c Geest. *American Geologist* 30 (6): 381–84.

1902d Germe industrie de la pierre en Amérique. *Bulletin et Mémoire Société d'Anthropologie* (Paris) 3: 82.

1902e Movements toward Union among Geographers. *Science,* new series, 15 (379): 549–51.

1902f The New Madrid Earthquake. *American Geologist* 30 (3): 200–1.

1902g Problems of the Pacific—The Great Ocean in World Growth. *National Geographic Magazine* 13 (9): 333–42.

1902h Proposed American Anthropologic Association. *American Anthropologist,* new series, 4 (2): 352–53.

1902i Proposed American Anthropologic Association. *Science,* new series, 15 (391): 1035.

1902j Regarding the Carnegie Institution. *Science,* new series, 16 (407): 611–13.

1902k Relation of the American Society of Naturalists to Other Scientific Societies. *Science,* new series, 15 (372): 246–50.

1902l Remarks on the Death of John Wesley Powell. *Science,* new series, 16 (411): 788–90.

1902m West Indian Disaster. *American Monthly Review of Reviews* 25: 676–86.

1903a Anthropology. In *Louisiana Purchase Centennial: Dedication Ceremonies, St. Louis, U.S.A. April 30th and May 1st–2nd, 1903,* 41–45. No imprint.

1903b John Wesley Powell As an Anthropologist. Proceedings of the Washington Academy of Sciences 5: 118–26.

1903c John Wesley Powell As an Anthropologist. In *Annual Report of the United States Geological Survey* 24: 283–87. Washington, D.C.: Government Printing Office.

1903d Review of Carl Lumholtz, "Unknown Mexico." *American Anthropologist,* new series, 5 (2): 345–48.

1904a The Anthropology Exhibit. *Harper's Weekly* 48 (April): 683.

1904b The Beginnings of Civilization. *World Today* 7 (September): 1210–13.

1904c Department of Anthropology. In *Official Catalogue of Exhibits, Universal Exposition, St. Louis, 1904,* 9–10. St. Louis: Official Catalogue Company.

1904d *Geography of Virginia.* 18 pp. Lincoln, Nebr.: University Publishing Co.

1904e   Opportunities in Anthropology at the World's Fair. *Science,* new series, 20 (503): 253–54.

1904f   Strange Races of Men. *The World's Work* 8: 5185–88.

1905a   Anthropology and Its Larger Problems. *Science,* new series, 21 (542): 770–84.

1905b   Anthropology at the Louisiana Purchase Exposition. *Science,* new series, 22 (573): 811–26.

1905c   Desert Cure. *Independent* 59 (2965): 669–72.

1905d   Prehistoric North America. In *The History of North America,* edited by Francis N. Thorpe, vol. 19. Philadelphia: George Barrie and Sons.

1906a   Climatology of Tinajas Altas, Arizona. *Science,* new series, 23 (593): 721–30.

1906b   Desert Thirst As Disease. *Interstate Medical Journal,* vol. 13, no. 3 [23 pp.]. St. Louis.

*1906c Glaciation in the Sonoran Province. *Science,* new series, 24 (606): 177–78.

1906d   Letter in the preface. In *Boas Anniversary Volume,* xi–xii. New York: G. E. Stechert and Co.

1907a   Our Great River. *World's Work* 13: 8576–84.

1907b   River Sediment As a Factor in Applied Geology (abstract). *Science,* new series, 25 (646): 765.

1908a   Bearing of the Proposed Appalachian Forest Reserve on Navigation. *Conservation* 14 (12): 661–63.

1908b   The Cult of Conservation. *Conservation* 9: 469–72.

1908c   Lafayette Deposits in Louisiana. *Science,* new series, 27 (690): 472.

*1908d Natural Movement of Water in Semi-Arid Regions. *Conservation* 14 (11): 596–99.

1908e   Our Dawning Waterway Era. *World's Work* 15: 10121–27.

1908f   Our Inland Waterways. *Popular Science Monthly* 72 (April): 289–303.

1908g   Outlines of Hydrology. *Bulletin of the Geological Society of America* 19 (September 4): 193–200.

1909a   Address to the Joint Conservation Conference. *Conservation* 15 (2): 93–94.

1909b   Current Progress in Conservation Work. *Science,* new series, 29 (743): 490–93.

1909c   New Union among the States. *American Monthly Review of Reviews* 39: 317–21.

1909d   Recent Steps in the Conservation Movement. *Science,* new series, 29 (744): 539–40.

1909e   Water As a Resource. *Annals of the American Academy of Political and Social Science* 33: 521–34.

1910a   The Five-Fold Functions of Government. *Popular Science Monthly* 77 (September): 274–85.

1910b   Notes on the Passenger Pigeon. *Science,* new series, 32 (835): 958–64.

1910c   Review of Edward S. Curtis, "The North American Indian. Volume 5: Mandan, Arikara, and Atsina." *American Anthropologist,* new series, 12 (3): 448–50.

1910d   Scientific Work of the Department of Agriculture. *Popular Science Monthly* 76 (June): 521–31.

1911a   The Agricultural Duty of Water. In *Yearbook of the United States Department of Agriculture for 1910,* 169–76. Washington, D.C.: Government Printing Office.

1911b   The Conservation of Natural Resources. *Proceedings of the Mississippi Valley Historical Association* 3: 361–79.

1911c   Primitive Copper Hardening. *Science,* new series, 33 (860): 963–64.

1911d   Principles of Water-power Development. *Science,* new series, 34 (885): 813–25.

1911e   Principles of Water-power Development. *Scientific American Supplement* 73 (1883): 66–67; (1884): 82–83.

1911f   Prospective Population of the United States. *Science,* new series, 34 (875): 428–35.

1911g   *Soil Erosion.* Bulletin of the Bureau of Soils, no. 71. Washington, D.C.: United States Department of Agriculture, Government Printing Office.

1911h   Soil Erosion (abstract). *Journal of the Washington Academy of Sciences* 1 (5): 161.

1912a   How One Billion of Us Can Be Fed. *World's Work* 23: 443–51.

1912b   Principles of Water-power Development; Reply to Professor Aldrich. *Science,* new series, 35 (901): 536–37.

1912c   Principles Underlying Water Rights. In *Official Proceedings of the 19th International Irrigation Congress,* pp. 309–20. Chicago.

1912d   Subsoil Water of the Central United States. In *Yearbook of the United States Department of Agriculture for 1911,* 479–90. Washington, D.C.: Government Printing Office.

1912e   Symptomatic Development of Cancer. *Science,* new series, 36 (924): 348–50.

1913a   *Field Records Relating to Subsoil Water.* Bulletin of the Bureau of Soils, no. 93. Washington, D.C.: United States Department of Agriculture, Government Printing Office.

1913b   *Wells and Sub-Soil Water.* Bulletin of the Bureau of Soils, no. 92. Washington, D.C.: United States Department of Agriculture, Government Printing Office.

1915a   Anthropology at the Louisiana Purchase Exposition (extract). In *Life of W J McGee,* by Emma R. McGee, 100–5. Farley, Iowa: privately printed.

1915b   The Conservation of Natural Resources (extract). In *Life of W J McGee,* by Emma R. McGee, 88–100. Farley, Iowa: privately printed.

1915c   The Cult of Conservation. In *Life of W J McGee,* by Emma R. McGee, 186–93. Farley, Iowa: privately printed.

1915d   Desert Thirst As Disease (extract). In *Life of W J McGee,* by Emma R. McGee, 178–86. Farley, Iowa: privately printed.

1915e   The Five-fold Functions of Government. In *Life of W J McGee,* by Emma R. McGee, 194–211. Farley, Iowa: privately printed.

1915f   Flood Plains of Rivers. In *Life of W J McGee,* by Emma R. McGee, 211–28. Farley, Iowa: privately printed.

1915g   In the Desert. In *Life of W J McGee,* by Emma R. McGee, 83–88. Farley, Iowa: privately printed.

*1915h   The Seri Indians (extract). In *Life of W J McGee,* by Emma R. McGee, 105–67. Farley, Iowa: privately printed.

1915i   Symptomatic Development of Cancer. In *Life of W J McGee,* by Emma R. McGee, 228–32. Farley, Iowa: privately printed.

1915j   The World's Supply of Fuel. In *Life of W J McGee,* by Emma R. McGee, 167–78. Farley, Iowa: privately printed.

1955   An Obsidian Implement from Pleistocene Deposits in Nevada. *Reports of the University of California Archaeological Survey,* no. 32; *Papers on California Archaeology,* no. 36, pp. 30–38. Berkeley: The University of California Archaeological Survey, Department of Anthropology, University of California.

*1971   *The Seri Indians*. Glorieta, N.Mex.: Rio Grande Press.

*1980   *Los Seris, Sonora, México*. México: Instituto Nacional Indigenista.

1987   The Conservation of Natural Resources. *The Amicus Journal* (Spring): 19–21.

1989a   Excerpt from an 1896 letter to Frank Hamilton Cushing. In *Key Marco's Buried Treasure: Archaeology and Adventure in the Nineteenth Century,* by Marion S. Gilliland, 99. Gainesville: University of Florida Press and Florida Museum of Natural History.

1989b   Excerpt from an August 24, 1990, letter to Stewart S. Culin. In *Key Marco's Buried Treasure: Archaeology and Adventure in the Nineteenth Century,* by Marion S. Gilliland, 117. Gainesville: University of Florida Press and Florida Museum of Natural History.

COAUTHORED PUBLICATIONS

Cattell, J. McKeen, W J McGee, Franz Boas, and William W. Newell

1899   Report of the Committee for the Study of the White Race in America. *Proceedings of the American Association for the Advancement of Science* 48: 355.

Evans, John, and W J McGee

1897   Hyde, J. *National Geographic Magazine* 8 (11): 358–59.

McGee, W J, and Richard E. Call

1882   On the Loess and Associated Deposits of Des Moines, Iowa. *American Journal of Science,* 3d series, 24 (141): 202–23, map.

*McGee, W J, and William Dinwiddie

1907   Untitled article [Description of the Papago hidden bean game]. In *Games of the North American Indians,* by Stewart Culin. Annual Report of the Bureau of American Ethnology, vol. 24, 354–55. Washington, D.C.: Government Printing Office.

McGee, W J, and William H. Holmes

1899a   The Geology and Archaeology of California. *American Geologist* 23 (2): 96–99.

1899b   The Geology and Archaeology of California (abstract). *Science,* new series, 9: 104–5.

1899c   The Geology and Archaeology of California (abstract). *Scientific American Supplement* 47: 19313.

*McGee, W J, and Willard D. Johnson

1896   Seriland. *National Geographic Magazine* 7 (4): 125–33.

McGee, W J, George H. Williams, Nelson H. Darton, and Bailey Willis

1891   The Geology of Washington and Vicinity. In *Guide to Washington and Its Scientific Institutions, Prepared by the Local Committee for the International Congress of Geologists,* 5th session, pp. 38–64, map. Washington, D.C.: Government Printing Office.

McGee, W J, G. H. Williams, Bailey Willis, and N. H. Darton

1893   The Geology of Washington and Vicinity. *Compte Rendu, International Congress of Geology,* 5th session, pp. 219–51. Washington, D.C.: Government Printing Office.

Muñiz, Manuel A., and W J McGee

1894   Primitive Trephining in Peru. *Bulletin of the Johns Hopkins Hospital* (Baltimore) 5: 1.

1897   Primitive Trephining in Peru. In *Annual Report of the Bureau of American Ethnology,* vol. 16, 3–72. Washington, D.C.: Government Printing Office.

Russell, Israel C., W J McGee, and others

1885   What Is a Glacier? *Bulletin of the Philosophical Society of Washington* 7: 37–39.

Thomas, Cyrus, and W J McGee

1903   *Indians of North America in Historic Times.* Vol. 2 of *The History of North America,* edited by Francis N. Thorpe. Philadelphia, George Barrie's Sons.

NOTES

INTRODUCTION

1. Biographical material concerning McGee and Willard D. Johnson is drawn principally from Hinsley (1976, 1981), Knowlton (1913), E. McGee (1915), and Washington Academy of Sciences (1916).

2. See Appendix D for a list of McGee's publications.

3. See Hovens (1989). Also see the references for a list of publications by ten Kate containing mention of Papagos (ten Kate 1883a, b, 1885, 1892, 1916, 1918, 1995).

4. Information concerning Dinwiddie is drawn largely from *Who Was Who in America* (Marquis Who's Who in America 1943: 326); from Dinwiddie entries in *The National Union Catalog Pre-1956 Imprints;* and from the *Readers Guide to Periodical Literature, 1900–1904* (no. 1, p. 392).

5. Information is from Brennan (1991: 459–60). Also see Appendix A.

6. Manuscript no. 1744, vols. 1–3; manuscript no. 2325, nos. A and B.

7. Most of the information concerning Johnson is from Hinsley (1976: 377–82).

8. Three letters by Johnson on this subject are in the National Anthropological Archives, Smithsonian Institution, in the Association of American Geographers Records, Administrative Records (General Corr.), Letters Received, Office of the Secretary, I–L, 1904–1966, Box 17 of 157 boxes.

9. Moser (1963: 25). Much of this history, including that concerning the Encinas War, is outlined by McGee himself (1898b: 55–94, 109–20). There is a more up-to-date summary in Spicer (1962: 105–17).

10. Also see Hinsley (1992).

11. See the asterisked items in Appendix D for publications resulting wholly or in part based on McGee's 1894 and '95 expeditions.

12. McGee's first child, his daughter Klotho, had been born the previous year. This inspired De Lancey Gill, the photographer and artist on the 1900 expedition, to name the highest peak in the Muggins Mountains east of Yuma, Arizona, "Klotho's Temple" (McGee 1901: 140). This name has survived on most modern maps, although on others the peak is labeled "Coronation Peak."

13. Summaries of McGee's role in the conservation movement are in Cross (1953) and Lacey (1979).

Papago Trip, 1894

1. Terrenate is located on the west side of the Río Magdalena approximately six miles south of Imuris. McGee was on the road that follows the course of the river along its west bank, immediately opposite the east-bank tracks of the Sonora Railway. Treasury agent and writer John Ross Browne traveled the same road in 1864 and penned a depressing picture of the region's people three decades before McGee met them:

> The inhabitants of Imuriz, Terrenati, San Ignatio, and the smaller villages or rancherias are miserably poor and lazy. Their cattle have nearly all disappeared, in consequence of the frequent raids of the Apaches; and their milpas, or fields, formerly cultivated with considerable success, have gone to ruin. Scarcely sufficient food to sustain life is now produced. The ground is rich and the climate unsurpassed, and with the rudest cultivation abundant crops of wheat, maize, pomegranates, and oranges might be produced; but all hope for the future seems to be crushed out of these miserable people. (Browne 1974: 168)

2. San Lorenzo is a very small community located about four miles south of Magdalena de Kino on the west bank of the Río Magdalena.

3. Something apparently happened to one of the wheels on the wagon. It was repaired in Magdalena.

4. He is almost certainly referring to *Stenocereus thurberi*, also commonly known as organ-pipe cactus or *pitahaya dulce* (Turner, Bowers, and Burgess 1995: 379).

5. The name of a ranch near Imuris; in more recent times the place was called Kino Hot Springs.

6. Probably the common cane, or *carrizo, Phragmites communis*.

7. McGee greatly underestimates the many uses to which *Phragmites communis* was put. The stalks were used for ceiling lathes (*latillas*) in houses and other buildings and for shades on the sides of *ramadas*. Various parts of the plant were also used for "shafts of arrows, Indian prayer sticks, weaving-rods, pipestems, mats, screens, cordage, nets, and thatching" (Kearney, Peebles, and collaborators 1960: 89).

8. San Ignacio de Cabórica was a Piman Indian community when it was first visited in 1687 by Jesuit missionary Eusebio Francisco Kino, who bestowed the patronage of St. Ignatius of Loyola on it. Adobe is a clayey soil commonly used in construction. In pre-Spanish times in the Southwest, adobe construction was generally of packed or rammed puddled adobe. The Spaniards introduced the method of forming puddled adobe into bricks with the use of forms. Left unfired, these bricks are sun-dried and commonly referred to as *adobes*. Fired, they are called either *burnt adobes* or simply *bricks*. The houses in San Ignacio were made of adobes; the mill was made of bricks; and unknown to McGee, the church, built of adobe before 1768, was remodeled from the ground up after 1772 by the addition of bricks to the original adobe fabric (Schuetz-Miller and Fontana 1996: 81–82).

9. Dinwiddie photographed her separately, however.

10. Now known as Magdalena de Kino, what was originally a settlement of Piman Indians became the mission visiting station of Santa María Magdalena when Father Kino founded it as such in 1690. Magdalena is now the hub city of an area of ranches, mines, and farms, and it is where Father Kino was buried in 1711. His remains are on display in a shrine in the city's main plaza (Fontana 1996; Olvera 1998; Schuetz-Miller and Fontana 1996: 82–84).

11. Camotes is a ranch in the *municipio* (county) of Santa Ana (Almada 1952: 131).

12. Baboquivari Peak is a 7,730-foot-high granite dome dominating the Baboquivari Mountains and surrounding desert landscape west of Tucson in southern Arizona.

13. This is from a Piman word that means "tuft-shaped," said of anything, such as the top knot on a quail's head or a fountain, that shoots up and falls outward (Mathiot n.d.: 166). The Sonoran town of Cibuta derives its name from this word.

14. Almost certainly the Spanish-introduced date palm, *Phoenix dactylifera*.

15. Old Santa Ana, or Santa Ana Viejo, is on the west side of the Río Magdalena opposite "new" Santa Ana, which lies along the railroad tracks on the river's east side. Never a mission settlement, it began as a ranch by at least 1739. By the 1990s it had become a small farming and ranching community regionally known for the fine racehorses raised by some of its inhabitants (see Schuetz-Miller and Fontana 1996: 84).

16. Rivers in the Sonoran Desert tend not to be perennial, but either intermittent, running only after rainstorms, or interrupted, running partly on the surface and partly underground. McGee tells us the Magdalena was running underground in late October 1894.

The Santa Ana "station" refers to the station for the Sonora Railway, an affiliate of the Atchison, Topeka & Santa Fe, which ran a line from Guaymas, Sonora, to Nogales, Arizona, between 1880 and 1882. Southern Pacific assumed management of the system in 1898, and it was later taken over by the Mexican government and continues in operation in the 1990s (Myrick 1975: 268, 288).

17. Caborca is about sixty miles west of Santa Ana. It was a Piman Indian settlement that became a mission community in 1694 and was christened La Purísima Concepción de Nuestra Señora de Caborca. A large mission church, one remaining largely intact in the 1990s, was built here by Franciscans between 1803 and 1809. The town's citizens defeated a group of American filibusters trying to take over Sonora in 1857, giving the community its modern name of Heroica Caborca. Due in part to construction of the Ferrocarril de Sonora a Baja California (the Sonora to Baja California railroad) completed through here in 1947, and because of good soils irrigated by pumping underground water, a century after McGee's visit Caborca had grown to become the major commercial center of the farming and ranching country of northwestern Sonora (Almada 1952: 124, 277; Schuetz-Miller and Fontana 1996: 73–74).

18. By the late nineteenth century, many Yaqui Indians, whose home villages were in southern Sonora, had scattered widely in their search for work as laborers on ranches and farms and in mines (see Spicer 1980).

19. The creosote bush, *Larrea tridentata*.

20. He may be referring to an extraordinarily large colony of harvester ants, either of the genus *Pogonomyrmex* or *Veromessor*, or to leaf cutter ants, either *Acromyrmex versicolor* or *Atta mexicana*. Also see n. 23 in "Second Expedition, 1895."

21. This is a wonderful description of a Yaqui *pascola* performance minus the pascola, a masked figure who presides as ritual host at religious and other fiestas. The pascola makes orations, gives out water and cigarettes, dances to the flute and drum, "tells comic stories, acts in humorous skits, and interacts with others at the fiesta" (Griffith 1980: 8). The man who plays the flute and drum is called the *tampaleo*. Both flute, *baka kusia*, and drum, *kubahe*, are illustrated in Fontana, Faubert, and Burns (1977: 23). The songs, including bird songs, are discussed in Painter (1986: 264–66).

22. Corn-hoy (corn today), is probably McGee's humorous way of referring to fresh corn.

23. Querobabi is an old ranching community between Santa Ana and Hermosillo where Los Otates arroyo drains into the streambed called El Zanjón. The station mentioned by McGee is the railroad station.

24. Llano is a railroad station about twelve miles south of Santa Ana.

25. In all probability these are markers memorializing persons who died at these locations. The tradition of erecting such markers is one that goes back in this region at least to the eighteenth century (Griffith 1992: 100–4).

26. McGee is describing the traditional Northern O'odham hammock cradle made by stretching two ropes and wrapping a hide, blanket, or other cloth between and around them. A third rope is attached to the hammock so it can be swung gently by someone while the child lies cradled inside. There is a traditional Tohono O'odham tale concerning these cradles, likening them to tiny brown curled leaves holding babies who have died (Wright 1929: 201–6).

27. A *metate* is a flat stone slab on which corn and other grains are ground with the aid of a flat, hand-sized grinding stone, or *mano*, as they are regionally labeled. There are many types of metates and manos (e.g., trough, slab, and basin metates and block trough, taper trough, and loaf trough manos; see DiPeso 1956: 463–747, 477–78). McGee initially tended automatically to believe such implements were prehistoric when, in fact, they remain in use in many parts of Mexico to the present.

28. O'odham earthenware pottery is made partly by the paddle-and-anvil technique in which the body of the pot being made is thinned and heightened. The potter holds a hand-sized flat stone in her left hand on the inside of the pre-fired vessel while paddling against it from the outside with a wooden paddle. When the pot is completely formed and the clay has dried slightly, the potter smoothes over the entire outer surface with small water-worn pebbles, other polished stones, or glass. The "olla stones" to which McGee refers probably include both the smooth polishing stones and the flat hand-stones or *anvils* (Fontana et al. 1962: 59, 65–66).

29. According to ethnobiologists Castetter and Bell (1942: 57–58), Tohono O'odham aboriginally cultivated about one-fifth of their total food supply annually, relying on wild plants and animals for the rest of their subsistence. Of the latter, they estimate that Tohono O'odham depended on plant foods (mesquite beans; cactus fruit and buds; seeds of saguaro, ironwood, horse bean, and paloverde; agave hearts; certain roots and bulbs; acorns; and greens) over game (deer, antelope, rabbits, a few species of birds, and the larvae of the lined sphinx moth) in a ratio of 4:1.

30. The O'odham shaman is called a *makai*. For a lengthy discussion of the subject, see Bahr et al. (1974).

31. Pozo Verde, or Ce:dagi Wahia, is a Tohono O'odham settlement on the northern Sonora border just southwest of Sásabe, Arizona. McGee had visited here earlier, before his diary commences, en route from the San Xavier Reservation. See Fontana (1981: 19–21, 23, 30–31, 68, 92).

32. By church law, any Catholic can perform the baptismal rites if a priest is not available. For a discussion of such folk baptisms among Tohono O'odham, see Joseph, Spicer, and Chesky (1949: 119) and King (1954: 72–78).

33. Carbó, a railroad station midway between Querobabi and Hermosillo, dates from 1888, when it was made a station on the rail line connecting Guaymas, Sonora, to Nogales, Arizona. It is named for General José Guillermo Carbó, who had helped quell a regional rebellion against the federal government in 1873 (Almada 1952: 143–44; Brito de Martí 1982: 203; Voss 1982: 266).

34. McGee uses *Fr* to indicate French pronunciation and *G* to indicate German pronunciation.

35. The root word in O'odham is *cuhuggia*, the *c* pronounced as *ch* (Mathiot 1973: 218). It is the term for wild spinach, or in Spanish, *quelite* (*Amaranthus palmeri* or *Amaranthus watsonii*). The O'odham word for a well is *vahia* (Mathiot n.d.: 242).

36. This kind of circumspection, manifesting itself in an unwillingness to approach others directly and abruptly, is a common feature of traditional cultures of many American Indian groups.

37. The verb is *maak* (Mathiot n.d.: 32).

38. In Sonoran Spanish *jacal* refers to structures whose walls are made of sticks, such as ocotillo stalks, reeds, or ribs from saguaro cacti. They are sometimes but not always stuccoed with mud to make a wattle-and-daub structure.

39. Possibly the ocotillo (*Fouquieria splendens*).

40. The relationship established here is the Spanish one of godmother, *comadre,* and female godchild, *ahijada*. This system of godparentage, or *compadrazgo,* can extend families beyond immediate ties of blood and marriage. The tradition was, and remains, strong throughout Hispanic America.

41. That is, Christian, or given, names.

42. O'odham traditionally use nicknames in referring to others, but never as terms of address. For a detailed discussion of the subject of O'odham names, see Fontana (1960: 67–82).

43. Yaqui relations with Spaniards and subsequently with Mexicans are characterized by a long series of episodes of violent resistance by Yaquis against outside intrusions. That being referred to here was headed by the Yaqui leader José María Leyva, known to Yaquis as Cajeme. The uprising led by Cajeme lasted from 1882 until his execution in 1887, although armed guerrilla resistance continued afterward (see Spicer 1962: 70–73).

44. Possibly the foothill paloverde, *Cercidium microphyllum,* and the blue paloverde, *Cercidium floridum,* respectively.

45. Possibly a distinct variety of the jumping cactus, *Opuntia fulgida* var. *mammillata.*

46. McGee is still on the road next to the railroad tracks. Pesqueira is a station approximately twenty miles north of Hermosillo.

47. El Zanjón is the major north-south drainageway in this part of Sonora. Its mouth is on the Río San Miguel south of Pesqueira and north of Hermosillo.

48. *Cis.-* is McGee's abbreviation for *cismontane,* meaning on this (the speaker's) side of the mountains. San Miguel refers to San Miguel de Horcasitas and to the Río San Miguel that flows past it.

49. Noria Verde (Green Well) is about eight miles north of Pesqueira.

50. Since 1879, Hermosillo has been the capital of the state of Sonora. Founded in the early eighteenth century as El Pitic, in 1828 it was renamed in honor of General José María González de Hermosillo, one of the heroes of Mexico's War of Independence (Almada 1952: 340–45).

51. Almost certainly the plant variously called *guayacán, árbol santo,* and *palo santo* (*Guaiacum coulteri*) (Turner, Bowers, and Burgess 1995: 227–28).

52. Possibly a plant known by many common names, including San Juan, San Juanico, San Juanito, and *palo de las ánimas* (*Jacquinia macrocarpa* subsp. *pungens*).

53. The mountain range to the east of the route McGee has been following is the Sierra Cucurpe, with the Río San Miguel running south along its opposite, eastern base. The blue mountains in the far distance are, indeed, the various ranges comprising a portion of Mexico's Sierra Madre Occidental.

54. *Tepetate* is Mexican Spanish for caliche, or calcium carbonate. It is also a term used by miners in referring to the waste that accompanies ore.

55. The Santa Ana to which he refers here is an *hacienda* in the judicial district of Hermosillo (Almada 1952: 727).

56. This is the Cerro de la Campana (Hill of the Bell), the city's symbol.

57. Quijotoa (O'odham for Burden Basket Mountain) was a village in Arizona on what today is the main reservation of the Tohono O'odham Nation. It is possible there may have been Mormons among the hundreds of miners who prospected and mined in the vicinity of Quijotoa during a brief silver-mining boom there that began in the spring of 1883 and lasted until April 1884 (Myrick 1993).

58. This one-sentence description of Tohono O'odham marriage practices foreshadows similar information gathered by anthropologist Ruth Underhill four decades later (1939: 31–56). She writes that the rules ideally were a bit more strict than McGee's note implies, but that "in practice . . . the Papago is not very assiduous in reckoning relationship" (p. 38).

59. Stories of blue-eyed and light-skinned Indians remain current throughout much of Mexico, the specific details varying from locale to locale. This particular tale of "Neago" Indians is unsubstantiated but like similar stories may have its basis in grains of fact: either occasional occurrences of albinism or groups of Indians among whom non-Indian genes have been introduced.

60. This may be the Tonuco Ranch directly west of Hermosillo a little less than half the distance to the coast. It lies immediately south of Cerro Cuevas.

61. The governor of Sonora in 1894 was Rafael Izábal. He was both preceded and, in 1895, succeeded by journalist and politician Don Ramón Corral (Almada 1952: 406–8). An intellectual, Corral published a history of the state of Sonora, 1856–1877, and a biography of Yaqui leader José María Leyva, known as "Cajeme." (Corral 1981).

62. Guaymas, located about eighty-five miles south of Hermosillo, is Sonora's principal port city. It has a fine bay and harbor on the Sea of Cortés (Gulf of California).

63. The judge may have been Conrado Pérez Aranda (Almada 1952: 562). J. Alexander Forbes, the former American consul, was living in Guaymas but apparently happened to be in Hermosillo on McGee's arrival there (McGee 1898b: 119).

64. This is amusing in view of McGee's published version of his trip: "Accordingly the party was reorganized at Hermosillo, and, with the sanction of the Secretary of State and Acting Governor, Señor Don Ramón Corral, proceeded to Rancho San Francisco de Costa Rica" (McGee 1898b: 12). In fact, he made the trip to Encinas's ranch without official sanction. He did, however, report to the governor and other officials on his return, "with no special event."

65. Pascual Encinas established a cattle ranch, San Francisco de Costa Rica, within Seri country in 1844. A biographical sketch of him and an outline of the history of his relationships with Seri Indians appear in McGee's published report on the Seri (1898b: 109–15). He is also memorialized in a book by a grandnephew (Thomson 1989).

The Costa Rica Ranch was sold by the Encinas heirs to Jim Blevins, who owned it in 1921 when it was visited by naturalist Charles Sheldon (1979: 84). Now abandoned, the old ranch headquarters and adjacent Indian campsites are today an archaeological site, Son. N:2:1, one examined in detail on February 14–15 by archaeologist Richard S. White working for the Centro Regional del Noroeste, Instituto Nacional de Antropología e Historia, Hermosillo. His surface collections gathered at the site were placed in Bolsa 138.

66. Felger and Moser (1985: 266–73) describe eleven distinct species of cholla (*Opuntia* spp.) for the Seri country.

67. Possibly *Opuntia fulgida* (Felger and Moser 1985: 268–70).

68. Probably the limberbush, *Jatropha cardiophylla* (Felger and Moser 1985: 295–96).

69. That is, quelite, *Amaranthus watsonii* (Felger and Moser 1985: 228–29).

70. Seris poisoned their arrows using the sap of the Mexican jumping bean, or *hierba de la flecha* (*Sapium biloculare*), sometimes in combination with the sap of *Marsdenia*. They also used the sap from limberbush (*Jatropha cinerea* and *Jatropha cuneata*) (Felger and Moser 1985: 128; Turner, Bowers, & Burgess 1995: 356–57). McGee (1898b: 25) had considerably more to say on the subject in his volume on the Seri Indians.

71. It is, of course, a canard to suggest the Seris were devoid of religion. The girls' puberty ceremony as it was still being carried out in 1953 is described in some detail by Hinton (1955).

72. There are good discussions of the Seri balsa rafts in Felger and Moser (1985: 131–33) and in McGee (1898b: 216–21).

73. This Tiburón Plain, or "eggshell," pottery is described in Bowen (1976: 53–54), Bowen and Moser (1968: 28, 120), Felger and Moser (1985: 80–81), and McGee (1898b: 183).

74. There is an excellent discussion of the various kinds of traditional Seri shelters in Felger and Moser (1985: 114–21). McGee mentions the Seris' use of shells of the green turtle (*Chelonia mydas*), but, in fact, they used the carapaces of other sea turtles as well, including the loggerhead, leatherback, hawksbill, and olive Ridley (Felger and Moser 1985: 43–44).

75. The black-tailed deer, *Odocoileus hemionis;* white-tailed deer, *Odocoileus virginianus;* collared peccary or javelina, *Tayassu tajacu sonorensis;* and desert cottontail (*Sylvilagus auduboni*), black-tailed jackrabbit (*Lepus californicus eremicus*), and antelope jackrabbit (*Lepus alleni alleni*).

76. Arturo Alvemar-León, "a young Mexican gentleman educated in the United States," lived in Hermosillo (McGee 1898b: 118).

77. Pelado (Shorn) was McGee's principal Seri informant. He is variously referred to as El Gran Pelado, Juan Estorga, Francisco Estorga, and the Seri "chief" or "subchief," Mashém (McGee 1898b: 18, 109–10).

As a youth, Pelado and another Seri boy were taken to Pascual Encinas's Costa Rica ranch to be educated in Spanish and in the Catholic faith, "in the hope that they might pass into priesthood and so form a future bond with their kin. One of these neophytes disappeared in the troublous times of a later decade, though tradition indicates that he became a tribal outcast . . . and slunk away to Pitiquito and Altar, and afterward to California; the other, christened Juan Estorga and nicknamed El Gran Pelado . . . survives as subchief Mashém, long since lapsed into his native savagery, save that he remembers the Spanish, affects a hat, cuts his hair to the neck (whence his nickname), and prefers footgear to the fashion of his fellows" (McGee 1898b: 109–10).

78. Seri customs connected with death and burial are discussed in Felger and Moser (1985: 7–8, 117, 254) and in Griffen (1959: 28–29, 43–46).

79. All Souls' Day, more formerly recognized by the Roman Catholic Church as The Commemoration of All the Faithful Departed, is observed on November 2. It is, as McGee, suggests, one of the more important events in the Yaquis' annual ceremonial calendar, although it is observed by O'odham and Mexicans as well.

The "tables spread with food and delicacies" were not primarily for worshipers but were intended for the dead. It is, however, true that certain of the Yaqui participants took food for themselves and their families (Spicer 1940: 213).

The two dancers "shaking gourd rattles in rhythm" were *matachin* dancers. Had they been deer dancers, McGee would have commented on their deer-head costumes. As for pascolas, concerning Pascua village in Tucson, Arizona, in 1937, Spicer (1940: 178) states unequivocally that pascolas "have no part . . . at the ceremonies centering about All Souls' Day in November." As seen in McGee's diary entry for November 3, they clearly performed at the Costa Rica ranch.

For details concerning the Yaquis' observance of All Souls' Day, see Spicer (1940: 117–28, 137, 178, 194–96, 211, 213, 246–47, 252, and pl. 12; 1954: 123–24) and Painter (1986: 86, 91, 312–13). For an understanding of the broader Mexican context in which these observances occur, see Griffith (1995: 13–33). Also see n. 21, above.

80. Seris fashioned kilts and robes from the pelts of both the brown pelican (*Pelecanus occidentalis californicus*) and winter-visiting white pelican (*Pelecanus erythrorhynchos*). From four to eight pelts were sewn together and used for clothing, sleeping mats, blankets, and items for trade or sale (Felger and Moser 1985: 50–51). McGee (1898b: 225) says such robes were worn to supplement the kilt-like skirt and short shirts usually worn by Seris and were "habitually carried to serve as bed or mackintosh, according to the chance of journey or weather, or as a shield in sudden warfare."

81. There are good illustrated discussions of Seri face painting in Burckhalter (1996), Felger and Moser (1985: 152–56), McGee (1898b: 164–69), and Xavier (1946). Some of the photographs taken by Dinwiddie on this occasion, including those of the reluctant Candelaria and bare-breasted Juana María, are published in McGee (1898b: pls. X–XI, XIII–XXVI, and XXVIII).

82. As graphic as this description is, McGee (1898b: 204 n. 1) embellished it further in his published version:

a starveling cur—a female apparently of nearly pure coyote blood and within a week of term—slunk toward the broken olla-kettle in the left center of the picture [pl. XI], in which a rank horse-foot was simmering; the woman bending over the kettle suddenly straightened and shot out her foot with such force and directness that the cur was lifted entirely over the corner of the nearest jacal, and the poor beast fell stunned and moaning, a prematurely born pup protruding from her two-thirds of its length. The sound of the stroke and the fall attracted attention throughout the group; the woman smiled and grunted approval of the well-aimed kick, and a dozen children gathered to continue the assault. Partially recovering, the cur struggled to its feet and started for the chaparral, followed by the jeering throng; at first the chase seemed sportive only, but suddenly one of the smaller boys (the third from the left in the group shown in pl. XVI) took on a new aspect—his figure stiffened, his jaws set, his eyes shot purple and green, and he plunged into the lead, and just before the harried beast reached cover he seized the protruding embryo, jerked it away, and ran off in triumph. Three minutes afterward he was seen in the shelter of a jacal greedily gorging his spoil in successive bites, just as the Caucasian boy devours a peeled banana. Meanwhile two or three mates who had struck his trail stood around begging bites and sucking at chance blood spatters on earth, skin, or tattered rags; and as the victor came forth later, licking his chops, he was met by half jocular but admiring plaudits for his prowess from the dozen matrons lounging about the neighboring jacales.

83. See Spicer (1940: 173–203) and nn. 21 and 79, above.

84. There are a La Palma Ranch in the municipio of La Colorada not far from Hermosillo, and an Aguaje Ranch in the municipio of Hermosillo; "Tonojo" may be Tonuco, a ranch in the municipio of Hermosillo north-northeast of Rancho Libertad on the Río Bacuache (Almada 1952: 19, 551, 789; McGee 1898b: 59).

85. The most comprehensive study of O'odham pottery is that by Fontana et al. (1962).

86. To my knowledge, Guardian Angel Island—Isla Ángel de la Guarda—awaits a systematic archaeological site survey. It is located in the Gulf of California some sixty kilometers west-northwest of Tiburón Island and between fifteen and thirty kilometers off the east coast of Baja California. While it is possible archaeological sites are on the island, it seems unlikely. Griffing Bancroft (1932: 354) has written of the island, probably correctly:

> In the northeastern corner lies a quite pretentious valley through which a temporary stream runs immediately after rains. Perhaps this is the foundation of the stories and legends that make of this island a site of romance second only to Tiburón. Rumors and tales of flowing water and weird occupants circulate all over the Gulf and even find their way into print. It is no pleasure to destroy a pretty story, no matter how fantastic, and there certainly would be satisfaction in finding an oasis in these incredibly inimical surroundings. The hard fact remains, however, that La Guarda is a desert, uninhabited and unwatered. With the exception mentioned long high ridges extend in a single line from end to end, their sides dropping directly into the Gulf. There are neither foothills nor benches nor valleys, and their slopes of high seawalls have no hiding places where secrets can be treasured.

87. McGee's use of the plant label "opoten" or "opeten" is one of the most perplexing in his 1894 field notes, the only place where he uses the word. Given his labeling of photos taken at Pozo Nuevo on November 7, 1894, however, it is probable the term was his misunderstanding of the generic term for *ocotillo,* which he uses regularly in 1895 (spelling it "okatillo") to the exclusion of "opeten." The ocotillo, *Fouquieria splendens,* is common in the areas traversed by McGee. The so-called tree ocotillo (*Fouquieria macdougalii*), however, has been recorded since McGee's day only in areas considerably to the south of his travels (Felger and Moser 1985: 35; Turner, Bowers, and Burgess 1995: 223–24).

The "cross" to which he refers here he labels in one of his photos as an "okatiya tree," lending further credence to equating "opeten" with ocotillo.

88. From Dinwiddie's photo of this structure, it would appear the horizontal members and door are split branches of the senita, *Lophocereus schottii.*

89. There is no sagebrush in Sonora. McGee could be referring instead to *Pluchea purpurascens.*

90. The Sierra Carnero (Ram Mountain), northwest of Hermosillo by what was once the main road between Hermosillo and Altar, Sonora, was the southernmost of several mining districts within what was referred to as the Altar goldfield (Waring 1897: 257).

91. Santa Rosa was another of the mining districts of the so-called Altar goldfield (Waring 1897: 257). It is almost due south of Trincheras.

92. Milpillas, on the west bank of the Río Bacuachito in the central-eastern extremity of the municipio of Pitiquito, is thirty-one miles south of Trincheras.

93. This set of geological observations is the first of those McGee made on this journey that later resulted in his published paper on sheetflood erosion (McGee 1897).

94. Ciénega started life as San Ildefonso de la Cieneguilla in January 1771, when soldiers discovered large deposits of gold here. Hundreds of eager miners and more than 1,500 Indian laborers poured into the area and, annually until 1779, extracted gold that on today's market would be worth millions of dollars. Father Pedro Font, the Franciscan priest who can be counted among those responsible for the founding of San Francisco, California, visited Cieneguilla in May 1776 after he had returned from California (Font 1931: 515).

There was a lesser gold discovery here in 1802, and between then and 1884, largely under the aegis of Teodoro Salazar and his descendants, there was considerable placer mining of gold, first through a winnowing process and, after 1875, with the aid of homemade dry-washing equipment, most notably a homemade version of the Hungarian dry washer. Between 1884 and 1894, at the time of McGee's arrival, the operation was in the hands of the Serna family. Cieneguilla, whose name had been shortened to Ciénega by 1894, was assaulted in 1849 by a party of more than thirty Americans, men possibly on their way to the California goldfields. They led the elderly parish priest around the town with a rope around his neck, like a leashed dog, and they rounded up other residents, stripped them of their possessions, and locked them in their houses (Merrill 1908; Officer 1987: 114–15, 1996: 51; Waring 1897: 257).

95. The operation of these dry washers is described in great detail by Waring (1897: 258):

> A crew of two adult Indians and three boys, and an overseer or *maquinista* is required to operate a dry washer. One of the men clears a piece of ground by removing shrubbery, trees, etc., and loosens the surface with a crowbar, which is the only tool used by him. The other shovels the earth through a portable sand screen with rods ½ in. apart. Two boys, with rawhide *tinates* or buckets, each holding 40 lbs. of earth, carry the alluvium as fast as it is screened, to the hopper, while the third boy turns the crank and regulates the flow of earth from the hopper. Such a crew can screen and jig from three to four tons of earth per hour.

The machine, a version of the Hungarian dry washer, and its operation are also described in Merrill (1908).

96. If the brush were indeed made of yucca leaves, unless imported from outside of Sonora it must have been of *Yucca arizonica,* Sonora's only known yucca species (Turner, Bowers, and Burgess 1995: 407–9). An authority on O'odham basketry reports: "Papago hair brushes are generally of agave fiber (*Agave* spp.); those of the Pima are of grasses, the tripled awn (*Sporbulus wrightii*); of grass roots; of yucca fiber (*Yucca baccata*); or agave fiber (*Agave* [spp.]).

"The crudest form of wrapped weaving occurs in the hair brushes of the locality. The technic is merely a winding and fastening, as the fiber, grasses, or roots are simply bundled together and wrapped toward one end, at times with crude craftsmanship, at other times more perfectly" (Kissell 1916: 145, 147, fig. 8).

97. There is little question that some O'odham built semi-subterranean houses while others did not. McGee's notes and Dinwiddie's photographs themselves offer some evidence of this fact. Questions relating to the geographic and temporal distribution of such houses,

as well as reasons for the choice between ground-level and semi-subterranean structures, remain to be answered (Castetter and Underhill 1935: 66–67; Underhill 1951: 14–19; Woodward 1933).

98. McGee (1898a: 367) incorporated this observation of a girl's washing a head scarf into a later article: "When garments require washing—and the Papago are a cleanly folk—they are taken to the waterside and rubbed with the hands and beaten with cobbles on a large stone, while the saponaceous lather of the soap agave is applied, and water is sprinkled or poured over them."

99. McGee's discussion anticipates a nearly identical description by Fontana et al. (1962: 68–73) of observations made more than a half-century later.

100. If McGee is correct in his identification, this is *Dasylirion wheeleri*.

101. Possibly the desert hackberry, *Celtis pallida*.

102. It is the Rancho Berruga—or Verruga—twenty-five miles south of Caborca (Almada 1952: 112).

103. The Santa Catalina Mountains immediately north of Tucson, Arizona.

104. The cottonwood, *Populus fremontii*, "is planted everywhere as a shade tree" (Kearney, Peebles, and collaborators 1960: 207).

105. San Diego del Pitiquito was a small O'odham settlement when it first came to the attention of Jesuit missionaries in the early eighteenth century. The church there was begun by Franciscans about 1776 and finished in 1781. Father Pedro Font, the diarist who accompanied the Anza expedition to California in 1775–76, died and was buried here in 1781 (Schuetz-Miller and Fontana 1996: 71–72). Pitiquito became a thriving agricultural community with good fruit orchards, but the orchards were devastated by nematodes and the town was bypassed by the railroad when it was built between Benjamin Hill, Sonora, and Baja California in the late 1930s and 1940s. These events relegated the community to a comparatively minor status.

106. McGee means by this that Caborca had been characterized this way to him by others, and that he had been greatly anticipating his visit here because of a reputedly large Papago presence. For a discussion of O'odham numbers in northern Sonora, see Fontana (1981: 86–96).

107. A *temporal* is a "field" village (*oidak* in O'odham), one occupied seasonally rather than permanently. Approximately a dozen miles downstream from Caborca on the Río Asunción would place the settlement at Santa María del Pópulo de Bísanig, a site that by the second half of the twentieth century had been abandoned and its mission ruins, dating from the eighteenth century, converted into a cemetery (Schuetz-Miller and Fontana 1996: 75).

108. *Pinole* is coarse flour typically ground from parched corn. It may also consist of ground wheat or mesquite pods.

109. These wooden "spoons" were probably ladles, which Tohono O'odham are known to have made from carved mesquite or paloverde (Russell 1908: 101, figs. 14b–c).

110. This was probably Arizona's Phoenix Indian Industrial Boarding School, a facility opened in 1891 and operated by the federal government until it closed in the 1980s (Trennert 1988).

111. For an illustrated and more detailed description of the identical process as it was carried out in the 1950s, see Fontana et al. (1962: 49–78).

112. The tortilla being described here may well be a Northern O'odham invention, one that has become popular in many parts of the United States. It is the flour tortilla, or *tortilla de harina*, made from wheat rather than corn flour (Griffith 1988: 14–16).

113. The church was intended as a replica of Mission San Xavier del Bac in southern Arizona, which McGee had already seen. It is, however, not typical of most other Pimería Alta churches, although it superficially resembles the church built much later in Hermosillo, which McGee had also seen.

114. Since McGee's day, archaeologists working in the Sonoran Desert have paid a great deal of attention to these so-called *cerros de trincheras* (entrenched hills), some of which, like that described here by McGee, were fortifications, while others were terraced and used for habitation and, possibly, for the cultivation of agaves. In 1930, thirty-six years after McGee's visit to this site, geographers Carl Sauer and Donald Brand (1931: 99) made an archaeological reconnaissance in the vicinity of Pitiquito and Caborca, noting: "On the hills south of the river between Pitiquito and Caborca is a series of faint trincheras. . . . On the isolated hill east of Caborca a trinchera is visible. At its base, among the rock waste normal to such a slope, there are shards in considerable amount with definite quartz and flint spalls, but without any traces of foundations." This is possibly the same site described here in greater detail by McGee.

More recent studies of Sonoran Desert prehistoric trincheras sites, in addition to that by Sauer and Brand (1931), include those by Downum (1986, 1993: 7, 36–38, 40, 53–95, 110, 123, 124); Downum, Fish, and Fish (1994); Fish, Fish, and Madsen (1992: 9, 20, 34–37, 44); Fontana, Greenleaf, and Cassidy (1959); Hoover (1941); Huntington (1913); Ives (1936); Stacy (1974, 1977); Wilcox (1979); and Woodward et al. (1993: 4–5, 83, 128).

115. Here McGee is referring to Las Trincheras, a very large hill immediately south of today's town of the same name. The hill has prehistoric stone-faced terraces on it from top to bottom, terraces that once supported habitations. The site has given its name to an entire prehistoric cultural complex that covers much of northwestern Sonora and parts of southern Arizona, the so-called Trincheras Culture, an agricultural and pottery-making people who seem to have thrived between about A.D. 1300 and 1450 (Johnson 1960, 1963–64; McGuire and Villalpando 1998; O'Donovan 1997). McGee visited Las Trincheras during his 1895 expedition and, with Willard D. Johnson, mapped the site (see pp. 60–63, below).

116. McGee arrived in Pitiquito on the vigil of the town's patron, San Diego de Alcalá or, as he is known in English, Saint Didacus. His feast day in the church calendar is November 14 (Thurston and Attwater 1956: IV:327–28).

117. Possibly McGee is describing the ashy limberbush, *Jatropha cinerea*, also known as *sangregrado* or *torotillo* in Spanish (Turner, Bowers, and Burgess 1995: 245–47). "Leatherwood" refers to the leatherplant or limberbush, *Jatropha cuneata* (Turner, Bowers, and Burgess 1995: 248–49).

118. This is an excellent description of the elephant tree, *Bursera microphylla*, also called *torote, torote colorado*, or *copal* in Spanish (Turner, Bowers, and Burgess 1995: 127–29).

119. Altar was begun as a Spanish military post, or *presidio*, about 1755 in the aftermath of the Piman Indian rebellion of 1751. Never an Indian town, it continued to have presidial status until 1848, after which it became a hub for surrounding farming and ranching enterprises (Williams 1991: 52–55).

120. McGee (1898a: 363) used the Spanish word *cajón* to mean "adobe mud, either mixed with stones or not, molded directly into walls."

121. Oquitoa, which McGee did not visit because he followed a more direct northerly route to Arizona, was a Piman (O'odham) community when Jesuit missionaries first came into contact with the people here in the 1690s. The Jesuits built a church dedicated to San Antonio del Paduano del Oquitoa in 1730, one later slightly remodeled by Franciscans and remaining standing and in use in 1997 (Schuetz-Miller and Fontana 1996: 70–71). Oquitoa remains a small farming community on the west side of the Río Altar.

122. Sonoyta (from the O'odham words meaning "spring field") was a Piman village on a river of the same name where in 1701 Father Eusebio Francisco Kino founded a mission dedicated to Nuestra Señora del Loreto de San Marcelo. A Jesuit priest, Enrique Ruhen, was martyred here by the Pimans in a general uprising in 1751 (Fontana 1994: 28, 98–99, 150–55, 157–59, 164–66, 207–10). By the late 1990s, Sonoyta had become a bustling Mexican town, a border crossing between Arizona and Sonora at the beginning of a highway leading to Puerto Peñasco, a popular resort community at the head of the Gulf of California (Ives 1989: 80–82).

Quitovac is a pre-Hispanic O'odham settlement at a desert oasis between Caborca and Sonoyta. The Mexican government opened a boarding school for Papagos in Quitovac in 1980, and the community has come to represent the largest concentration of Papagos in Sonora, lands here being reserved for their use (Fontana 1981: 68, 96, 99–101).

123. The "rather new church," which replaced the earlier presidial chapel and remained in use in Altar in 1997, was eight years old when McGee saw it. It had been built in 1886 (Olvera 1998: 154). The palm is almost certainly the introduced date palm (*Phoenix dactylifera*).

124. This is Rancho Paredones de Apalategui north of Altar (Almada 1952: 556; Lumholtz 1912: map of southwestern Arizona and northwestern Sonora).

125. It is shown as the Río Seco on the map in Lumholtz (1912).

126. This is C. T. Gedney of Culiacán, Sinaloa, Mexico. McGee makes no mention of him in his published reports and there is but scant mention of him in the field notes. Dinwiddie's photographs show that Gedney was with the party south of Caborca in the vicinity of Santa Rosa, as well as here on the trail to Arizona. He may well have joined McGee in Hermosillo to accompany him to Tucson.

127. One of these "modern ranches" was the Rancho de Félix photographed by Dinwiddie.

128. On later maps these mountains are called the Sierra de Moreno.

129. These are mounds raised in the tract of land between the confluence of two drainageways.

130. Actually, the rainbow (*kiohod*) occurs in many O'odham myths and legends. Wright (1929: 209–14) tells an O'odham story of the origin of the rainbow, and the rainbow is mentioned in Gila River Pima stories as well (Bahr et al. 1994: 74, 146, 259), none precisely the tale told here.

131. Clouds, as bearers of rain, feature prominently in O'odham legends and ritual (see indices in Bahr 1975 and in Underhill et al. 1979). Clouds as directional markers—white clouds for east, black for west, green for south, and red for north—were used in Tohono O'odham drypaintings made for the cure of wind sickness (Wyman 1983: 236–41).

132. Corn appears in later-told Northern O'odham myths to have been, if anything, a young man; in some versions of the story, he married a human woman with whom he had a child that later became the saguaro (Bahr et al. 1994: 75–77). In another version, Corn seduced a Papago woman with whom he lived for a long time, teaching her songs, before she returned to her husband (Underhill 1946: 78). The story of corn is also related in Rea (1997: 344–47).

133. This is a greatly over-simplified account of the annual Tohono O'odham *nawait*, or saguaro wine, ritual intended to "bring down the clouds" (make rain). It has since been described in great detail by Crosswhite (1980) and Underhill et al. (1979: 17–35) as well as other investigators (see Fontana 1980). The alcoholic beverage consumed was wine fermented from saguaro fruit, not mescal, which is distilled from agave.

The "doctors," or shamans, are called *mamakai* in O'odham. Their roles in Piman culture are outlined in Bahr et al. (1974). The eagle feather wands, *mámcwidag*, used by mamakai for divination are also discussed, and illustrated, in Bahr et al. (1974: 201, 203–6). Underhill (1946: 270) writes that the wand consisted "of the two top feathers of an eagle's wings. . . . To get them, [the shaman] either killed an eagle himself or traded for plumes with some old man who had been guardian to an eagle killer. . . . The feathers had to be fitted with a handle, and for this purpose the shaman inserted a small stick in the quill end of each, cementing it with gum." The eagle most readily available to the Tohono O'odham is the golden eagle, *Aquila chrysaëtos*.

134. The etiology of O'odham sicknesses, including those that involve such animals as rattlesnakes, is described in great detail in Bahr et al. (1974), with specifics concerning rattlesnake disease on pp. 26, 29, and 296. The account of rattlesnake disease among the

Pima given by Russell (1908), that "it causes kidney and common stomach troubles in children," and that it is "cured by singing the rattlesnake song and pressing the parts affected with an image in wood or stone of the rattlesnake" is much like that in an unpublished manuscript of Jose Lewis Brennan (1897): "The rattlesnake disease being only among the infants, when having this usually cry & seems to complain in their stomach, so the Indian doctor says. Therefore one sing the rattle snake's song to cure the disease. They [have] little board cut like r. snake."

Underhill (1946: 294) describes the curing fetish as a snake carved from a crooked creosote branch. No later investigator mentions a dance or rattles cut from the snake, living or dead.

135. Underhill (1939: 42, 113) made the same observation some forty years later: "Papago had no avoidances and no joking relationships," and, "instead of avoiding particular individuals, they avoided harsh words or open disagreements with anyone."

136. McGee makes no mention of the fact, but this day he crossed from Mexico back into the United States. There obviously was neither fence nor official entry point on the road. According to Bryan (1925: 408), "The old Ventana ranch is 4 miles northwest of San Miguel, on the road to Vamori. This American cattle ranch, dependent on a drilled well, was occupied as late as 1893 but has since been abandoned." The abandonment could have been caused in part by Papagos who were helping themselves to the livestock of Anglo cattlemen (Wagoner 1952: 114).

Carl Lumholtz (1912: 335) visited the site of Ventana Ranch in 1909–10. Approaching from the south, he saw "numbers of potsherds" lying on the ground.

137. This hill with a natural window (Spanish: *ventana*) in it is the feature giving its name to the nearby ranch. Lumholtz (1912: 41) wrote that three miles from the ranch "there rises a small hill, four hundred feet high, called La Ventana. On the west side it has been fortified by ancient people with half a dozen or more stone walls." This trincheras site is Ariz. DD:6:1 in the Arizona State Museum Archaeological Site Survey System (Stacy 1977: 12).

138. Although an O'odham named Miguel may have had something to do with this summer field village, its full name is San Miguel (Saint Michael). Lumholtz (1912: 38) referred to the place as "a lately established summer rancheria." A few years later, in 1925, Kirk Bryan (1925: 408, 179) wrote that San Miguel was "a comparatively modern rancheria, [and] has fields that extend from the represo and well more than 4 miles south to the international boundary. With the possible exception of Topahua [Topawa] it has larger fields than any of the other summer rancherias. There is a Catholic and a Protestant church here, and an Indian Service well" drilled in 1917. Griffith (1974: 235, 237–39, 242, 244, 250, 255) tells the story behind construction of the Catholic church, Our Lady Queen of Angels, that was built here in 1913.

139. Situated east of Topawa on the west side of the Baboquivari Mountains, Fresnal, according to Bryan (1925: 407), was "probably one of the oldest settlements of the Papagos. In 1863 it had 250 inhabitants, in 1864 385, and in 1912 about 500. There are three parts of this community in Fresnal Canyon. The western village is Pitóikam ('where there are ash trees'), and from this comes the Spanish name Fresnal ('grove of ash trees'). The middle village is Tshíuliseik ('willow forest'), and the upper village Kóxikux ('where the mulberry tree stands'), now known as Ventana. It seems likely that Fresnal was visited by Father Kino and [Captain] Mange, for Mange speaks of a flowing stream near a high square 'peñasco' visible for 18 leagues, which they visited in 1699. . . . They [*sic*] are now 18 wells dug in the canyon at Fresnal, and three more at Ventana."

An English translation of the 1699 account by Manje, in which he labels Baboquivari Peak *Arca de Noé* (Noah's Ark), has since been published (Manje 1954: 109).

Traditionally a winter "well" or "spring" village for the O'odham, in 1864 Fresnal also boasted a small Mexican town, "a collection of adobe hovels built at this point in the last two years, on account of the convenience afforded by the Indian wells for the reduction of ores stolen from the Cahuabia mines. . . . Fresnal contains some ten or a dozen rude adobe hovels, roofed and partially walled with the favorite building material of the country, oquitoia—a kind of hard, thorny cactus [*sic*] which grows on the deserts. We found here about twenty vagabond Sonorians, who were engaged in grinding and smelting the ores which they had stolen from the Cahuabia mines" (Browne 1974: 281, 282).

World traveler Raphael Pumpelly spent more than two weeks among Papagos at Fresnal in 1860 with a wounded companion who had accidentally shot himself (Wallace 1965: 78–81).

140. There are, in fact, a great many O'odham coyote tales (e.g., those in Bahr et al. 1994: 39, 49, 67, 70–71, 73–74, 106–7, 228; and in Saxton and Saxton 1973: 65–127), but given the story of ice fishing, this is not likely to have been one of them. Coyote trickster tales are told by all North American Indians, and this particular story, like others told by Jose Lewis Brennan (1991), is one influenced by his association with non-O'odham.

141. These are startling observations for a time when the term *ecology* had not yet become widely incorporated into the language of scientists. These observations also form the basis of a prophetic article written by McGee (1895) on the beginnings of agriculture, one in which he correctly concludes that agriculture is likely to have had its beginnings in arid lands.

142. This may be the earliest written account of the Tohono O'odham *vikita* ceremony, one about which a great deal has been written since (Fontana 1987; Galinier 1991; Hayden 1987).

143. An account of Apache warfare written in 1897 by Jose Lewis Brennan (1959) has been published. Detailed information concerning traditional Tohono O'odham warfare has also been compiled in print (see *Papago* in index in Kroeber and Fontana 1986).

144. McGee seems simply to have appended this note concerning Gedney to his field notes as some kind of reminder to himself.

145. This ranch, situated northwest of Rancho San Francisco de Costa Rica on the west side of the Rio Bacuache, was begun by Pascual Encinas about 1874 and was abandoned by 1894 (McGee 1898b: 58, 19, 40 n. 1). Twenty-seven years later, however, it was again a working ranch where there were "forty cows for milking and making cheese. There are several families living here. . . . The people live a camping life on only a bare subsistence.

"Four families of Seri Indians are camped at Rancho La Libertad. They wear rags and appear primitive with half-wild, fierce faces (Figs. 5-2, 5-3). . . . This evening the Seris came to my camp and danced. . . . It was a strange sight with the Mexicans sitting around the fire urging them on" (Sheldon 1979: 86–87).

146. Rancho Santa Ana, fifteen miles from Rancho San Francisco de Costa Rica and between there and Rancho Libertad, was begun by Pascual Encinas about 1870 (McGee 1898b: 16, 19). It was visited by naturalist Charles Sheldon (1979: 85–86, fig. 5-1) in December 1921, and its elaborate *malacate,* an animal-driven windlass used to extract water from a deep well, was photographed.

147. Opodepe is the Mexican village on the Río San Miguel from which a priest occasionally visited Querobabi.

Second Expedition

1. I have been unable to identify a ranch by this name in southern Arizona.

2. The entire Santa Cruz River basin is literally strewn with prehistoric archaeological sites, some of them dating from Archaic times more than 3,000 years ago. Most, however, are sites of a prehistoric agricultural people whom archaeologists have labeled the Hohokam. These are the sites that attracted McGee's attention. Some of the sites between Tucson and San Xavier have since been excavated and reported on by archaeologists. See, for example, Doelle (1985), Greenleaf (1975), and Ravesloot (1987).

3. Now a National Wildlife Refuge, at one time the Buenos Aires was one of the larger and more important ranches in southern Arizona. It was begun by Pedro Aguirre in the early 1870s. A post office was established here in 1892 (Barnes 1935: 66; Sheridan 1986: 52; Wagoner 1952: 40).

4. The San Luis Wash is a tributary of the Altar Wash.

5. Whether a map McGee and Johnson were making or a map McGee was using is impossible to say.

6. El Grupo was apparently a mining camp or cluster of small mines in northern Sonora.

7. The location of Sásabe, by the late nineteenth century an official border crossing between the United States and Mexico, seems to have moved from time to time. The present Sásabe, Arizona, has been in its location only since 1916, when "old Sásabe" was abandoned because of the lack of water. At one time an O'odham settlement, Sásabe is believed to be derived from the O'odham word for "echo," *shashawk* (Granger 1960: 280–81; Lumholtz 1912: 393).

8. Nogales was, and remains, the principal point of entry between Arizona and Sonora.

9. Whether McGee was aware of it or not, he was engaging in a traditional negotiation with a Mexican border official, one involving payment of a bribe, or *mordida,* disguised in the form of some other kind of payment.

10. If a mimosa, it's most likely to have been the catclaw mimosa, *Mimosa aculeaticarpa* (Turner, Bowers, and Burgess 1995: 271–72). It could also have been a small *Acacia greggii* or the fairy duster, *Calliandra eriophylla* (Turner, Bowers, and Burgess 1995: 21–22, 142–43).

11. I have been unable to identify this plant.

12. Possibly the fairy duster, *Calliandra eriophylla,* or *Mimosa aculeaticarpa.*

13. McGee passed by here on November 15, 1894, when Dinwiddie photographed some part of the ranch (see "Papago Trip, 1894" n. 127).

14. This could be either the blue paloverde (*Cercidium floridum*) or foothill paloverde (*C. microphyllum*).

15. Here he may be referring to the Jerusalem-thorn, *Parkinsonia aculeata.*

16. Apaches remained a serious threat to non-Apaches in northern Sonora at least until the final surrender of Geronimo in 1886. Isolated groups of Apaches continued to trouble ranchers in northeastern Sonora into the early parts of the twentieth century.

17. This is the trinchera between Pitiquito and Caborca that attracted McGee's attention and which he described on November 12, 1894, during his previous expedition. See "Papago Trip, 1894" n. 115.

18. This man is described by McGee (1898b: 255) as, "a distinguished sportsman citizen of Caborca, the local authority on the Seri." He may be the same "Mexicanized Frenchman" who in 1909 owned an up-to-date flour mill in Caborca (Lumholtz 1912: 145–46).

19. The "football" is presumably stone, although McGee is not explicit. Northern O'odham played kicking ball races, the balls being variously made out of wood, wood covered with gum, stone, and stone covered with gum (Culin 1907: 666; Russell 1908: 173–74; Underhill 1939: 146–48). In prehistoric times, such balls were made out of rubber (Haury 1937, 1976: 78–79) and used in a game played in courts especially constructed for the purpose.

20. I have been unable to identify the beans or the game Norris mentions.

21. Las Cruces is twenty-six miles due south of Trincheras near the southern limit of the municipio of Trincheras.

22. The desert prong-horn, *Antilocapra americana sonorienses.*

23. The small reddish brown, crater-building ants are possibly *Acromyrmex versicolor;* the small black ants, *Pheidole* spp. or *Veromessor* spp.; and the large-headed red ants are probably *Atta mexicana.* Both of the latter produce chaff rings about neat openings. Also see n. 20 in "Papago Trip, 1894."

24. If the plants are indeed mimosas, they could be the catclaw, *Mimosa aculeaticarpa*, and garabatillo, *Mimosa distachya* (Turner, Bowers, and Burgess 1995: 271–73).

25. These could be either the western turkey vulture, *Cathartes aura*, or the black vulture, *Coragyps atratus*.

26. See McGee (1897).

27. This is most probably the cliff fig, *Ficus petiolaris* (Felger and Moser 1985: 347–48).

28. While specimens twelve feet tall would be unusual, this may be the desert lavender or bee sage, *Hyptis emoryi* (Turner, Bowers, and Burgess 1995: 239–41).

29. This may be one of the spurges, *Euphorbia* spp.

30. The expedition picked up guides at various points along the route. This is Don Ramón Noriega of Pozo Noriega (McGee 1898b: 258).

31. "Mr. Griggs" was said by McGee to be Jesús Omada [Amado?], but he was Jesús Contreras, a water guide the party acquired at Bacuachito. He was in Bacuachito when Seri Indians once attacked the ranch. "'They killed my father. They killed my brother! They killed my brother's wife!! They have killed half my friends!!!' As he spoke he was feverishly baring his breast; displaying a frightful scar over the clavicle, he exclaimed, 'There struck a Seri arrow'; then he stripped his arm with a single sweep to reveal a ragged cicatrix extending nearly from shoulder to wrist, and added in a tone tremulous with pent bitterness, 'The Seri have teeth!'" (McGee 1898b: 116).

32. In his published account, McGee (1898b: 120–21) writes:

according to apparently trustworthy press accounts, two small exploring parties entered Seriland; the first consisted of seven prospectors, who kept well together until about to leave the territory, when one of their number fell behind—and his companions saw him no more, though they carefully retraced their trail beyond the point at which he had stopped; the other was a German naturalist-prospector with two mozos (servant-companions), purporting to hail from Chihuahua, who started across the delta-plain of Rio Bacuache and Desierto Encinas with saddle animals, and never reappeared.

33. It is difficult to know just what press accounts are being referred to here. McGee (1898b: 117–22) offers a good résumé of Seris' fights with non-Seris during the period 1894 to 1896.

34. This is *hierba de la flecha*, the Mexican jumping bean, *Sapium biloculare*. For its use by Seris, see Felger and Moser (1985: 300–1).

35. "Bara-prieta" should be *vara prieta* (black rod). McGee's description suggests he is actually describing the coral bean, *Erythrina flabelliformis*. The *vara prieta*, in contrast, is *Cordia parvifolia*.

36. Ecologist Paul Martin has suggested this may be the mistletoe, *Phoradendron californicum*.

37. Here are some more of the observations that resulted in McGee's (1897) publication on sheetflood erosion.

38. This old man came from Visnaga, a ranch southwest of Hermosillo about midway between there and the coast. He was visiting grandchildren at Costa Rica. His Spanish name was Juan; his name in O'odham, according to McGee, was O'-â-si'-tu' (Sifting). The separately recorded notes McGee took while conducting this interview appear in the last half of Appendix B.

39. Thompson is Louis Keith Thompson, of Scottish descent, who was born on Prince Edward Island, Canada. During the Civil War Thompson moved to Maine, and subsequently he and a brother, Horace, moved to California. Horace and Louis operated a stage between San Diego, California, and Tucson, Arizona, for several years around 1869. In 1878 or 1879 Louis moved to Hermosillo to work for Pascual Encinas, having been recommended to Encinas by the Mexican consul in San Diego. In 1879 he married Concepción Encinas, daughter of Ignacio María Encinas, a brother of Pascual Encinas's.

About 1884 Thompson returned to Arizona, this time going to Flagstaff, where he acquired some land and worked helping to lay a railroad bed. A son, Robert Thompson, was born in Flagstaff on October 18, 1888. Many years later this son—who changed the spelling of the family name to Thomson—became an interpreter for anthropologists Edward N. Davis and Alfred L. Kroeber during the latter's studies among Seri Indians (Davis 1965: 141–218; Kroeber 1931: 1, 7). Roberto Thomson died in 1969.

About 1890, at the insistence of his wife, Louis Thompson took his family back to Hermosillo. He died there in late December 1898, three years after having worked with McGee (Thomson 1962, 1989: 18).

40. This is the Barranca Salina on Johnson's map of Seriland (McGee 1898b: 16).

41. Milpillas, small fields capable of cultivation, especially of corn.

42. This is probably the vessel described and illustrated in the published report on the Seris by McGee (1898b: 175, pl. XXXII).

43. While the literal meaning of *tinaja* is an earthenware jar, the term is used in Sonora to denote a stone or other natural water catchment basin.

44. This is *Pachycereus pringlei*, an enormous columnar cactus variously known to Sonorans as *cardón, cardón pelón,* or *sahueso.*

45. O'odham who were working for Pascual Encinas at the Costa Rica ranch.

46. This is 3,490-foot-high Pico Johnson, the name applied by McGee "in commemoration of the first and only ascent of the peak, and of its occupation as a survey station, December 7 and 8, 1895, by Willard D. Johnson, accompanied by John Walter Mitchell and Miguel (Papago Indian)" (McGee 1898b: 18). Charles Sheldon (1979: 90–106) spent several days in the Seri Mountains and on Pico Johnson in December 1921.

47. McGee later surmised that this "debility of malaria" was the first symptom of the prostate cancer that eventually killed him. His account of this episode, published posthumously, is far more detailed than are his field notes:

During my second expedition to Seriland in the autumn of 1895 my party had occasion to climb Sierra Seri, the culminating range of the region. After leaving the wagon camp the party moved on foot (with two pack animals) over some ten miles of gently upsloping plain to the foothills, where the real climb began; the pace taken was rather rapid and I was somewhat but not excessively tired on reaching the foothills, where the pack horses were to be sent back. Within a few minutes after starting the climb I observed a condition novel in my experience, *i.e.,* inability to lift the feet (especially the left) more than a few inches above the level at which I stood. There was no pain, scarcely any discomfort—merely the inability to raise the feet without any help from the hands. Assuming it a manifestation of exhaustion, I halted the party for a time and ate lunch; but, on resuming, the condition almost immediately returned. Greatly puzzled, I abandoned the climb and started back with the Indian in charge of the pack-horses, finding no difficulty in going down-slope. Within fifteen minutes I was startled by a call from one of the remainder of the party making the climb, "El Gringo es muerto" [the American is dead]. Even without explanation I knew this referred to W.D. Johnson, topographer of the expedition; and stimulated by the apparent tragedy I immediately returned to resume the climb to the point of the disaster—but despite the intense excitement, I had not climbed fifty steps before the former inability to lift the feet returned. So I remained in a virtually helpless condition (sending my Indian up to the climbing party with specific inquiries) for perhaps half an hour; when the Indian returned with the gratifying intelligence that "El Gringo" had come to life and gone on up the mountain—for it appeared he had merely swooned under the stress of the long walk and the early stages of a stiff climb, and, recovering, had gone on with his accustomed persistence. This episode marked the first observed abnormality in locomotory powers which had been above the average (McGee 1912).

48. They are discussing the prickly pear cactus (*Opuntia* spp.), which the Mexicans refer to as the *nopal* and whose fruits they call *tunas*.

49. The desert bighorn sheep, *Ovis canadensis mexicana*.

50. Don Andrés Noriega, of Costa Rica, was credited with killing seventeen Seri Indians. "When he pointed out the site of his last exploit, a mile or two south of Rancho Libertad, and some incredulity was expressed, he immediately galloped to the spot and brought back a silent witness in the form of a bleached Seri skull" (McGee 1898b: 113). The skull was examined at the Smithsonian Institution by physical anthropologist Ales Hrdlicka and described in considerable detail in McGee (1898b: 140–41, n. 1).

51. McGee (1898b: 14, 19) says that Millard is "of Los Angeles," presumably Los Angeles, California, although there is a Los Ángeles in Sonora as well. Millard died in 1897.

52. M. M. Rice, who apparently for the moment was at the mining camp of Minas Prietas south of Hermosillo, was a resident of Phoenix, Arizona, who in 1895 "intimated a strong desire to join the . . . expedition of the Bureau of American Ethnology for the express purpose of personally ascertaining the fate and seeking the remains of [R. E.] Robinson who was extensively known in southern California and southwestern Arizona" (McGee 1898b: 117 n. 1). Robinson and a man named James Logan had purportedly been killed on Tiburón Island by Seri Indians in May 1894, an allegation that caused a sensation in the newspapers in California and the southwestern United States (see the San Francisco *Examiner,* June 6, 1894, p. 3, col. 1).

53. The entry for this day and those following through December 28 have been previously published (Fontana and Fontana 1983: 29–55).

54. This is labeled "Poso Escalante" on Johnson's map of Seriland (McGee 1898b: pl. I).

55. Just as John Wesley Powell had christened one of the boats he used in his first trip through the Grand Canyon in 1869 the *Emma Dean* in honor of his wife, so did McGee name the *Anita* after his wife, Anita Newcomb. By a happy coincidence, Anita was also the first name of Señora Pascual Encinas.

56. This Papago's sister, who was also a spouse of one of the men used as a supporter at the supply station, supposedly was so horrified over her husband's and brother's venturing into Seri country that she "broke under the strain, and died of her terrors" (McGee 1898b: 131). He is probably the same Antonio Castillo described twenty-six years later by naturalist Charles Sheldon (1979: 133) as "a fine old fellow, but too old to do much."

57. The best guide to these marine shells is that by Brusca (1973). For the significance of these and other large shell deposits observed by McGee, see R. L. Ives's essay in Appendix C, and Bowen (1976), Foster (1975), and Ives (1963).

58. One of these is illustrated in McGee (1898b: fig 37a).

59. The skin was probably from the California sea lion, *Zalophus californicus*.

60. If the bird Mitchell shot was indeed a curlew, it was an over-wintering long-billed curlew (*Numenius americanus*). The gulls may have been the western gull (*Larus occidentalis*) or Heerman gull (*Larus heermanni*).

61. For virtually the entire time of McGee's stay on the Sonoran and Tiburón coastlines, the party was plagued by "The 'Pestiferous Winds' of the Northern Gulf of California" (Ives 1962).

62. According to McGee (1898b: 131), Norris's illness was occasioned by "the mere entrance into Seriland at Poso Escalante."

63. This is indicated as Punta Antigualla on Johnson's map (McGee 1898b: pl. I).

64. Although McGee refers to this place as "Kino pt." in his field notes, it is actually Punta Ygnacio on Johnson's map of Seriland, and Punta Kino is located in its proper place (McGee 1898b: pl. I).

65. On modern maps, Punta San Miguel is referred to as Punta Santa Rosa (e.g., Bowen 1976: 8).

66. The Infiernillo Channel (little hell) between Tiburón Island and the Sonoran mainland, a strait often made treacherous for travelers because of strong winds and rising seas.

67. This is probably a brand of mineral water.

68. McGee later christened this spring, one of only nine reliable water sources on Tiburón, "Tinaja Anita." Seris called this water hole Pazj Hax. The canes growing here were the giant reed, *Arundo donax* (Felger and Moser 1985: 82–84, 305–7; McGee 1898b: 16, 19).

69. McGee was obviously aware that the liquid extracted from this barrel cactus could provide an emergency source of drinking water.

70. No desert bighorn, *Ovis canadensis,* are known to have lived on Tiburón (Sheldon 1979: 123).

71. The Seris call this settlement Zozni Cmiipla (Felger and Moser 1985: 5). It is probably the place called "Armen" by Charles Sheldon and where he stayed with Seris in December 1921 (Sheldon 1979: 109–25, fig. 5-11).

72. Seven of Mitchell's photos are published in McGee (1898b: figs. 3, 5; pls. IV–VII, IX).

73. The Tiburón Island subspecies was subsequently named for Mitchell: *Dipodomys merriami mitchelli* Mearns.

74. He is referring here to a water source at the southern end of Tiburón, possibly that called Xacacj by the Seris (Felger and Moser 1985: map 6.1).

75. Because they ended up spending Christmas here, in his published report McGee refers to this place as Campo Navidad (Nativity Camp) (McGee 1898b: 18).

76. The map to which McGee refers is one prepared as a result of surveys conducted for the U.S. Hydrographic Office by the USS *Narragansett,* captained by Commander George Dewey, U.S.N. "These surveys resulted in trustworthy and complete geodetic location of all coastwise features, in geographic placement of the entire coast-line, in soundings of such extent as to determine the bottom configuration, in tidal determinations, in recognition of the currents, in definition of harbors and anchorages, and eventually a series of elegant and accurate charts (dated 1873–75) available for cartographers and navigators of the world" (McGee 1898b: 105).

77. This is Punta Narragansett, the principal ranchería of Seri Indians in 1873, when George Dewey and the USS *Narragansett* paid them a visit (Belden 1880: 45; McGee 1898b: 18). McGee (1898b: 288) also observed "a scant half-dozen perceptible graves" near here.

78. *Tegua,* in Sonoran parlance, refers to homemade leather footwear akin to Apache moccasins (Sobarzo 1984: 233–34).

79. Johnson's map of Tiburón is a remarkable achievement (McGee 1898b: pl. I).

80. Although unable to determine its purpose, McGee describes this cone-shaped rock cairn—which was eighteen to twenty feet wide at the base and seven feet high—in some detail in his report (McGee 1898b: 289). It seems not to have occurred to him that it may have been made by non-Indians.

81. This word could be *skunk* rather than *shark,* but the latter seems far more likely inasmuch as skunks have not been reported from Tiburón in the scientific literature, and a skunk would not have provided the quantity of meat implied by McGee's comments about its being eaten. Tiburón, on the other hand, is the Spanish word for shark, and sharks were "said by some explorers to have been seen by thousands along its coasts" (McGee 1898b: 38).

82. As with many other pieces of Seri property, McGee helped himself—and the Smithsonian Institution—to this beautiful watercraft. It is illustrated in McGee (1898b: pl. XXXI) as well as in Felger and Moser (1985: fig. 10.6).

83. Seri graves are discussed in Felger and Moser (1985: 7–8).

84. This skull and skeleton are minutely described by physical anthropologist Ales Hrdlicka in McGee (1898b: 140–47). McGee neglects to mention in his published report that he actually robbed a Seri grave and merely states: "The skeletal characteristics of the Seri are known only from a single specimen obtained in the course of the 1895 expedition

in such manner as to establish the identification beyond shadow of question." The detailed description he gives of Seri burial practices (pp. 289–91) is based on this single excavation.

Bowen (1976: 46–50) reports on other burials uncovered in Seri country.

85. Kolusio, also known as Fernando, was purported to be a full-blooded Seri Indian. He lived in Hermosillo at the Pueblo Seri and served as a Seri interpreter. A linguistic informant for U.S. Boundary Commissioner John R. Bartlett (1854: I: 463–64) in December 1851, Kolusio had left Tiburón and Seri country when he was about six years old never to return any nearer than "the Seri border. . . . He was . . . a fine-looking man of noble stature and figure, and of notably dignified air and manner, dressed in conventional attire; his hair was luxuriant, iron-gray in color, and trimmed in Mexican fashion. His looks indicated an age of about 70, but in his own opinion (which was corroborated by that of Señor Pascual Encinas and other old acquaintances) he was at least 75. . . . He was in the employ of the state as a trustworthy attaché of the governor's palacio, where his services were nominal; his real function was that of Seri interpreter in case of need. . . . He was aware that he was regarded as a tribal outlaw, and admitted that no consideration could induce him to approach Seriland, since he would be slain by his tribesmen more eagerly than any alien" (McGee 1898b: 98).

Kolusio is mentioned frequently in the report by McGee (1898b: 14, 96–99, 102, 107, 296).

86. If the group returned via Sonoyta and Quijotoa, they did much more than cover the former route. Sonoyta, perhaps the westernmost O'odham settlement, is on the south side of the Arizona-Sonora border some 110 air miles west of Tucson, while Quijotoa is about 65 miles west of Tucson. During his journey up the Baboquivari Valley in 1894, McGee was never more than 50 miles west of Tucson.

87. There is no evidence the Seri ever had clans of any kind, including gens, which is to say, patrilineally exogamous clans.

88. *Chief* is a concept attributed to Seris, or in some cases imposed upon them, by outsiders who had no idea of traditional Seri leadership mechanisms. "Like most people with very low population density, the Seri had essentially no political organization other than a local, temporary war chief. There were no leaders or spokesmen until interactions with Spanish and Mexican authorities created a need for them.

"The extended family formed the center of Seri social life. . . . Several obligatory customs associated with the Seri kinship system placed strict social controls on the members of the extended family" (Felger and Moser 1985: 3).

89. Felger and Moser (1985: 165–67) describe ten occasions traditionally celebrated by a feast (*fiesta*), including the boys' and girls' puberty feasts and the marriage feast. Traditional marriage customs, which include the payment of a bride price, are also described by Felger and Moser (1985: 6). An impromptu fiesta is described by Edward H. Davis (1965: 195).

90. The floating gourd drum was only one of a dozen musical instruments used by the Seri (Felger and Moser 1985: 169).

91. Based on fieldwork among the Seri in 1955, Griffen (1959: 22–23) stated:

Every Seri basically has two names, one in Seri and one in Spanish. The Seri name, which later should never be spoken, is given when the child begins to acquire the faculty of speech and is the first word he repeatedly pronounces that can be understood. This is the only formal Seri name he will have during his lifetime. However, the tribe members are extremely fond of nicknames, and each male or female may have one or many. These nicknames usually refer to some special characteristic and are dropped or changed as readily as they are given.

The Spanish name is generally conferred soon after birth. It almost invariably consists of a first and a last name, and many times of a middle name. . . . Informants stated that until some twenty years ago a baptism was performed by putting salt in the child's mouth and sprinkling his head with fresh water. No reason could be offered why this practice has dropped out today.

92. More up-to-date discussions of Seri traditions associated with death, including disposal of the dead, are in Felger and Moser (1985: 7–8, 117, 135, 254) and Griffen (1959: 28–29, 45–46). Burials above ground, whether in trees or in such giant cacti as the cardón, seem to have been limited to stillborn infants, a situation that may well have been especially common among Seris in the nineteenth century.

93. This is perhaps the strangest assertion of all. Even Kolosio must have been aware of the rich nature of Seri oral tradition and their ability, through myths, to account for nearly everything in their surroundings. Fragments of many of these stories can be found in Felger and Moser (1985).

94. Shamans and shamanism are discussed in Felger and Moser (1985: 102–6).

APPENDICES

1. This statement is false; colors and directions *are* known.

2. This text was written by Ives in December 1961 for inclusion with publication of the McGee field notes. The references he cites for these notes are Hubbs and Miller (1948) and Ives (1951). To these, however, should be added Ives (1963).

REFERENCES

Adams, Henry

1961   *The Education of Henry Adams: An Autobiography*. Boston: Houghton Mifflin.

Almada, Francisco R.

1952   *Diccionario de historia, geografía y biografía sonorenses*. Chihuahua, México: Francisco R. Almada. Reprint, Hermosillo: Gobierno del Estado de Sonora, 1983.

Alvarez de Williams, Anita

1975   *Travelers among the Cucupá*. Baja California Travel Series, no. 34. Los Angeles: Dawson's Book Shop.

Anderson, Keith

1986   Hohokam Cemeteries As Elements of Settlement Structure and Change. In *Anthropology of the Desert West: Essays in Honor of Jesse D. Jennings*. University of Utah Anthropological Papers, no. 110, edited by Carol J. Condie and Don D. Fowler, 179–201. Salt Lake City: University of Utah Press.

Anderson, Keith, Fillman Bell, and Yvonne G. Stewart

1982   Quitobaquito: A Sand Papago Cemetery. *The Kiva* 47 (4): 215–37.

Bahr, Donald M.

1975   *Pima and Papago Ritual Oratory*. San Francisco: The Indian Historian Press.

Bahr, Donald M., Juan Gregorio, David I. Lopez, and Albert Alvarez

1974   *Piman Shamanism and Staying Sickness (Ká:cim Múmkidag)*. Tucson: University of Arizona Press.

Bahr, Donald M., Juan Smith, William Smith Allison, and Julian D. Hayden

1994   *The Short Swift Times of Gods on Earth: The Hohokam Chronicles*. Berkeley: University of California Press.

Bancroft, Griffing

1932   *The Flight of the Least Petrel*. New York: G. P. Putnam's Sons.

Barnes, Will C.

1935   *Arizona Place Names*. University of Arizona Bulletin, vol. 6, no. 1 (January 1), General Bulletin, no. 2. Tucson: University of Arizona. Reprint, Tucson: University of Arizona Press, 1988.

Bartlett, John R.

1854   *Personal Narrative of Explorations and Incidents in Texas, New Mexico, California, Sonora, and Chihuahua Connected with the United States and Mexican Boundary Commission, during the Years 1850, '51, '52, and '53.* 2 vols. New York and London: D. Appleton Co.

Belden, Samuel, comp.

1880   *The West Coast of Mexico from the Boundary Line between the United States and Mexico to Cape Corrientes, including the Gulf of California.* Reports of the U.S. Hydrographic Office, Bureau of Navigation, no. 56. Washington, D.C.: Government Printing Office.

Bowen, Thomas

1976   *Seri Prehistory: The Archaeology of the Central Coast of Sonora, Mexico.* Anthropological Papers of the University of Arizona, no. 27. Tucson: University of Arizona Press.

Bowen, Thomas, and Edward Moser

1968   Seri Pottery. *The Kiva* 33 (3): 89–132.

Brennan, Jose Lewis

1897   Papago Language. Manuscript, July 1897. No. 1744, vol. 3, National Anthropological Archives. Smithsonian Institution, Washington, D.C.

1959   Jose Lewis Brennan's Account of Papago "Customs and Other References." Edited by Bernard L. Fontana. *Ethnohistory* 6 (3): 226–37.

1991   Gold Placer of Quijotoa, Ariz. *Journal of the Southwest* 33 (4): 459–74.

Brito de Martí, Esperanza, ed.

1982   *Almanaque de Sonora, 1982.* México, D.F.: Almanaque de México.

Brown, C. B.

1960   Who Was Hugh Norris? *Arizona Daily Star* (Tucson), February 19, sec. D, p. 12.

Browne, J. Ross

1974   *Adventures in the Apache Country: A Tour through Arizona and Sonora, 1864.* Re-edition edited by Donald M. Powell. Tucson: University of Arizona Press.

Broyles, Bill

1982   Desert Thirst: The Ordeal of Pablo Valencia. *Journal of Arizona History* 23 (4): 357–80.

Brusca, Richard C.

1973   *A Handbook to the Common Intertidal Invertebrates of the Gulf of California.* Tucson: University of Arizona Press.

Bryan, Kirk

1925   *The Papago Country, Arizona: A Geographic, Geologic, and Hydrologic Reconnaissance with a Guide to Desert Watering Places.* United States Geological Survey Water Supply Paper, no. 499. Washington, D.C.: Government Printing Office.

Burckhalter, David

1996   Seri Face Painting: The Traditional Art of Adornment. *Native Peoples* 9 (3): 70–74.

Castetter, Edward F., and Willis H. Bell

1942   *Pima and Papago Indian Agriculture*. Inter-Americana Studies, no. 1. Albuquerque: University of New Mexico Press.

Castetter, Edward F., and Ruth M. Underhill

1935   *Ethnobiological Studies in the American Southwest. II. The Ethnobiology of the Papago Indians*. The University of New Mexico Bulletin, no. 275 (October 15), Biological Series, vol. 4, no. 3. Albuquerque: University of New Mexico Press. Reprint, New York: AMS Press, 1978.

Corral, Ramón

1981   *Obras históricas*. Prologue by Horacio Sobarzo. Hermosillo: Publicaciones del Gobierno del Estado de Sonora.

Cross, Whitney R.

1953   W J McGee and the Idea of Conservation. *The Historian* 15 (2): 148–62.

Crosswhite, Frank S.

1980   The Annual Saguaro Harvest and Crop Cycle of the Papago, with Reference to Ecology and Symbolism. *Desert Plants* 2 (1): 2–61.

Culin, Stewart

1907   Games of the North American Indians. In *Annual Report of the Bureau of American Ethnology*, vol. 24, 1–846. Washington, D.C.: Government Printing Office.

Davis, Edward H.

1965   *Edward H. Davis and the Indians of the Southwest United States and Northwest Mexico*. Arranged and edited by Charles Russell Quinn and Elena Quinn. Downey, Calif.: Elena Quinn.

Davisson, Lori

1986   Arizona Law Enforcement: A Survey from the Collections of the Arizona Historical Society. *Journal of Arizona History* 27 (3): 315–48.

Dinwiddie, William

1899a   *Puerto Rico: Its Conditions and Possibilities*. New York and London: Harper & Brothers.

1899b   Staging through Mountain and Desert. *Outing* 34 (1): 48–54.

DiPeso, Charles C.

1956   *The Upper Pima of San Cayetano del Tumacacori: An Archaeological Reconstruction of the Ootam of Pimería Alta*. Amerind Foundation Publication, no. 7. Dragoon, Ariz.: Amerind Foundation.

Doelle, William H.

1985   *Excavations at the Valencia Site. A Preclassic Hohokam Village in the Southern Tucson Basin*. Anthropological Papers, no. 3. N.p.: Institute for American Research.

Downum, Christian E.

1986   The Occupational Use of Hill Space in the Tucson Basin: Evidence from Linda Vista Hill. *The Kiva* 51 (4): 219–32.

1993   *Between Desert and River: Hohokam Settlement and Land Use in the Los Robles Community*. Anthropological Papers of the University of Arizona, no. 57. Tucson: University of Arizona Press.

Downum, Christian E., Paul R. Fish, and Suzanne K. Fish

1994   Refining the Role of *Cerros de Trincheras* in Southern Arizona Settlement. *The Kiva* 59 (3): 271–96.

Eckhart, George B.

1960   The Seri Indian Missions. *The Kiva* 25 (3): 37–43.

Felger, Richard S., and Mary B. Moser

1985   *People of the Desert and Sea: Ethnobotany of the Seri Indians*. Tucson: University of Arizona Press.

Fish, Suzanne K., Paul R. Fish, and John H. Madsen, eds.

1992   *The Marana Community in the Hohokam World*. Anthropological Papers of the University of Arizona, no. 56. Tucson: University of Arizona Press.

Font, Pedro

1931   Font's Complete Diary of the Second Anza Expedition. Translated and edited by Herbert E. Bolton. In *Anza's California Expeditions,* by Herbert E. Bolton, vol. 4. Berkeley: University of California Press.

Fontana, Bernard L.

1960   Assimilative Change: A Papago Indian Case Study. Ph.D. diss., The University of Arizona.

1975   Introduction to the Re-edition. In *The Pima Indians,* by Frank Russell, ix–xv. Tucson: University of Arizona Press.

1980   Ethnobotany of the Saguaro: An Annotated Bibliography. *Desert Plants* 2 (1): 62–78.

1981   *Of Earth and Little Rain: The Papago Indians*. Photographs by John P. Schaefer. Flagstaff, Ariz.: Northland Press. Reprint, Tucson: University of Arizona Press, 1989.

1987   The *Vikita*: A Biblio History. *Journal of the Southwest* 29 (3): 258–72.

1994   *Entrada: The Legacy of Spain and Mexico in the United States*. Tucson: Southwest Parks and Monuments Association.

1996   Finding Father Kino. In *The Pimería Alta: Missions and More,* edited by James E. Officer, Mardith Schuetz-Miller, and Bernard L. Fontana, 40–41. Tucson: Southwestern Mission Research Center.

Fontana, Bernard L., Edmond J. B. Faubert, and Barney T. Burns

1977   *The Other Southwest: Indian Arts and Crafts of Northwestern Mexico*. Phoenix: Heard Museum.

Fontana, Bernard L., and Hazel M. Fontana

1983   A Search for the Seris, 1895. In *Tales from Tiburon: An Anthology of Adventures in Seriland,* edited by Neil B. Carmony and David E. Brown, 23–55. Phoenix: Southwest Natural History Association.

Fontana, Bernard L., J. Cameron Greenleaf, and Donnelly D. Cassidy

1959   A Fortified Arizona Mountain. *The Kiva* 25 (2): 41–inside back cover.

Fontana, Bernard L., William J. Robinson, Charles W. Cormack, and Ernest E. Leavitt, Jr.

1962   *Papago Indian Pottery*. Seattle: University of Washington Press.

Foster, John W.

1975   Shell Middens, Paleoecology, and Prehistory: The Case from Estero Morua, Sonora, Mexico. *The Kiva* 41 (2): 185–94.

Gaillard, David D.

1894   The Papagos of Arizona and Sonora. *American Anthropologist,* old series, 7 (3): 293–96.

1896   The Perils and Wonders of a True Desert. *The Cosmopolitan* 21 (6): 592–605.

Galinier, Jacques

1991   From Montezuma to San Francisco: The Wi:gita Ritual in Papago (Tohono O'odham) Religion. *Journal of the Southwest* 33 (4): 486–538.

Gilliland, Marion S.

1989   *Key Marco's Buried Treasure: Archaeology and Adventure in the Nineteenth Century*. Ripley P. Bullen Monographs in Anthropology and History, no. 8. Gainesville: University of Florida Press and Florida Museum of Natural History.

Granger, Byrd H.

1960   *Will C. Barnes' Arizona Place Names*. Tucson: University of Arizona Press.

Greenleaf, J. Cameron

1975   *Excavations at Punta de Agua in the Santa Cruz River Basin, Southwestern Arizona*. Anthropological Papers of the University of Arizona, no. 26. Tucson: University of Arizona Press.

Griffen, William B.

1959   *Notes on Seri Indian Culture, Sonora, Mexico*. Latin American Monographs, no. 10. Gainesville: University of Florida Press.

Griffith, James S.

1974   Franciscan Chapels on the Papaguería, 1912–1973. *The Smoke Signal* 30 (Fall): 233–56.

1980   *Old Men of the Fiesta: An Introduction to the Pascola Arts*. Phoenix: Heard Museum.

1988   *Southern Arizona Folk Arts*. Tucson: University of Arizona Press.

1992   *Beliefs and Holy Places: A Spiritual Geography of the Pimería Alta*. Tucson: University of Arizona Press.

1995   *A Shared Space: Folklife in the Arizona-Sonora Borderlands*. Logan: Utah State University Press.

Gruber, Jacob

1970   Ethnographic Salvage and the Shaping of Anthropology. *American Anthropologist* 72 (6): 1289–99.

Haury, Emil W.

1937   A Pre-Spanish Rubber Ball from Arizona. *American Antiquity* 2 (4): 282–88.

1976   *The Hohokam: Desert Farmers & Craftsmen. Excavations at Snaketown, 1964–1965*. Tucson: University of Arizona Press.

Hayden, Julian D.

1987   The Vikita Ceremony of the Papago. *Journal of the Southwest* 29 (3): 273–324, pls. I–XI.

Hinsley, Curtis M., Jr.

1976   The Development of a Profession: Anthropology in Washington, D.C., 1846–1903. Ph.D. diss., University of Wisconsin–Madison.

1981   *Savages and Scientists: The Smithsonian Institution and the Development of American Anthropology, 1846–1910*. Washington, D.C.: Smithsonian Institution Press.

1992   Collecting Cultures and Cultures of Collecting: The Lure of the American Southwest. *Museum Anthropology* 16 (1): 12–20.

Hinton, Thomas B.

1955   A Seri Girl's Puberty Ceremony at Desemboque, Sonora. *The Kiva* 20 (4): 8–11.

Hoover, J. W.

1941   Cerros de Trincheras of the Arizona Papaguería. *Geographical Review* 31 (2): 228–39.

Hovens, Pieter

1989   Herman F. C. ten Kate, Jr. (1858–1931) en de antropologie der Noord-Amerikaanse Indianen. Ph.D. diss., Katholieke Universitet te Nijmegen, The Netherlands.

Hubbs, C. L., and R. R. Miller

1948   The Great Basin, with Emphasis on Glacial and Postglacial Times. II. The Zoological Evidence. *Bulletin of the University of Utah* 38: 103–13.

Huntington, Ellsworth

1913   The Fluctuating Climate of North America. In *Annual Report of the Smithsonian Institution, 1912*, 283–412. Washington, D.C.: Smithsonian Institution.

Ives, Ronald L.

1936   A Trinchera near Quitovaquita, Sonora. *American Anthropologist* 38 (2): 257–59.

1951   High Sea Levels of the Sonoran Shore. *American Journal of Science* 249 (3): 215–23.

1962   The "Pestiferous Winds" of the Northern Gulf of California. *Weatherwise* 15 (5): 196–201.

1963   The Problem of Sonoran Littoral Cultures. *The Kiva* 28 (3): 28–32.

1989   *Land of Lava, Ash, and Sand: The Pinacate Region of Northwestern Mexico*. Compiled by James W. Byrkit; edited by Karen J. Dahood. Tucson: Arizona Historical Society.

Johnson, Alfred E.

1960   The Place of the Trincheras Culture in Northern Sonora in Southwestern Archaeology. Master's thesis, University of Arizona.

1963–64   The Trincheras Culture of Northern Sonora. *American Antiquity* 29 (2): 174–86.

Joseph, Alice, Rosamond B. Spicer, and Jane Chesky

1949   *The Desert People: A Study of the Papago Indians*. Chicago: University of Chicago Press.

ten Kate, Herman F. C.

1883a   Quelques observations ethnographiques recueilles dans la presqu'ile Californienne et en Sonora. *Revue d'Ethnographie* (Paris) 2: 89–90.

1883b   Visite chez les Pàpagos. *Revue d'Ethnographie* (Paris) 2: 89–90.

1885   *Reizen en Onderzoekingen in Noord Amerika*. Leiden: E. J. Brill.

1892   Somotological Observations on Indians of the Southwest. *Journal of American Ethnology and Archaeology* 3 (2): 117–44.

1916   Dynamometric Observations among Various Peoples. *American Anthropologist* 18 (1): 10–18.

1918   Notes on the Hands and Feet of American Natives. *American Anthropologist* 20 (2): 187–202.

1995   Ten Kate's Hemenway Expedition Diary, 1887–1888. Translated, with an introduction by Pieter Hovens. *Journal of the Southwest* 37 (4): 635–99.

Kearney, Thomas H., Robert H. Peebles, and collaborators

1960   *Arizona Flora*. 2d edition with supplement. Berkeley: University of California Press.

King, William S.

1954   The Folk Catholicism of the Tucson Papagos. Master's thesis, The University of Arizona.

Kissell, Mary L.

1916   *Basketry of the Papago and Pima*. Anthropological Papers of the American Museum of Natural History, vol. 16, part 4. New York: Trustees of the American Museum of Natural History. Reprint, Glorieta, N.Mex.: Río Grande Press, 1972.

Klinkenborg, Veryln

1988   The West Indies As Freshly Seen in the Sixteenth Century. *Smithsonian* 18 (10): 89–96, 98.

Knowlton, F. H.

1913   Memoir of W J McGee. *Bulletin of the Geological Society of America* 24: 18–29.

Kroeber, Alfred L.

1931   *The Seri*. Southwest Museum Papers, no. 6. Los Angeles: Southwest Museum.

Kroeber, Clifton B., and Bernard L. Fontana

1986   *Massacre on the Gila: An Account of the Last Major Battle between American Indians, with Reflections on the Origin of War*. Tucson: University of Arizona Press.

Lacey, Michael J.

1979   The Mysteries of Earth-making Dissolve: A Study of Washington's Intellectual Community and the Origins of American Environmentalism in the Late Nineteenth Century. Ph.D. diss., George Washington University.

Lumholtz, Carl

1912   *New Trails in Mexico: An Account of One Year's Exploration in North-western Sonora, Mexico, and South-western Arizona, 1909–1910.* New York: Charles Scribner's Sons; London: T. Fisher Unwin.

Manje, Juan M.

1954   *Luz de Tierra Incógnita: Unknown Arizona and Sonora, 1693–1701.* Translated by Harry J. Karns. Tucson: Arizona Silhouettes.

Marquis Who's Who in America

1943   *Who Was Who in America, 1897–1942.* Chicago: Marquis Who's Who in America.

Mathiot, Madeleine

n.d.   *A Dictionary of Papago Usage.* vol. 2: *Ku–?u.* Language Science Monographs, vol. 8, no. 2. Bloomington: Indiana University.

1973   *A Dictionary of Papago Usage.* vol. 1: *B–K.* Language Science Monographs, vol. 8, no. 1. Bloomington: Indiana University.

McGee, Emma

1915   *Life of W J McGee.* Farley, Iowa: privately printed.

McGee, W J

1895   The Beginnings of Agriculture. *American Anthropologist,* old series, 8 (4): 350–75.

1897   Sheetflood Erosion. *Bulletin of the Geological Society of America* 8 (Feb. 13): x, 87–112, pls. 10–13.

1898a   Papaguería. *National Geographic Magazine* 9 (8): 345–71.

1898b   The Seri Indians. In *Annual Report of the Bureau of American Ethnology,* vol. 17, part 1, 1–344. Washington, D.C.: Government Printing Office. Reprint, as *The Seri Indians of Bahia Kino and Sonora, Mexico,* with an introduction by Bernard L. Fontana, and added plates of color photos taken in 1971, Glorieta, New Mexico: Río Grande Press, 1971.

1901   The Old Yuma Trail. *National Geographic Magazine* 12 (3): 103–7; (4): 129–43.

1906   Desert Thirst As Disease. *Interstate Medical Journal* 13 (3) [23 pp.]. St. Louis.

1912   Symptomatic Development of Cancer. *Science,* new series, 36 (924): 348–50.

McGuire, Randall H., and Elisa Villalpando C.

1998   Cerro de Trincheras: A Prehispanic Terraced Town in Sonora, Mexico. *Archaeology in Tucson* 12 (1): 1–5.

Merrill, F.J.H.

1908   Dry Placers of Northern Sonora. *Mining and Scientific Press* (September 12): 360–61.

Morgan, Lewis H.

1851   *League of the Ho-dé-no-sau-nee, or Iroquois.* Rochester: Sage & Brother; New York, M. H. Newman & Co.

1870   *Systems of Consanguinity and Affinity of the Human Family.* Smithsonian Contributions to Knowledge, vol. 17, Smithsonian Institution Publication, 218. Washington, D.C.: Smithsonian Institution.

1877   *Ancient Society: Or, Researches in the Line of Human Progress from Savagery through Barbarism to Civilization.* Chicago: C. H. Kerr.

Moser, Edward

1963   Seri Bands. *The Kiva* 28 (3): 14–27.

Myrick, David F.

1975   *Railroads of Arizona.* Vol. 1: *The Southern Roads.* Berkeley: Howell-North Books.

1993   Quijotoa: Boom and Bust in the Arizona Desert. *Journal of Arizona History* 34 (2): 117–54.

National Union Catalog

1968–81   *The National Union Catalog, Pre-1956 Imprints: A Cumulative Author List Representing Library of Congress Printed Cards and Titles Reported by Other American Libraries.* Compiled and edited with the cooperation of the Library of Congress and the National Union Catalog Subcommittee of the Resources Committee of the Resources and Technical Services Division, American Library Association. 754 volumes. London: Mansell.

O'Donovan, Maria J.

1997   Confronting Archaeological Enigmas: Cerro de Trincheras, Cerros de Trincheras and Monumentality. Ph.D. diss., State University of New York at Binghamton.

Officer, James E.

1987   Yanqui Forty-Niners in Hispanic Arizona: Interethnic Relations on the Sonoran Frontier. *Journal of Arizona History* 28 (2): 101–34.

1996   Government, Mining, and Agriculture. In *The Pimería Alta: Missions and More,* edited by James E. Officer, Mardith Schuetz-Miller, and Bernard L. Fontana, 47–53. Tucson: Southwestern Mission Research Center.

Olvera H., Jorge

1998   *Finding Father Kino: The Discovery of the Remains of Father Eusebio Francisco Kino, S.J., 1965–1966.* Tucson: Southwestern Mission Research Center.

Painter, Muriel T.

1986   *With Good Heart: Yaqui Beliefs and Ceremonies in Pascua Village.* Edited by Edward H. Spicer and Wilma Kaemlein. Tucson: University of Arizona Press.

Powell, John W.

1897   Report of the Director. In *Annual Report of the Bureau of American Ethnology,* vol. 16, xv–xcix. Washington, D.C.: Government Printing Office.

1898   Report of the Director. In *Annual Report of the Bureau of American Ethnology,* vol. 17, part 1, xxvii–lxxiii. Washington, D.C.: Government Printing Office.

Ravesloot, John C., ed.

1987   *The Archaeology of the San Xavier Bridge Site (Az BB:13:14), Tucson Basin, Southern Arizona.* Archaeological Series, 171. Tucson: Cultural Resource Management Division, Arizona State Museum, University of Arizona.

Rea, Amadeo

1997   *At the Desert's Green Edge: An Ethnobotany of the Gila River Pima.* Foreword by Gary Paul Nabhan. Tucson: University of Arizona Press.

Readers Guide to Periodical Literature

1905   *Readers Guide to Periodical Literature, 1900–1904*. Minneapolis: H. W. Wilson.

Russell, Frank

1908   The Pima Indians. In *Annual Report of the Bureau of American Ethnology,* vol. 26, 3–389. Washington, D.C.: Government Printing Office. Reprint, with an introduction by Bernard L. Fontana, Tucson: University of Arizona Press, 1975.

Rydell, Robert W.

1984   *All the World's a Fair: Visions of Empire at American International Expositions, 1876–1916*. Chicago: University of Chicago Press.

Sauer, Carl O., and Donald D. Brand

1931   Prehistoric Settlements of Sonora with Special Reference to Cerros de Trincheras. In *University of California Publications in Geography,* vol. 5, no. 3, 67–148. Berkeley: University of California Press.

Saxton, Dean, and Lucille Saxton

1973   *O'othham Hoho'ok A'agitha: Legends and Lore of the Papago and Pima Indians*. Tucson: University of Arizona Press.

Schuetz-Miller, Mardith, and Bernard L. Fontana

1996   Mission Churches of Northern Sonora. In *The Pimería Alta: Missions and More,* edited by James E. Officer, Mardith Schuetz-Miller, and Bernard L. Fontana, 61–95. Tucson: Southwestern Mission Research Center.

Sheldon, Charles

1979   *The Wilderness of Desert Bighorn & Seri Indians*. Phoenix: Arizona Desert Bighorn Sheep Society.

Sheridan, Thomas E.

1982   Seri Bands in Cross-Cultural Perspective. *The Kiva* 47 (4): 185–213.

1986   *Los Tucsonenses: The Mexican Community in Tucson, 1854–1941*. Tucson: University of Arizona Press.

Sobarzo, Horacio

1984   *Vocabulario sonorense*. 2d ed. Hermosillo: Gobierno del Estado de Sonora.

Spicer, Edward H.

1940   *Pascua: A Yaqui Village in Arizona*. Chicago: University of Chicago Press.

1954   *Potam: A Yaqui Village in Sonora*. Memoirs of the American Anthropological Association, no. 77. Menasha, Wis.: American Anthropological Association.

1962   *Cycles of Conquest: The Impact of Spain, Mexico, and the United States on the Indians of the Southwest, 1533–1960*. Tucson: University of Arizona Press.

1980   *The Yaquis: A Cultural History*. Tucson: University of Arizona Press.

Stacy, Valeria K. P.

1974   Cerros de Trincheras in the Arizona Papaguería. Ph.D. diss., The University of Arizona.

1977   Activity Patterning at Cerros de Trincheras in Southcentral Arizona. *The Kiva* 43 (1): 11–17.

Thomson, Roberto

1962   Notes of interview by Bernard L. Fontana with Roberto Thomson at the University of Arizona Library, Tucson, on April 2, 1962. Copy on file with Bernard L. Fontana, Tucson.

1989   *Pioneros de la costa de Hermosillo (la hacienda de Costa Rica 1844)*. Hermosillo: Artes Gráficas y Editoriales Yescas.

Thurston, Herbert, and Donald Attwater

1956   *Butler's Lives of the Saints*. Complete edition. 4 vols. New York: P. J. Kenedy & Sons.

Trennert, Robert A.

1988   *The Phoenix Indian School: Forced Assimilation in Arizona, 1891–1935*. Norman: University of Oklahoma Press.

Turner, Raymond M., Janice E. Bowers, and Tony L. Burgess

1995   *Sonoran Desert Plants: An Ecological Atlas*. Tucson: University of Arizona Press.

Underhill, Ruth M.

1939   *Social Organization of the Papago Indians*. Columbia University Contributions to Anthropology, vol. 30. New York: Columbia University Press.

1946   *Papago Indian Religion*. Columbia University Contributions to Anthropology, no. 33. New York: Columbia University Press.

1951   *People of the Crimson Evening*. Riverside, Calif.: Department of the Interior, United States Indian Service, Branch of Education. Reprint, Palmer Lake, Colo.: Filter Press, 1982.

Underhill, Ruth M., Donald M. Bahr, Baptisto Lopez, Jose Pancho, and David Lopez

1979   *Rainhouse and Ocean: Speeches for the Papago Year*. American Tribal Religions, vol. 4. Flagstaff: Museum of Northern Arizona Press.

Voss, Stuart F.

1982   *On the Periphery of Nineteenth-Century Mexico: Sonora and Sinaloa, 1810–1877*. Tucson: University of Arizona Press.

Wagoner, J. J.

1952   *History of the Cattle Industry in Southern Arizona, 1540–1940*. University of Arizona Bulletin, vol. 23, no. 2 (April); Social Science Bulletin, no. 20. Tucson: University of Arizona.

Wallace, Andrew, ed.

1965   *Pumpelly's Arizona*. Tucson: Palo Verde Press.

Waring, W. George

1897   The Gold Fields of Altar, Mexico. *The Engineering and Mining Journal* (March 13): 257–58.

Washington Academy of Sciences (Washington, D.C.)

1916   *McGee Memorial Meeting of the Washington Academy of Sciences Held at the Carnegie Institution, Washington, D.C., December 5, 1913*. Baltimore: Williams and Wilkins.

Wilcox, David R.

1979   Warfare Implications of Dry-Laid Masonry Walls on Tumamoc Hill. *The Kiva* 45 (1–2): 15–38.

Williams, Jack S.

1991   Architecture and Defense on the Military Frontier of Arizona, 1752–1856. Ph.D. diss., The University of Arizona.

Woodward, Arthur

1933   Ancient Houses of Modern Mexico. *Bulletin of the Southern California Academy of Sciences* 32 (part 3, September–December): 79–98.

Woodward, Arthur, Scofield DeLong, Leffler B. Miller, and George A. Grant

1993   *The Missions of Northern Sonora: A 1935 Field Documentation*. Edited by Buford Pickens. Tucson: University of Arizona Press.

Wright, Harold B.

1929   *Long Ago Told (Huh-kew Ah-kah): Legends of the Papago Indians*. New York and London: D. Appleton & Co.

Wyman, Leland C.

1983   *Southwest Indian Drypainting*. Santa Fe: School of American Research; Albuquerque: University of New Mexico Press.

Xavier, Gwyneth H.

1946   Seri Face Painting. *The Kiva* 11 (2): 13, 15–20.

INDEX

Numbers in italics refer to illustrations

A

adobe, 128n. 8

agave (*Agave* spp.), 65

Agua Amarilla, Sonora, 74–76, 82, 85, 92, 95, 96, 97, 98–99, 144n. 54

Agua Caliente, Sonora, 6, 128n. 5

Agua Nueva, Sonora, 29–30

Alcatraz Island (Gulf of California), 76–77, 88

Altar, Sonora, xxiv, xxv, 41–42, *42*, 55, 57–58, 137n. 119; church, 42, 138n. 123

Alvarez, Ruperto, 75, 76, 77, 79, 80, 85, 86, 87, 88, 89, 90, 91, 92, 93, 96, 99

Alvarez, Rupuelto. *See* Alvarez, Ruperto

Alvemar-León, Arturo, 22, 26, *26, 28, 29,* 132n. 76

Amado, Arizona, xxii, xxv

American Anthropological Association, xxvii

American Anthropologist, xxvii

Ángel de la Guarda (island in the Gulf of California), 28, 40, 134n. 86

Anita (sloop), 74–76, *76,* 77, 78–80, 82, 85, 86, 87, 88, 90, 92, 94, 97, 98, 144n. 55

antelope *(Antilocapra americana sonorensis),* 64

antelope jack rabbit *(Lepus alleni),* 86

Anthropological Society of Washington, xxvii

Anton (Papago Indian), 70–71, 73, 75, 77, 80, 81, 82, 88, 91, 92, 93, 99, 143n. 45

ants, 9, 11, 55, 64, 129n. 20, 141n. 23

Apache Indians, 8, 47, 55, 58, 128n. 1, 140n. 143, 141n. 16

Archaeological Institute of America, xxvii

Arivaca, Arizona, xxi–xxii

arrow-weed (*Pluchea* spp.), 134n. 89

B

Baboquivari Mountains, xxiv, 128n. 12

Baboquivari Peak, 8, 43, *48,* 54, 55, 56, 57, 128n. 12, 139n. 139

Baboquivari Valley, xxiv, 45, 146n. 86

Bacuache, Sonora, 49, 65–66, 69, 109–10. *See also* Río Bacuache

Ballestere, Mariano, *xxiii*

balsas. *See* Seri Indians, rafts

Ban Dak, Arizona. *See* Coyote Sits, Arizona

barrel cactus (*Ferocactus* spp.), 56, 86, 145n. 69

Bartlett, John Russell, 100

bee sage *(Hyptis emoryi),* 66, 142n. 28

Berger, John M., xvi, *xvii*

Berruga, Sonora (ranch), 36, 136n. 102

Bísanig, Sonora, 136n. 107

blacksmith shop, *9*

blue paloverde *(Cercidium floridium),* 16, 20, 57, 131n. 44, 141n. 14

Brennan, Jose Lewis. *See* Lewis, Jose

About the Transcriber and Editor

Bernard Fontana and Hazel Fontana have collaborated on several publications since their marriage in 1954. Hazel, a graduate of the University of California at Berkeley whose art has illustrated such books as Edward Spicer's *Cycles of Conquest* and Herbert R. Hislop's *An Englishman's Arizona,* has often been her husband's amanuensis.

Now retired, Bernard Fontana received his Ph.D. in anthropology at the University of Arizona, where he was formerly ethnologist in the Arizona State Museum and field historian in the University of Arizona Library. A past president of the American Society for Ethnohistory and of the Society for Historical Archaeology, he is author, coauthor, editor, and co-editor of many books concerning the anthropology and history of the American Southwest.